Art,
Expression,
and Beauty

Arthur Berndtson

UNIVERSITY OF MISSOURI–COLUMBIA

Art, Expression, and Beauty

HOLT, RINEHART and WINSTON, INC.

NEW YORK   CHICAGO   SAN FRANCISCO   ATLANTA
DALLAS   MONTREAL   TORONTO   LONDON   SYDNEY

Copyright © 1969 by Holt, Rinehart and Winston, Inc.

All rights reserved

Library of Congress Catalog Card Number: 69-14249

03-073590-4

Printed in the United States of America

1 2 3 4 5 6 7 8 9

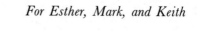

For Esther, Mark, and Keith

Preface

This book has been written with the hope that it may be of interest to the specialist in aesthetics, the student, and the reflective layman, and with the belief that what may be of primary interest for one of these groups will be of some value for the others.

For the aesthetician, the book undertakes extended analysis of a number of topics and theses, from the phases of sensation and the modes of representation to tragedy as power and the morality of art as liberal activity. The special concern of the book is a theory of art as expression of emotion: the theory is stated in Part Two, adumbrated in the chapters on emotion and contemplation in Part One, and applied in each of the chapters of Part Three. I have tried to fill in major gaps of preceding theories of expression and to purge the theories of some apparent errors.

The student at the upperclass and graduate levels will find in the book the full range of general aesthetics, including three basic hypotheses about the essential nature of art. The book may be used alone or with an anthology. No book can combine the virtues of a systematic study and an anthology: but the former can excel in unity, and it can offer detailed criticism when other writers are considered.

For the reflective layman, who may be any other person with an interest in general ideas, the book emphasizes the experience of value in art, and with it the humanistic nature of art. I have attempted to convey the concrete and imaginative nature of aesthetic experience, and to do so with the clarity but not the limitations of ordinary language.

My indebtedness in aesthetics is to Schopenhauer, Nietzsche, Santayana, and Croce among the classics, and to Collingwood, Ducasse, Susanne Langer, and Parker among more recent writers. Despite a predilection for it where it is appropriate, I have filtered out a good deal of the speculative metaphysics of the earlier writers in the context of aesthetics.

In another direction, I am grateful also to the University of Missouri Research Council for considerable support of the writing of this book.

Arthur Berndtson

Columbia, Missouri
November 1, 1968

Contents

PART II: THE INTERPRETATION OF ART

PART III: ART AND VALUES

List of Plates

Art,
Expression,
and Beauty

PART I

The Analysis
of Art

CHAPTER 1

Introduction

Aesthetics is an inquiry into an experience of a certain kind, which occurs often and with a constant sense of value, but in a striking variety of conditions. Aesthetic experience embraces works of art, such as a painting, and products of nature, such as a fortunate tree. It includes the creative activity of the artist, which terminates in the work of art, and the contemplative activity of the appreciator, which originates with the object provided by art or by nature. The object may be as ponderous and enduring as stone or as subtle as sounds that vanish in the air. It may consist almost entirely of sensations, as in music, or of representations, as in a novel. The emotion expressed in the object may be of joy, as in almost any part of Beethoven's *Seventh Symphony,* or of sorrow, as in the second movement of his *Third Symphony,* or of a nature that seems to lie beyond that polarity, as in not a little of the later work of Mozart. And the aesthetic experience may vary greatly in perfection and scope: from a novel by Dreiser to a sonnet by Shakespeare, and from a flower that raises no questions to the stars that answer none.

From this variety it is perhaps natural to conclude that aesthetic experience is radically plural, admitting of no term or unified set of terms that applies to the experience in all of its conditions. Then there would be no general aesthetics, apart from impressions and platitudes; instead there would be an aesthetics of art and another of nature, and the aesthetics of art would frac-

3

ture into separate systems for each art or for the major groupings of arts, such as the visual arts, the auditory arts, and the literary arts. It is possible to go a step further and hold that aesthetics is not so much plural as impossible, since the aesthetic experience may be thought to lie beyond the province of conceptual under-standing. Aesthetic structure has no logic; emotion is private and fluid; value is relative to man or men, and has its source in desire rather than reason; and the radiance of beauty is dimmed by analysis.

These statements are true, or mainly true, but they do not entail the conclusion that aesthetics is impossible. Aesthetic struc-ture has an order, which observes a number of general principles that can be stated clearly. Emotion can be made relatively public and fixed in the aesthetic object, which alone can achieve that result. Human nature and human desire give some evidence of uniformity and system, which allow values to be shared and under-stood. And though beauty can be grasped only in a living intui-tion, it has a describable structure that distinguishes it for analysis from other experiences of pleasure. These matters will be discussed in some detail in the following text, where evidence will accumulate that aesthetic experience can be known concep-tually.

The evidence will not lead to the conclusion that aesthetic experience can be quantified, controlled experimentally, or sub-sumed under predictions applying to the creator or to the appre-ciator. Aesthetics is not a science like astronomy, to mention a model, or psychology, to mention an aspirant. It has elements which derive directly from one or another of the sciences, and these elements should be encouraged and may be expected to grow. But they are not of commanding importance at this time, and it is not likely that they will be in the future, since they miss the individual intimacy, the organic wholeness, and the critical inde-pendence of the aesthetic experience. A painter sees colors better than does a physicist or a psychologist, and he consults no science in deciding how to unite colors on a canvas. A novelist probes the particulars and currents of human nature more fastidiously than does a psychologist and projects them in words by a process that cannot be duplicated in the laboratory. For the most part, therefore, the special methods of the sciences do not truly engage the aesthetic experience.

Those methods rest upon a broad base of ordinary experience, which precedes experiment, and of common reason, which precedes measurement. Philosophy is the systematic analysis and use of this base, as well as of the general findings of science, and it is in philosophy that aesthetic experience is brought to conceptual understanding. A philosopher may observe a color, a contrast, or an emotion as acutely as any other human being, excepting usually the artist, whom the philosopher is wise enough to take as his model in this matter. He is a specialist in abstract and dialectical analysis. This he brings to the study of aesthetic experience with suitable modifications in view of his understanding, as a student of methods, of the intuitive and imaginative aspects of the experience. He has some competence in the study of value and aesthetic value, since philosophy alone makes a general inquiry into the distinction between existence and essence on the one hand, and between existence and oughtness on the other. With these methods the philosopher takes a position between the scientist and the artist or appreciator. He comes as close to the aesthetic experience as conceptual understanding will permit, practicing neither the language of the statistical laboratory nor that of image and metaphor, though willing to use either when the occasion warrants.

Since the aesthetic experience may be understood in general terms, aesthetics is possible; and the question is then in order whether aesthetics is one or many. The role of philosophy in aesthetics establishes a presumption that aesthetics is one; for philosophy not only contributes a unified method as do the sciences, but it seeks a greater degree of unity of subject than do the sciences. Method, however, does not determine subject matter, if only because method is less specific and more flexible than subject matter: so unity of method does not guarantee unity of subject matter; and both unities are required if aesthetics is to be a single inquiry. The stress on unity in the goal of philosophy does not mean that unity is adequately achieved: philosophy has its disappointments. The presumption that aesthetics is one must therefore be examined from the standpoint of subject matter. The subject matter of aesthetics is aesthetic experience, and the use of that term confers a nominal unity of subject. The question then arises whether a further term can be found that is coextensive with the field of aesthetic experience, and that gives substantial unity to the field and to the inquiry. The exposition, interpretation, and criticism of such a term should be the major occupation of any book in aesthetics and cannot be undertaken in an introductory chapter. It may be sought for, however, and stated in this place in order to establish the unity of aesthetic inquiry, to clarify the boundaries of a complex field, and to indicate the point of view governing the present inquiry.

The term most frequently used in aesthetic discourse is *art*. That term is fully justified if the purpose is to indicate the most important part of aesthetic experience, or, from that importance, to have a shorthand term for the experience. It does not, however, serve to define the subject matter of aesthetics. It suffers from ambiguity, which in this instance is not severe and can in any event be corrected by decision, as well as from excesses of width and narrowness, which are serious defects.

Apart from what might be called the administrative meaning of *art*, which confines the word to the visual arts in naming certain kinds of museums, academic departments, and pages of newspapers, *art* has three meanings. The most common usage makes it equivalent to *work of art*, such as a poem, painting, or musical composition. A less common but more basic and appropriate use of the word is to signify a certain kind of activity, usually of making. The activity has an end or purpose; it is skilled, achieving its end and doing so efficiently; it is learned rather than innate or instinctive; it is conscious, except where repetition makes it automatic; and it is self-critical, adjusting itself and the object being made in the light of the end in view. This activity may occur as much in the making of a chair for sale and use as in the writing of a poem for aesthetic motives. It has its basis in a third meaning of *art*, which is a habit within the maker. Since the habit is good and is thought to qualify the intelligence or cognitive power, it is classed as an intellectual virtue by Aristotle, who called it "a state concerned with making, involving a true course of reasoning,"[1] and by Aquinas, who characterized it as "right reason about things to be made."[2] The three meanings of

---

[1] Aristotle, *Nicomachean Ethics*, trans. W. D. Ross (Vol. 9 in *The Works of Aristotle*, ed. by J. A. Smith and W. D. Ross, Oxford: Clarendon Press, 1925), 1140a.

[2] Thomas Aquinas, *Summa Theologica*, Vol. VII (London: R. and T. Washbourne, 1915), Ques. lvii, Art. iii.

art are distinct but closely related, being three stages or aspects of an area defined by the notion of learned, purposive skill. Of the three stages, the second appears to be most important for the concept of art, as distinct from that of aesthetic experience. A *work of art* is so-called because it is literally a "work of" art, and the habit of art is a potential for the activity in which it is completed. The ambiguity of *art* may thus be resolved by emphasis on the second meaning, an activity of a certain kind.

This activity is not adequate for the definition of aesthetic experience. It occurs not only in writing a poem, which is an aesthetic art, but in carpentry, which is a practical art, and in making a mathematical demonstration, which is a conceptual art, or, in the medieval curriculum, a liberal art. Something must be added to the notion of art if it is to describe the activity of the poet, painter, or musician. A notion of creation, spontaneity, and genius is required to distinguish the art of the poet from that of the carpenter; and it will be found that the two factors of art and genius will be somewhat at war with each other, though genius cannot dispense with art, however much it may dominate and absorb art. Still a further conception is needed to distinguish the art of the poet from that of the creative mathematician. The difference between the two arts appears to be that the mathematician formulates thought, while the poet formulates emotion, and thought as a vehicle of emotion. Thus the activity of art must be supplemented in two significant ways if it is to describe the activity of the person who, in aesthetic discourse, is called an artist.

The activity of the aesthetic artist does not, however, exhaust aesthetic experience. The experience of the appreciator or contemplator of the work of art is different from that of the artist or creator and must be considered in any definition of the aesthetic experience. The position of the appreciator may seem to be less significant for aesthetics than that of the artist, since the artist alone creates, and undergoes a depth of love and fury that the contemplator does not, and knows more of the work of art that he has made than the most acute critic or learned historian. But the contemplator is far more numerous than the artist and constitutes the larger part of the audience that the artist (and aesthetician) is trying to reach. It is only in the moment of contemplation that the work of art is truly known. Despite its rare intrinsic value, the act of creation exists mainly for the sake of its result, the work of art. In the act of creation, however, the work of art is not known in its entirety, in its full scope and unity. The artist is absorbed in one part or another, since he does not create in a flash; and he deals in tentatives which later are discarded or confirmed. Only when creation is over does the artist fully see what he has made, and gather the reward of his exertion. Then, however, he has left the position of the artist or creator and taken the position of the appreciator or contemplator, which is not fundamentally altered by the immediate history of creation or by the special expertness of the creator. The concept of the activity of the artist therefore does not do justice to the whole experience of the work of art.

That experience, in turn, does not include all that is available to aesthetic experience. Beyond art is nature, by which may be understood whatever is not art, and in particular the nonhuman world presented to the senses. Nature supplies objects to the aesthetic experience, and aesthetics should account for their aesthetic character as well as for that of works of art. The judgment on nature as an aesthetic object varies among writers on aesthetics and among artists. Most aestheticians are oriented toward art: compare Aristotle on drama, Nietzsche on music and drama, and Croce on literature. Some philosophers who take aesthetic experience seriously think rather of nature, as Kant and Whitehead, and especially Emerson, who expressed some scorn for art despite his regular practice of it.

Artists almost necessarily prefer art to nature, since otherwise they would be content to contemplate nature rather than to create works of art, which are never made for the reasons of a traveling photographer. But romanticism in all of the arts finds a profound stimulus in nature, and painting of most schools is inconceivable without nature as the source and target of the will to form. Art and nature have complementary virtues. Art is human, but nature offers refreshing release from the pressure of man. Art is highly organized, but finite, and nature is somewhat random, but infinite. Art reflects the most complex intelligibility available to man, but nature seduces or overpowers. It is difficult to choose between the two, and perhaps it is not necessary: art may be said to be nature refined in thought and valuation. It is therefore appropriate for aesthetics to stress art, but not to take art as its fundamental term. The concept of art has a unique and explanatory character only when construed as the art activity: but that activity is progressively deficient in accounting for the aesthetic experience of the artist, of the contemplator of works of art, and of the contemplator of nature.

A term that may be applied to both works of art and products of nature is *beauty,* which competes with *art* for primacy in aesthetic discourse. Tradition and popular belief seem to agree that beauty is the fundamental character of aesthetic experience. From Plato to Bosanquet, Santayana, and Croce, beauty is accepted as the aesthetic essence, though these writers do not agree on the nature of beauty or its relation to art. In the tradition, the main objection to identifying beauty with aesthetic experience is that beauty may be coordinate with other aesthetic values, such as the sublime in Kant,[3] or the sublime, grace, and the "characteristic" in Schopenhauer.[4] This objection disappears if it is agreed that the beauty that is differentiated from the sublime, or other aesthetic values, is a specialization within the more general beauty referred to by these writers when discussing aesthetic experience as such. But a far more serious objection to beauty appears in contemporary aesthetics and art. Bell[5] and Collingwood[6] believe that the term is more fitting outside of art, and Ducasse thinks that it may be applied within the realm of art but only under certain conditions: for Ducasse, though apparently not for Bell and Collingwood, genuine art may be ugly.[7] It is hard to be as convinced of the relevance of beauty in contemporary art as in older art: consider the women of de Kooning, the distortions and monsters of Picasso, and the nightmares of Albright. Despite these current views and practices, beauty can be assigned an essential role in the aesthetic experience of both art and nature, and this book will undertake to do so.

[3] Immanuel Kant, *Critique of Judgment,* trans. J. H. Bernard (New York: Hafner, 1951), Pt. I, Sec. 23.

[4] Arthur Schopenhauer, *The World as Will and Idea,* Vol. I, trans. R. B. Haldane and J. Kemp (London: Routledge & Kegan Paul, 1957), Bk. III, Secs. 39, 45.

[5] Clive Bell, *Art* (New York: Frederick A. Stokes, n.d.), pp. 12–15.

[6] R. G. Collingwood, *The Principles of Art* (Oxford: Clarendon, 1950), pp. 37–41.

[7] Curt J. Ducasse, *The Philosophy of Art* (New York: Dial, 1929), pp. 16–18.

Beauty will be defined in a later chapter as "the emergent quality of embodiment,"[8] and embodiment will be predicated of all consummated aesthetic experience. But beauty is the terminus of embodiment, and embodiment is the terminal phase of expression. Beauty is the final stage in the goal of the artist in creating and of the appreciator in contemplating, but it is not the whole goal; and it does not engage these activities in their developmental processes. Beauty therefore may be taken as necessary but not as sufficient to the definition of aesthetic experience, in contrast to art in the strict and explanatory sense, which is neither necessary nor sufficient.

The term that now suggests itself is one that was used in indicating limitation in both art and beauty. That term is *expression*. Expression consists in a very close relation between form and emotion, which will be set forth at length in the central chapters of this book. Expression occurs in the act of aesthetic contemplation, for in that act an emotion is experienced in a state of fusion with, or embodiment in, an object or form. The object may be a work of art or a product of nature: what makes the object aesthetic is not its source in art or nature, but its function in expressing emotion. When an object expresses emotion, a third term emerges in their relation. That term is beauty, which takes its place as a part of expression. And expression engages the creative making of the artist as well as the contemplative activity of the appreciator. The artist is a poet or painter or musician, as distinct from being simply an artisan or creator, because he uses art to create a form that expresses emotion. He is an artist in the full sense of the word because he creates a form of a certain kind: a kind that is appropriate for the expression of emotion. In the process of creating the form, however, emotion and form are closely related to each other in a common development, which is also a phase of expression. The concept of expression therefore embraces all of the terms that have arisen in the attempt to define aesthetic experience. It occurs as development in artistic creation and as completed state in aesthetic appreciation. Its object may come from art or from nature. It flowers in beauty. Expression therefore has the breadth required for the term that should give substantial unity to the variety of

[8] Below, Chap. 9, "Beauty: Embodiment and Emergence."

aesthetic experience. It is not so wide as to go beyond the aesthetic into other fields, since the requirement of emotion and the specification of the "very close relation" between form and emotion are sufficient to prevent overlap of related but nonaesthetic fields. Given the concept of expression, it is possible to make a brief and adequate definition of aesthetic experience: the experience consists of the creation or contemplation of form as the expression of emotion.

The theory that aesthetic experience is expression is complex: it draws upon all basic factors in the experience and relates them with greater intricacy than is suspected in most accounts of the subject. It is controversial, since it has rivals in other theories which purport to give an equally fundamental explanation of art, if not of aesthetic experience as a whole. It has special affinity with the conception of values, including both the values peculiar to art and other fields of value; for the emotion that is central to expression is closely related to value, being value in a condition of immediate awareness. These attributes of the theory of expression define the subject matter of this book, and to some extent its organization into three parts.

Part I is an analysis of the basic factors of aesthetic experience, with emphasis on the work of art in the moment of contemplation. The factors are (1) an object, such as a poem or rock; (2) an emotion experienced in connection with the object; and (3) contemplation, which comprises the awareness and attitude with which the appreciator confronts the object and emotion. The object in turn is divisible into three factors: (1) sensation, as of a blue color present on a canvas or in the sky; (2) representation, as of a blue-colored sky by the blue color on canvas, or of God by the three-lettered sound; and (3) structure, which is a unified relation among elements drawn from sensation, as in music; or from representation, as in a novel; or from both sensation and representation, as in most painting. Aesthetic experience will thus be considered to draw upon five factors: sensation, representation, structure, emotion, and contemplation. These factors will be set forth without regard to any particular theory of the fundamental nature of aesthetic experience. The aim of Part I is to clarify and give content to the terms used in aesthetics, to suggest their relations on a level more basic and neutral than that specified by a particular theory, and to establish the data of which any theory must take account if it is to be adequate. In a value activity such as aesthetic experience, there are no rigorous data, for the evaluations within a given theory may rule out as irrelevant one factor or another, even though the factor may be present in the experience of many persons. In a value context, the interplay of fact and theory is such that fact may become apparent rather than real, and theory prescriptive rather than false. But some sort of line may be drawn between datum and theory, lest theory have no content to draw upon.

Part II is an interpretation of the aesthetic experience. It will discuss three theories of the basic nature and function of art: (1) the theory of art as representation, for which the function of art is to represent a world outside of art; (2) the theory of art as form, for which the function of art is to present "pure forms" or sensory designs without regard to the world and its values and emotion; and (3) the theory of art as expression. Whereas the representational theory emphasizes representation, and the formalist theory sensation, the expressional theory admits both representation and sensory design as sufficient objects, but conceives of the object as vehicle for the expression of emotion, and of expression of emotion as distinct from representation of emotion. In setting forth these theories, Part II will go further into the basic factor or factors favored by each theory.

Part III will discuss the relation of aesthetic experience to values. It will deal with the problem of criticism or comparative value in regard to individual works of art, the problem of pain or negative value in art, and problems of the relation of art to the values of morality and religion. For all but the first of these problems the formalist theory has a position of indifference or rejection, the representational theory one of moderate interest, and the expressional theory one of decided interest and strength. If Part I prepares the way for the theory of expression and Part II sets it forth by contrast with its rivals, Part III puts the theory to work in the study of art and values, which is the part of aesthetics that makes the greatest demands on the synoptic vision and dialectical coolness of the philosopher.

CHAPTER 2

The Aesthetic Object
Sensation and Representation

Sensation and Art

Of the basic factors of art, sensation is the most characteristic,
though it is not thereby shown to be the essence of art. Representation occurs in science and in ordinary discourse. Mathematics
traces a complex structure of definitions, postulates, and theorems,
which are tightly connected. Emotion dominates human life from
the first discomfort of the infant to the last fear or regret at
death. Contemplation perhaps is rare, but it occurs in liberal
science as the act of understanding for its own sake. Art, however, has an emphasis on sensation that has no parallel elsewhere.
The sciences begin and end with sensation, in the observation of
data and the verification of hypotheses; but even at those extremes sensation is taken as a clue to things and events which are
construed in abstraction from the qualities of sensation, as in the
physicist's replacement of colors by light waves. Practical action
uses sensation as a sign of useful things, as when someone reaches
for a white pill to relieve a headache. Ethics often frowns on
sensation as a temptation to evil or as a distraction from the
proper business of decision and responsibility. Religion frequently
regards the world of sense as an appearance, or a transition to a
better estate in the next life, or a place of trial. But art steeps

itself in the senses as though sensation were life, or the gateway to life: one of which it is.

Sensation appears to be at its maximum in painting, perhaps because of the qualitative diversity of which color, line, and shape are susceptible. In contemporary painting, which emphasizes more than most periods of art the freedom of sensation from service to representation, the maximum is supported by subtle probing of color in Matisse, by line in Picasso, and by colored shapes in Cézanne that thrust themselves against the act of vision. Sensation is basic in music, where it is only incidentally tied to representation. In music, sensation seems more readily to disappear into structure than it does in the visual arts: partly because sounds vanish on entry and endure in patterned relation to their successors, and partly because sounds have less diversity in themselves and therefore depend largely on combination for scope. Musical structure is nothing, however, without sound, which is a heard quality that expands through structure; mobile sound makes a work of art, but the sound of motion does not. In literature, sensation is at its minimum, since the sounds of words are dispensable in the novel and share attention with representation and idea in the medium of poetry. Sensation comprises the presented vehicle of the literary arts as it does of the other arts, but its weight as vehicle is comparatively slight. To compensate for this deficiency in sensation, literature echoes sensation in the representation of sensory values in image and metaphor. It does this not in the interest of technique, but to express the mode of awareness of the literary artist, which is seldom separated from sensation. For examples of that mode, consider Keats, who expressed in a letter his preference for "a Life of Sensations rather than of Thoughts";[1] or Pater, whose meditative novel, *Marius the Epicurean,* is subtitled "His Sensations and Ideas"; or John Cowper Powys, whose sensory acuteness overflowed from his novels into *In Defence of Sensuality.*

The importance of sensation in the arts is due to many causes. Sensation is a primary source of quality, as distinct from relation, in human experience, and it offers qualities in amazing abundance according to the aptitude of the sense and, it may be

---

[1] John Keats, *Letters,* Vol. I, ed. M. B. Forman (New York: Oxford, 1931), No. 29.

observed, of the person who senses. Sensation is vital, immediate, concrete, and convincing. It is clear and intense: by extension, a thinker may say that he sees a point that has become clear; and a person in grief may say that when his emotion is intense, it is as sharp as sensation. Sensation is spared the labor of abstraction, as in conceptual thought, and of decision, as in moral experience. Moreover, sensation has striking flexibility. It ranges from a sensual pole, where it serves the body in food, drink, and lust, to an ideal pole, where body becomes a vehicle or disappears entirely from view. It is no paradox of the life of sensation that Leonide Massine used the body, in the ballet *Saint Francis,* to express redemption from the body. The flexibility of sensation allows sensation to unite with thought and emotion: on that union art depends.

The Constituents of Sensation

If thought is taken as any awareness of relation and is not restricted to comparatively advanced relations involving generalization, abstraction, inference, and the use of signs, the contribution of thought to sensation is almost as extensive as sensation itself and helps to define the nature of sensation. From the standpoint of the student of art, the contribution of thought to sensation may be divided into two areas, one pre-aesthetic, the other intra-aesthetic. In the pre-aesthetic area thought organizes sensation in relations of identity, of time and space, and of causality and substance. The result is the common world of sense perception, an assemblage of such things as trees, tables, and human bodies. This world is the scene of practical human action, such as planting crops and waging wars. It furnishes data and problems to the sciences, which investigate it with the help of comparatively refined relations. And it supplies the artist with sensory materials which, though sufficient as the sensory basis for practical action and scientific thought, are not adequate for the aesthetic consciousness. The color and shape of a tree are sufficient to a general if they help him to identify camouflage, or to a botanist if they help him to identify a species of tree: but they may not be adequate for an artist, who is interested in sensory experience as far as it will take him.

Thought therefore assumes an intra-aesthetic function, starting with sensation as organized by the earlier function, but selecting from it, modifying it, and organizing it further in structures which serve the purpose of the artist, whether that purpose be the sheer enjoyment of sense, or representation, c. the expression of emotion. The intra-aesthetic function of thought in sensation, which is to develop sensation in complex and carefully controlled structures, is a concern of aesthetics generally. The pre-aesthetic function is the concern of this section, where it will take its place in the exposition of sensation as a whole.

Sensation comprises whatever occurs in existential connection with the stimulation of the senses. The phrase *existential connection* serves to distinguish sensation from memory, imagination, and conception, which depend heavily on sensation for their content or essences, but may exist when stimulation of the senses does not. It covers aspects of sensation that are not normally experienced as well as aspects that are experienced. These aspects of sensation may be summarized in five stages, which have a logical succession and may or may not have a temporal succession. The stages may be called (1) reception and development of stimulus, (2) production of quality, (3) sensory feeling, (4) sensory intuition, and (5) sense perception. The activities of the last three stages are modes of awareness of their objects, and the activities can themselves be objects of introspection. The last two stages involve thought.

For the purposes of aesthetics, as distinct from those of psychology and theory of knowledge, it is not necessary to dwell on the first two stages, since they do not enter aesthetic experience proper. Reception of stimulus becomes the ordinary basis for distinguishing between what is sensed and what is represented in art: a sensed object stimulates the senses, and a represented object does not. Reception is not purely passive, a mere event or process rather than an activity, for reception is a physiological act according to the nature of the receptor: the eyes do not receive sound waves, and the ears do not receive light waves. Subsequent neural development is also active.

Considerably more active is the next stage, of qualitative production. What reaches the eye is a light wave, and what occurs in the brain is an electrochemical process, neither of which is a color; but in sensation a color occurs. If we accept the quantitative emphasis of physics, which ascribes no color to the external thing from which the light wave is reflected, or if we accept the instrumental emphasis within theory of knowledge, for which the purpose of awareness is to create rather than to reproduce, it will be clear that in sensation quality is produced. On the other hand, if we maintain that color does exist in the external object, apart from our awareness, it must still be granted that color is in some way a possession of consciousness. A color may be found in consciousness when the eyes are closed or the external object is removed. It appears, then, that a color is produced in consciousness, since it may be found there apart from any color that may exist in the external world. Memory reproduces or revives the color possessed by mind, and imagination manipulates it. But sensation alone produces it; it does not occur in a person who has never received the appropriate stimulus, such as a person born blind.

Sensation as an act of qualitative production seems to stand at the border of neural and conscious activity. Quality is not produced in the body, where the most minute physiological investigation does not claim to find it, but in the field or medium of awareness, where it stands at full blaze. Awareness, however, does not reach the activity of production, and that activity is not a mode of awareness of the quality produced. Sensation as an act of awareness starts with sensory feeling of the quality deposited by sensation as production, and continues with sensory intuition and sense perception. These three stages are of direct concern to aesthetics.

Sensory feeling is the simplest awareness of sensory quality, in which the act of feeling and the content felt are not distinguished, and the content felt has hardly any relations to give it order. Sensory feeling occurs without benefit of memory: it is sheer presentness. It is similar to Schopenhauer's "dull, plant-like consciousness of the changes of the immediate object,"[2] though it may be more vague than dull. It resembles Santayana's "im-

---

[2] Arthur Schopenhauer, *Die Welt als Wille und Vorstellung,* Vol. I, *Sämmtliche Werke,* Vol. II (Leipzig: F. A. Brockhaus, 1891), Bk. I, Sec. 4, pp. 13–14. *The World as Will and Idea,* Vol. I, trans. R. B. Haldane and J. Kemp (London: Routledge & Kegan Paul, 1957), p. 14.

mediate continuum" and "irreparable flux," which he describes as predecessors of ideas and things.[3] It is akin to Collingwood's "psychical" level of apprehension.[4]

The content of sensory feeling has five characteristics. The first is a quality or group of qualities, such as a red color or a sound of a certain pitch. The defining character of quality, in contrast to other types of character, nature, or essence, is the irreducibility of a given quality: its stubborn uniqueness which makes it impossible to experience or to state the quality as a function of other qualities or characters. This means that red, orange, and yellow, though closer to each other than any of them is to blue, are inherently distinct. Orange as sensed is not a mixture of the sensory qualities of red and yellow, and a person who had seen red and yellow, but not orange, could not apprehend the quality of orange. This is in contrast with the possibility of mixing pigments, or light rays, which are causes of qualities but are not themselves qualities. The irreducibility of qualities extends to classes of qualities, such as colors and sounds. The irreducibility of such classes, or generic qualities, evidently is the ultimate basis of the untranslatability of the several arts into each other. What is done or expressed in music cannot be duplicated in painting, for the sensory departments of sound and color are radically distinct.

The second trait of sensory feeling is intensity, which is an attribute of quality. Intensity may be exemplified in color, where it occurs in two ways: as saturation, or quantity of hue in relation to gray, and as value, or quantity of white in a color. Value is visibility as such, and saturation is visibility in regard to a given hue. Intensity is intensive magnitude and is the characteristic magnitude of quality. Like extensive magnitude, which occurs in number and in space, intensive magnitude admits of more and less; unlike it, intensive magnitude cannot be stated in multiples of some elementary unit, for no unit can be found. The dichotomy of intensive and extensive magnitude is basic in philosophy, for it affords a clue to the dualisms of creation and repetition, organism and atomism, voluntaristic idealism and

---

[3] George Santayana, *Reason in Common Sense* (New York: Scribner, 1929), p. 163; *Reason in Science* (New York: Scribner, 1928), p. 28.

[4] R. G. Collingwood, *The Principles of Art* (Oxford: Clarendon Press, 1950), p. 164.

classical materialism. The position of art in this dichotomy is quite clear.

The third characteristic of sensory feeling is emotion, such as the gaiety of yellow and the dark sorrow of violet. The emotive characters of sensation appear to be innate or unlearned, rather than to be based on association. If they are innate, it remains to be seen whether they are identical with sensory quality in whole or in part, or are effects of it. These questions will be considered in Chapter 4, the third section, as part of the general analysis of emotion.

The fourth characteristic of sensory feeling is temporality of an incomplete and fugitive kind. Time involves two factors: passage, or coming to be and ceasing to be in some respect, and endurance or duration, which is extent or interval between coming to be and ceasing. The element of passage predominates in sensory feeling, as it does in all sensation and all human experience; but it is greater in sensory feeling than in later stages of sensation. Sensory feeling is an awareness so simple that memory makes no contribution to it. Sensory feeling thus occupies the present moment, without recollection of the past or anticipation of the future. The present moment yields to another, without identity, continuity, or inheritance from one moment to another. Each moment therefore is new and distinct, as is the feeling identified with that moment, and the feeling is as brief as the moment with which it is identified. Stimulus may change, as in music, or it may persist, as in painting; but this difference between temporal and spatial art is canceled for sensory feeling, in which every moment of feeling in response to a persisting stimulus is a new feeling.

But the predominance of passage in sensory feeling does not mean absolute flux; it does not mean instantaneity with no endurance at all. Nothing actual is instantaneous, and a mere point of time is as fictitious as a point of space. A single pulsation in an advancing wave of light energy or sound energy occupies some time, however slight. A moment of sensory awareness must occupy at least as much time if it is to be a response to such a stimulus, and it will inevitably spread over more time than that because of the organic character of awareness. Without embracing the past, which is gone in default of memory, or the future, which is unavailable in the absence of anticipation, the presentness of sensory feeling has a span of its own. The length of this interval is not fixed by the sensory stimulus, nor by any general a priori factor; as Royce showed in his analysis of the specious present, it may vary greatly.[5] In human awareness the span of the present is very short, and sensory feeling is restricted entirely to that span. But it is restricted not because it is sensation, but because it is feeling: not because it is an awareness occasioned by passing stimuli, but because it is an awareness without memory.

The final trait of sensory feeling is spatiality of a very primitive sort. It may be objected that only visual contents are in space and that sounds are located in time only. But the spatial character of colors in ordinary experience is not yet in view. What is intended here is a more rudimentary character which occurs in all sensory classes as a diffuse massiveness or voluminousness. It may be found in low-pitched tones, and seems restricted almost to a point in high-pitched, bright tones; but even as an approximate point its spatial relevance is evident. Space occurs whenever there is some degree of separateness or externality of coexistent parts in relation to each other. Such separateness may vary greatly. It is at a minimum in the space of sensory feeling, and at a maximum in the space of mathematical physics, which lies well beyond any sensory space.

Sensory feeling passes into sensory intuition when memory enters the experience and contributes a basis for identity and when the temporal and spatial characters become well-defined. In sensory intuition, content and activity are distinct, so that the content can be spoken of as an object. *Object* here does not signify thing, such as a table or tree, or independence of awareness, such as may be ascribed to a color if it is thought to exist in things apart from awareness. *Object* signifies merely the condition of standing over against the act of awareness, as the goal or target of the awareness. Sensory intuition has a quality as its object, such as a red color or a tone of a certain pitch. But it intuits the quality instead of merely feeling it. In contrast with feeling, intuition implies a high degree of relation, organization, or forming. In contrast with perception, it implies in this sensory context an absence of sign function and inference. Sensory intuition in-

[5] Josiah Royce, *The World and the Individual,* Vol. II (New York: Macmillan, 1904), pp. 115–143.

volves thought, or awareness of relation, on a presymbolic level; though thought here has a certain simplicity, it also achieves an order of perfection on which it will not improve in the realm of signification, inference, and abstraction. Sensory intuition should not be confused with the more complex intuition that will be described in the theory of art as expression.[6]

The process by which sensory feeling passes into sensory intuition is complex, and accounts of it are as speculative as they are interesting. What is important for aesthetics is not the process, which appears in no aesthetic experience and influences neither the artist nor the interpreter of art, but the result, which enters the experience and bears upon the theory of art. The first half of the result is the awareness of identity in the quality, which fixes and stabilizes it for aesthetic contemplation and artistic use. The quality in sensory feeling was shown to be highly fluid, coming anew with each moment because of the absence of memory, and incapable of relation with itself or other qualities because of its novelty. Through memory, a given sensory feeling is enlarged by consolidation with traces of earlier sensory feelings that are similar in quality. The earlier feelings are not signified, as when we remember a conversation that took place yesterday or a person now dead: instead, they are present to the given feeling in the form of faint survivals. From this elementary relation of a present feeling to past feelings, the present quality is stabilized, recognized, and identified: it achieves identity, or status as being itself and not some other quality. The quality may now be detached from the moment of feeling that brought it into awareness and may endure as the stable object of an awareness that continues as long as the stimulus and interest permit. The quality may be further identified by naming and by subsumption under the concept or class of that quality, but this action goes beyond the scope and need of sensory intuition.

The second half of the intuition is the awareness of definite temporal and spatial relations in the quality. If it is a sound, the quality is intuited as having the duration just noted, which has within it relations of before and after. The enduring interval has a beginning and an end, which limit it, contain it, and set it off from other intervals that precede and follow it. If the quality

---

[6] Below, Chap. 9, "Aesthetic Intuition."

is a color, it is intuited as having a given extent in two-dimensional space. The extent has within it relations of coexistence, and it has a boundary which contains it and sets it off from other coexisting extents. What is required for the intuition of a given color or sound is not that it be placed within a spatial or temporal structure of colors or of sounds, as in a given work of art, but that it have the spatial or temporal determinateness that makes it negotiable for such structure.

Colors acquire both kinds of determinateness in visual intuition; but temporal definiteness drops out of the intuition when it does not affect structure, as in the static shapes of painting, while retained when it does influence structure, as in the mobile shapes of the dance. Sounds acquire temporal but not spatial determinateness. The spatiality of sounds does not become an object of intuition, as distinct from feeling, and the relations in space of different sounds are not intuited. Sound thus is not intuited spatially and therefore is not negotiable for spatial structure.

Sensory intuition moves into sense perception when an intuited quality, or intuited sensum as it may be called, is interpreted in an activity that involves signification and inference. A colored shape, when perceived, functions as a sign of characters that are not intuited, but which have so immediate a connection with the intuited color that they enter vicariously into sensation in the form of sense perception. The total of the connected characters is a perceptual object, or thing of ordinary experience, such as a tree or human face. The characters are known from past experience to occur together; the occurrence of one of them leads to an inference of the occurrence, or possible occurrence, of the others; and the character that occurs to sensory intuition is a perceptual sign of the others.

The various characters that may be objects of sense perception may be distinguished in an order that may be arbitrary for science and philosophy, but highly relevant for the analysis and interpretation of art. If we are looking at a human face and take as our sign an arrangement or design of colored shapes in plane space, it seems that the first inferred, or perceived, item is shape in depth. We do not perceive the face as two-dimensional: the nose stands forward in space; the cheek is rounded off backward; and we expect to find something at the rear of the head. The second perceived character is some degree of resistance and of smoothness, which we may confirm in tactile intuition if we extend our hand. The third object of perception consists of the objects of the remaining senses, such as sounds and odors. If other sense qualities are intuited at the same time that the plane color is intuited, the function of perception is merely to unite them for awareness as though they were parts or effects of one thing. The fourth item consists of the defining physical and biological properties of things, which distinguish coal from ice, life from inert matter, and one kind of tree from another. The fifth object consists of psychological or spiritual characters, such as an emotion or a virtue, which may be the main object of perception in the ordinary course of human affairs. The sixth item is substance as the ground or cause of the preceding characters and of their unity as one thing. The last object is existence in some respect and asserted at the level of any of the preceding items.

The number and range of these objects of perception testify to its complexity, which will have a bearing on the subsequent interpretation of formalism in art.[7] Perception is as extensive as the concepts or universals that thought can bring into close connection with sensory intuition. But when universals are apprehended and combined on their own, in abstraction or separation from the awareness that starts with sensory reception, thought passes beyond perception, and thus beyond sensation, and becomes conception.

The range of sensation from sensory feeling to sense perception can be summarized under the interplay of two important factors, scope and immediacy. Scope is amount or wealth of content or character in an object. Scope is at a minimum in sensory feeling. It is greater in sensory intuition, due to the addition of memory and spatial and temporal relations. It appears to be at its sensory maximum in perception, particularly when all types or levels of perceptual character are involved. But there may be some loss of scope in perception. The use of a color to signify a thing may very well attract perception from the color to the thing, of which the color is only one part or effect. The result may be a loss of scope in regard to the quality of the color, its intensity, and its emotional character. Of this trio, the last suffers most readily. Loss of scope in this way is of interest to the interpretation of art, particularly for the formalist, as will appear later.

[7] Below, Chap. 7, "Formalism in Painting: Bell."

Immediacy is priority of position in an order of some kind. Logical immediacy is priority in an order of simple and complex, of part and whole, of premise and consequent. Temporal immediacy is priority in an order of time. For sensation, temporal immediacy may be genetic, concerned with the development of any given act of sensation, or attentional, concerned with the play of attention in a sensory act. Logical immediacy is in inverse proportion to scope, so it belongs primarily to sensory feeling and secondarily to sensory intuition. Genetic immediacy has the same order. A quality must be felt, or registered in bare awareness, before it can be identified through memory and discriminated in space and time; and it must be identified before it can be interpreted to mean a thing, and be intuited in two dimensions of space before the mind can make the leap to the third dimension. Through repetition and the formation of sensory habits, the transition may be so rapid as to make genetic immediacy negligible: but the causal relation of feeling, intuition, and perception appears to make a relation of temporal succession inevitable.

The transition cannot in any case be attended to completely, for the stage of sensory feeling escapes attention. Attention implies direction and control of awareness, which in turn require some identification of the objects of attention. Moreover, attention also implies some sustained character to awareness, in the course of which a preceding moment of awareness influences the immediately present moment. Sensory feeling therefore cannot have attentional immediacy. The latter appears to be commonest for perception, for ordinarily we attend to an object as a face, or other thing, before we attend to it as a color, or other intuited sensum. But attentional immediacy is influenced by interest. When the aesthetic consciousness is highly developed, it is quite possible to attend to something in the environment as simply a colored shape, and to do so on first awareness of the object.

The Constituents of Sensation in the Arts

The analysis of sensory feeling, sensory intuition, and sense perception makes it possible to state with some understanding the place of sensation in the work of art. The role of sensation varies from art to art, occupying in each art a fairly definite and appropriate part of the spectrum defined by the constituents of sensation. Sensed objects comprise the presented part of the aesthetic object, and may be called a vehicle since they are the bearers of the structure into which they enter and of any representation that may occur. An exception to the general condition of sensation as furnishing the presented vehicle of art occurs when images take the place of sensed objects in the absence of a stimulus. The tones of music may be apprehended in image rather than in sensation, as by the deaf Beethoven. This function of images in the presented vehicle of any of the arts should be distinguished from the representational function of images, such as occurs in poetry when the meaning of a word has been executed in images which may draw upon the contents of any sense. Images in the presented vehicle are drawn from the department of sense that is appropriate to the particular art, for they are copies of the objects that sensation would present if the stimulus occurred; they may be described in the same terms as sensation as far as the stages of sensory awareness are concerned. This being so, we may confine our attention to sensation in discussing the presented part of the work of art.

Of the three stages of sensation, sensory feeling is necessarily excluded from the presented object, which draws on nothing simpler than the intuited sensum. A quality must have achieved identity if it is to enter into complex and fixed structures, and it must have been assimilated spatially or temporally if the structures involve relations in space or time. Art as a learned skill depends on memory. But sensory feeling functions to some extent as an ideal to the aesthetic imagination, for in it quality, intensity, and emotion are found in their pristine state before they have been organized in relations that lead to their attrition, as in perception, or that discipline them, as in intuition. Although the nature of sensory feeling cannot be recovered, since memory cannot be thrown off, it can be approached by a movement of awareness that melts away at least part of the work of thought and thus yields an intimation of what would result if that movement were completed. For the movement to occur, an actual structure must be subtly devised to give the illusion of the dissolution both of itself and of the separateness of its parts.

Sensation makes its appearance in the realm of art in the form of sensory intuition, which governs the presented object in the literary arts, music, and painting. And it continues as perception in defining the presented object in sculpture, architecture, the dance, and the theatre.

The novel, the drama read in the "closet," and poetry, have for their vehicle sounds intuited temporally. The same is true of music. The difference between these arts, as concerns sensation, is one of scope and capacity for organization. In music, the sounds have specific qualities, defined by pitch and timbre; specific intensities, defined by volume and brightness; and specific durations. All of these occur with great variety, as exemplified in the range of pitches and diversity of timbres that an orchestra can produce. The specificity and variety of musical tones make them candidates for complex organization. These attributes are greatly diminished in the literary arts, and particularly in the novel and drama as ordinarily written. Poetry has the strongest sensory position of the literary arts, but it is far inferior to music in the realm of sensation. The sounds of vowels and consonants do not have the specificity and variety of quality, intensity, and duration that are common in music.

Painting has a presented character made of colored shapes, which are colors intuited in a two-dimensional plane. If the shapes are regarded as having depth, representation takes place, since only the plane surface of the canvas is used. The canvas and the pigments on it are perceived, not intuited, for they are known only for an interpretation that embraces deep space and specific physical and chemical properties. But the canvas and pigments as such are not parts of the aesthetic object and are not sensed by the appreciator of the painting, though they must be sensed by the artist in the process of creation and by the student of techniques. The contemplation of a painting involves, apart from representation and structure, only the intuition of colors and of the lines, masses, and shapes that they define in a plane.

The remaining arts require the perception of things in deep space. For sculpture, architecture, the dance, and the drama as staged, perception by the appreciator takes as its clue intuited sensa, which are colored shapes in sculpture and architecture, and colored shapes associated with sound in the dance and theater. How far perception may go in the discernment of the content or character of the perceived thing depends on the art and on the aesthetic theory of the percipient. Formalism holds a tight rein on perception; and representationalism, or an aesthetics of maximum meaning or content, permits a wide interpretation of the thing in question. This will be evident in Part II of this book. But some minimum of perceptual interpretation is required in each art, in order to establish a perception and presentation appropriate to distinct arts.

In sculpture and architecture, the thing is at least a physical thing, or thing characterized by resistance and weight. The colored shape yields to a shaped volume, and the volume becomes the scene of forces which play and thrust. Architecture differs from sculpture in the magnitude of the volume, in the magnitude and character of the forces involved, and in the greater emphasis in sculpture on the surface of the volume. These differences in regard to the thing as physical do not seem sufficient to distinguish the two arts. Short of representation, which opens up the entire realm of the human body for sculpture, architecture must be differentiated from sculpture by a perception of the thing as having a function: the thing as a shelter or as a place of certain human actions and rites.

In the dance, the thing once more is physical, but forces contained in a static volume give way to forces in motion, which follow a rhythm set by the accompanying sounds of the music. The motion is not merely that of a physical thing, but of a living thing which is conscious of its motions. The human body with its motions and consciousness of motion thus is the minimal perceived object in the dance. The dance may enlarge perception to embrace every item in the consciousness perceived in the dancing body: but this is not required to distinguish the dance perceptually.

In the theater, the human body again is perceived in motion accompanied by sounds, which are now derived from speech. The moving body, however, yields in perception to the consciousness perceived through it, a consciousness that may embrace any content of human emotion, desire, or thought. But the consciousness of the actor is not his own: it represents the consciousness of the person whose part is being played. That derived consciousness does not fall within the chain of perception. What the theater adds to the closet drama is visual sensation. But visual intuition of colored shapes on the plane of the stage yields to visual perception of subtly conscious human beings, and that perception yields in value to the representation of an absent consciousness. What theater adds to the drama as read therefore is insufficient in its visual content to make it a visual art, just as the sounds of drama, fiction, and even of poetry are insufficient in auditory content to make any of them an auditory art. The title of literary art is appropriate to these arts, for what distinguishes them is not the use of sensation in some department, but of words, which are occurrences in which sounds are subordinate to meaning or representation.

Representation and Meaning

Representation enters the aesthetic object when the sensed object is deemed insufficient in scope and is taken as a sign of some other object, which becomes the represented content of the aesthetic object. The intuited sounds of a poem may signify ideas or things, and the perceived physical thing in sculpture may refer to a human body. In this way the world enters art, and art is enriched if it does not lose sight of the sensed object that represents the world. It is not the only way in which the world enters art, for aesthetic experience may add to sensation through the expression of emotion, which does not require representation. Music expresses the inward character of human experience without representing anything. But if art embraces the world more intimately in expression, it views it with greater scope through representation.

Representation furnishes the major instance of meaning in art, and its nature may be approached from the standpoint of the concept of meaning. When meaning is taken specifically as sign-function, rather than loosely as value, it involves three terms: an object that functions as a sign, or vehicle of meaning; a further object that is meant by the sign; and an interpreter, or activity of interpretation, for which alone the two objects are united by the relation of meaning. This relation may be divided into three kinds. The referential meaning or function of a sign is a relation between the sign and a further object of any sort, of which the sign enables the interpreter to "take account"; the sign refers to or signifies the object, and the object is the referent of the sign. Thus the word *war* refers to a situation of organized violence among nations. The syntactical meaning or function of a sign is a relation between the sign and other signs that may assist the initial sign in its task of referring. The word *war* bears a logical relation of equivalence to the complex sign "situation of organized violence among nations," and it bears a grammatical relation of subject to the word *evil* in the complex sign "war is evil." The pragmatic meaning of a sign is a relation between the sign and effects upon the interpreter that result from the referential function. The pragmatic meaning of *war* may be an impulse to fight, a feeling of anxiety, or an attitude of moral outrage, depending upon the nature of the interpreter. None of these effects is referred to by the word.

Representation is meaning in the referential function, and its general nature may be developed by considering the attributes of referential meaning. Some of these attributes belong to meaning as a whole, and others only to reference; all will be stated in relation to reference, for concreteness and ready application to representation.

1. Reference involves a distinction and duality of sign and referent. In representational painting, there is a duality of the colored shape on the canvas and the tree or other object in nature. If representation is as faithful as Leonardo's was praised for being, the tree may seem to be so "real" as to appear to be present rather than represented. The duality remains, however, as the extended hand would show. The value of a sign depends on the fact that the sign differs in some respect from the referent.

2. The sign is known with genetic immediacy, the referent mediately and through the mediation of the sign. The color must be intuited before it can be interpreted as meaning a tree. But through habit the process of interpretation may become so rapid that the referent may have attentional immediacy. In both instances awareness becomes schismatic through dominance of sign or referent at the expense of the other.

3. The referent may exist, or it may not exist. The sign does not, as sign, influence the nature or existence of the referent. For artistic representation, as distinct from historical and scientific representation, the existence of the referent is irrelevant.

4. The referent is in some way absent as concerns the sign and interpreter. It may not exist; or it may be at another place; or it

may have features inaccessible to observation; or it may have features not yet noticed; or a given feature may be subsumed under a concept which implicitly relates it to similar features of absent objects.

5. Awareness shifts from the sign to the referent. The movement of awareness is one-directional, from sign to referent, any other direction being incidental. The movement is purposive, and the purpose is consummated in the lodgment of awareness at the referent.

6. The sign is subordinate to the referent, since awareness and the interest that governs awareness come to rest at the referent. The sign serves the interpreter in regard to whatever it is that is absent concerning the referent.

7. An ideal sign is transparent: it attracts no attention to its own nature except as an instrument of reference.

These traits of referential meaning define the general nature of representation. To the extent that they are qualified or absent from the aesthetic experience, the object does more than represent or does not represent. Every work of art that represents, and that has an aesthetic as distinct from a documentary value, does more than represent. The principle of transparency therefore is modified in art: no matter how well a color, shape, or sound is suited for the representation of an object, it will attract some attention for its own sake. Representation thus sets up a rivalry in art, which purely formal art is intent on avoiding, and which the representational artist tries to overcome by further modifications, this time illusory: the use of icons and symbols to make it appear that the represented object is one with the sign and present with it.

The referential character of representation clarifies the relation of representation to two adjoining terms: perception and expression. In perception, the intuited sensum refers to the perceptual object in much the same way that the color on canvas refers to a tree in the forest. The special characteristic of perception is that the referent is judged to exist and the sign is apprehended as a part of the referent. The shape of a leaf passed in the forest is regarded as part of a leaf that exists; but the shape of a leaf on canvas is not regarded as part of the represented leaf, and the latter is not judged to exist.

Expression differs from representation in most or all of the seven traits listed. The contrast of the two methods will be developed under the theory of art as expression.[8] Here it may be sufficient to say that the expression of emotion implies a much closer connection between form and emotion than representation envisages: where representation of emotion starts with a duality of form and emotion, expression starts with their "mutual immanence." If expression involves meaning in the strict sense, the meaning is pragmatic rather than referential. But pragmatic meaning also is inadequate for the concept of expression.[9]

Modes of Representation

Artistic representation varies from art to art, and from one work of art to another, in the nature of the relation between the sensed vehicle and the thing or idea that is represented. The relation always is one of reference, but reference may be engaged in under a variety of conditions which specify the relation of art to its subject matter and the freedom of the artist in representing his world. Four modes of representation may be singled out for emphasis. Artistic representation may use arbitrary or natural signs; it may be passive or active; it may be literal or symbolic; and it may be concrete or abstract. The duality involved in each of these four ways of representing should be thought of not as a sharp antithesis, of which only one of the two terms may be present, but as a distinction admitting of more or less. Thus a given work of art may be highly abstract, but still have a degree of the concreteness which may be dominant in another work of art.

A sign is arbitrary if another object might as readily have been chosen to signify the referent in question. A sign is natural if the relation of the sign and referent, independent of the act of interpreting, disposes the interpreter to use the one as a sign of the other. Meaning is not natural in the sense that it inheres in things after the fashion of shape, motion, or causal relation: it occurs only in the act of interpretation, and the interpreter may use any object to signify any other object. But the interpreter may be influenced by the relations of objects in deciding which object shall be used to signify another. The relations that make

---

[8] Below, Chap. 9, "Form as the Sign of Emotion."
[9] Below, Chap. 9, *Ibid.*

reference natural are resemblance and contiguity. If an object is similar to another in some respect, or if it occurs at the same time and place, it functions more readily as a sign of the other. A causal relation also provides a tendency toward reference, but it may be classed with contiguity: causes and effects usually are contiguous, and a marked interval between them reduces the tendency to use one as a sign of the other. If reference is based on resemblance, the sign may be called iconic; if reference is based on contiguity, the sign may be called a contiguous sign.

Contiguous signs do not occur in the sensed vehicle of art, for a work of art does not share the time and place of the objects it may represent, and it has no causal relation to those objects. A colored shape on canvas does not share the space and time of the tree that it may represent, and it is neither cause nor effect of the tree. But contiguous signs may occur when a represented object signifies a further object, as in symbolic representation; the cross represents Christianity by virtue of the contiguity of the two terms in the Crucifixion.

Art uses arbitrary signs and icons in the sensed vehicle: arbitrary signs when it must, and icons when it can. Arbitrary signs, such as most word sounds, have a high degree of transparency when mastered, since attention passes right through them to their referents: in using the word *two,* we hardly notice the sound, but dwell immediately on the meaning. But the process of mastering the sign requires a dictionary of some kind, which may not be available, and which makes the meaning mediate for attention. Arbitrary signs give no information about their objects, since they have no points of resemblance to yield clues. They do not appear to present their objects and thus to provide maximum vividness of meaning. They are most effective in representing general, abstract, relational, and nonsensory objects, but least effective in representing the concrete wealth of the world of sensible nature.

Icons are opposites of arbitrary signs in all of these respects. They may seem to be similar in regard to transparency, since a form on canvas may be noted more readily as meaning a tree than as being a shape and color. Though this awareness implies attentional immediacy for the referent, it does not imply transparency for the sign, for the attention that focuses on the tree retains the color and shape among its objects, thereby making the tree more vivid than an arbitrary sign could make it. In iconic representation, the duality of sign and referent is aggravated by the intrinsic interest of the icon, but the resemblance between sign and referent makes it possible to lessen the duality by partial identification of the two terms: the color of the icon and the color imputed to the tree on the authority of the icon are the same color.

Icons are used universally in the sensed vehicle of all but the literary arts, in which they are secondary to arbitrary signs. If it is true that the function of a building is perceived and the emotional content of the building is expressed, architecture has virtually no represented content. But when representation does occur, it is through icons, as in the resemblance to the cross of the intersecting long nave and short transept of many Christian churches. The perceived physical thing of sculpture resembles the human body, or occasionally some other organic body, and the intuited color and shape of painting resemble any perceptual thing of nature and of human existence. In both painting and sculpture, the representation of psychological states belonging to represented persons is accomplished through the use of sensed forms that resemble those that are visible in the face and body when emotion is being expressed: the facial lines of a smile or scowl are represented iconically.

The tones of music sometimes, though rarely, resemble sounds of nature, and this slight relation exhausts the representative, as distinct from the expressive, character of music. If the composition is said to represent a specific situation or event, such as the death of a great man or the antics of a clown, it is not the tonal pattern that does so, but the emotion expressed in the pattern; and the emotion is so interpreted because of a title or program consisting not of music, but of arbitrary verbal signs. These signs guide the interpreter in reference to situations whose emotional content is similar to the emotion expressed in the tones. The dance follows the principles observed by program music, in conjunction with the iconic value of moving visual forms in determining the nature of the event being represented.

The literary arts alone make use of arbitrary signs, and this is the fate of the novel and of the closet drama. The point of staging a play is to present icons that mere sounds cannot. Poetry, however, develops as far as possible the limited iconic potential of its verbal vehicle. The resemblance of what is sensed to what is meant is a leading part of the poet's art. It occurs most commonly in onomatopoeia, or the echoing of referents by sound: "adamantine chains," "murmur of maternal lamentation," and "fast thick pants." It may occur also in rhythm, as in the resemblance to the rise and fall of waves of certain lines in Part IV, "Death by Water," of *The Waste Land* of Eliot. And it may even be found at a distant outpost, when the visual form of the printed lines resembles the subject, as in Herbert's "The Altar."

A distinction that applies with equal force in every art insofar as it represents is that of passive and active. Art is passive to the degree that it reproduces, without change, the characters of things and events as found in ordinary experience. It is active when it modifies the object that is represented. The modification may be called an interpretation, and representation is active to the extent that it interprets what is represented. Some degree of interpretation is inevitable in art, for however admiringly the artist may look upon his subject, he looks from the standpoint of a system of ideas and values that belongs rather to him than to the subject, and of a medium that demands as well as it enables. It is a virtue in art, for it is through artistic interpretation that the infinite wealth of nature is combined with the defining and organizing skill of human intelligence.

Interpretation begins with selection of subject matter and within subject matter, which even the most photographic or realistic art must undertake. This selection is governed by the limitations of human attention, by the resources and limitations of a given artistic medium in representing specified objects, by the requirements of artistic structure, and by the character of the artist and his time. Interpretation continues with those transformations of a selected subject that are required in a given medium if the representation is to render, in some fairly direct fashion, the characters that are found in ordinary experience. A photograph of a house or mountain may not give as accurate an impression of the object as a painting that changes hues and light and shade, lengths and directions of lines, relations of objects in space, and apparent depth in space. A third aspect of interpretation is concerned with the relations of what is more obvious in a subject to what is less obvious but fundamental and causal. A novelist explores motives that lie behind actions, and recesses of character and feeling that are involved with motives. He may even take the whole of this literal content and make it a symbol of something of a different order.

Interpretation also seeks what is essential and universal in the subject. This may be found in the given or the obscure, though usually by passing from the first to the second. And interpretation must relate the object being represented to the values and emotion of the artist or appreciator, since nothing is represented without a reason, and the reason lies at least partly in the nature of the artist or appreciator: a nature in which value and emotion are the driving force. An artist represents external nature or his fellow men in order to fulfill himself, and his representation of the world is a covert representation of himself. But perhaps it is better to describe this as an expression of himself, and to stipulate that the self that is expressed is ideally as universal as intelligence itself.

An aspect of interpretation that has had a leading role throughout the history of the arts is one concerned with the distinction between literal and symbolic representation. A white color may be a symbol of purity of spirit, a satyr of self-conscious lust, a stair of the ascent of the soul, and a slaying of the victory of good over evil. Any of these eight terms is in itself a literal content; but the first term of each pair is a symbol if, in addition to signifying the second term, it is invested with some of the content of its referent. A symbol is a sign that has four characteristics. It must have a nature of its own, or intrinsic content, that has some interest and is readily identifiable. It must be an icon or contiguous sign. It must reflect the nature of its referent. And it must "absorb" or fuse with the nature thus reflected.

These requirements may be illustrated by a comparison of the symbolization of purity by a white color, with the signification of purity by the sound of the word *purity,* and the signification of snow by a white color. The word sound is of little intrinsic interest and is comparatively hard to identify in the sea of word sounds; it is an arbitrary sign; and it does not reflect, and thus does not absorb, the character of purity. It is a literal arbitrary sign. White is a literal icon of snow. It meets the first two requirements, and it reflects, by its resemblance, the nature of snow: not merely the whiteness of snow, but the solidity, texture, and coldness of snow. But these reflected characters do not coalesce with the white sign, any more than they do with each other in the white snow: they are united with the sign in an association that leaves them distinct from the sign. This distinction, or cool observance of boundaries, is fundamental to logical synthesis and to the formation of conceptual systems. It stands in contrast to what happens in the symbolization of purity by the white color. White is a symbolic icon of purity. The character of purity is reflected in the white sensum and coalesces with it: it seems to inhere in the sensum rather than to be juxtaposed with it. The same is true of the cross as a symbol of Christianity: the cross is a contiguous symbol of Christianity and is not a mere proxy or associate of its referent, but carries some of the content and value of what it stands for. This transfer beyond boundaries, or merging of distinctions, is fundamental to imaginative synthesis and to the formation of aesthetic structures.

The aspect of transfer and imaginative synthesis links symbol to metaphor. Metaphor involves a similar duality and transfer of terms, as in "flaming youth," "the white radiance of eternity,"[10] and "The fog comes / on little cat feet."[11] It requires resemblance in the relation of the two terms and states both terms. Symbol states only the term that is used to elucidate or describe: if it were to borrow from the metaphors listed, it would confine itself to a flame or a white radiance. Symbolism thus requires terms that speak for themselves, except insofar as the term can be clarified in the remainder of the work, or in a title (as in some paintings), or in notes (as in *The Waste Land*). The need for clarification delays the functioning of the symbol and may weaken it, since the purpose of a symbol is to convey concretely and intuitively a meaning that otherwise would fall apart, and perhaps disappear, in discursive analysis and literal reference. A symbol usually represents an object that sensation does not reach, but which introspection, abstract conception, and evaluative functions may reach. Sometimes it represents objects that lie at the fringes of human awareness and understanding: objects that are perpetually dark, except for the moment that a difficult symbol vividly realized lifts the veil. That lifting is the profoundest function of a symbol. But whether the object may be reached in its own terms

[10] Percy B. Shelley, "Adonais."
[11] Carl Sandburg, "Fog," *Selected Poems* (New York: Harcourt, 1926), p. 64.

or not, the function of a symbol is to convey the unfamiliar in the familiar, the abstract in the concrete, the discursive in the intuitive, and the spiritual in the physical: in general, to communicate the nonsensory through the sensory.

Symbols are as appropriate to poetry as are metaphors, which are close relatives, and images, which furnish the sensory content of symbols but may also have a poetic life of their own. Symbolism is least appropriate to painting. The difference of the two arts in regard to the use of symbols arises from the basic difference between these arts in regard to signs and referents. Poetry uses arbitrary signs which refer initially to abstract concepts or universals. Some of these concepts, such as father and white, admit of images, which are relatively intuitive and concrete; others, such as God and purity, do not. There is a gain in concreteness when symbolism permits the second kind of concept to be implemented by the first. But painting uses icons which refer initially to particular things or situations, which are eminently intuitive and concrete in their own right. Symbolism does not increase the vividness of these objects, but makes the objects means for the representation of concepts which frequently remain distant and pale in comparison with the objects.

This is evident in much of the allegorical painting that flourished in the Middle Ages with Christian subjects and in the Renaissance with secular and classical themes. Tintoretto's *Minerva Pursuing Venus* represents literally two female figures engaged perhaps in combat, and symbolically the rightful subjugation of erotic desire by wisdom. The figures are objects of a living intuition; the ethical import and admonition are appendices that would draw attention from the work of art if they were not so pale. We may agree with Schopenhauer that the artistic value of such painting is entirely independent of its allegorical status,[12] and with Croce that the allegory is "an expression externally added to another expression."[13]

More can be said for symbolic representation in the visual arts when the idea is more directly suggested by the symbol. In Michelangelo's *Moses* (Plate 1), the horns and tablets are minor symbols of

[12] Arthur Schopenhauer, *Die Welt als Wille und Vorstellung*, Vol. I, Bk. III, Sec. 50, pp. 280–281. *The World as Will and Idea*, Vol. I, p. 307.
[13] Benedetto Croce, *Aesthetic*, trans. Douglas Ainslie (London: Macmillan, 2nd ed., 1929), p. 34.

mystical illumination and the law received in it. Their function as symbols depends on knowledge of the title of the sculpture, the Old Testament, and other sources. Provided with these symbols, the powerful figure of Moses, with its expression of controlled and righteous wrath, becomes a major symbol of august law and of measured punishment of evil. Dali's *Persistence of Memory* (Plate 2) is a lesser achievement in art but its symbolism is autonomous, needing no knowledge of the title or literary sources or conventions: the symbolization of spent time remaining accords intimately with the emotion expressed in the limp watches. It is significant that of these two works, the greater has complete value in its literal content and the lesser depends on symbols to complete its value.

It should be noted that symbols have uneven value in literature also, despite their greater appropriateness in verbal art. In *Everyman,* the abstract moral ideas so dominate the action that the symbol virtually disappears, and with it the art. In Maeterlinck's *Pelléas and Mélisande,* action and character are much more important, but still are sacrificed to the abstract idea of man's loss and helplessness. The special merit of Ibsen's *Wild Duck* is in the mutual enhancement of action and symbolic content: this appears to be due to the fact that the wild duck stands apart from the action and adds, somewhat lyrically and meditatively, a further meaning and unity to a play that already is highly complex and unified.

Like symbolism, abstraction is an important tool of artistic interpretation; unlike symbolism, it does not use levels of meaning or content, and its role in painting and sculpture is of special importance. Representation is concrete when it renders an object, or aspect of an object, in the context of other objects or aspects, which nature usually provides. Representation is abstract when it renders an object apart from its context. The aim of abstraction is to get at the essential in the object, which abstract art conveys without the distraction of contingent elements. Abstract art applies the principle of selection, which all art must, as far as the principle can be applied. It does not simply focus on one subject rather than another, but focuses on one aspect or closely related set of aspects of the chosen subject. Its first tendency is to reduce the concreteness of space by attenuating or eliminating depth in space. This may be done to suggest more essential relations of objects in space, or to convey the immediacy of visual intuition rather than the mediateness of visual perception, or to eliminate the causal and purposive aspects of perceptual objects that have three-dimensional space as their theater, or because of that "mental fear of space" that Worringer imputed to cultures that feel "a great inner disturbance of man due to the appearances of the outer world."[14] The second tendency of abstraction is to eliminate physical detail, sometimes by schematic or stylized line, sometimes by a diffuse impression that reduces line in favor of mass, color, and light. In the third place, abstraction reduces individual physiognomy and expression in the human subject, emphasizing generic features instead. And finally, abstraction becomes quite serious and self-conscious when it focuses the forming impulse on elementary and abstract forms, such as "the cylinder, the sphere, the cone" of Cézanne,[15] and recasts the object out of such forms.

Abstraction has many degrees, depending on the extent to which any one of the four tendencies is developed, and on the extent to which the tendencies are combined. No painting is as concrete as an object in nature, and no abstraction can go so far as to eliminate the object of which it is an abstraction. Fra Angelico's *Madonna of Humility* (Plate 18), Rembrandt's *Bathsheba* (Plate 3), Manet's *Olympia,* and Picasso's *Woman in White* (1923) are relatively concrete, though differing in spatialization and in individuation of the female subject. Picasso's *Seated Woman* (1909) and *Seated Woman* (1953), Archipenko's *Woman Combing Her Hair* (Plate 4), Duchamp's *Nude Descending a Staircase,* and Lipchitz's *Figure* (1926–1930) (Plate 5) are relatively abstract. These works have a common reliance on elementary abstract forms, which are used in the earlier Picasso to portray a highly individuated face, in the Duchamp to convey an abstraction of motion, and in the Lipchitz to express a chained anguish which belongs equally to women and men. In landscapes, the range from concrete to abstract may be illustrated in Corot's *Forest of Fontainebleau* and Inness' *Delaware Water Gap,* which are highly concrete; in Hsü Tao-ning's *Fishing in a Mountain Stream* (Plate 6), El Greco's *Toledo,* and Rousseau's *Cascade,* which are more abstract but substantially concrete; and in Monet's *Bordighera Trees* (Plate 7), Van Gogh's *Crows Over the Wheat Fields*

[14] Wilhelm Worringer, *Abstraktion und Einfühlung* (Munich: R. Piper, 1921), pp. 19–20.

[15] Quoted in Alfred H. Barr, Jr., *Cubism and Abstract Art* (New York: Museum of Modern Art, 1936), p. 30.

(Plate 19), Cézanne's *Forest of Tholonet* (Plate 12), and Klee's *Landscape with Yellow Birds* (Plate 8), which involve different degrees and motives of modern abstraction.

The question may fairly be raised whether Klee's *Landscape,* apart from the birds, is abstract art, which is representative, or formal art, which is a structure of sensory elements without representational content. Abstract and formal art are frequently confused, owing to their common removal from the objects of ordinary experience. Formal art, however, does not represent or attempt to represent. Instead of starting with a thing, person, or event, on which interpretation may shed light, it starts with colored shapes or with sounds and constructs them without reference to nature. This is the usual procedure of music. It has also become a standard option of recent painting and sculpture. Widely differing examples of formal art may be found in Mondrian's *Composition in White, Black and Red* (Plate 9) and in de Kooning's *Excavation* (Plate 10). Works of this kind do not lead the imagination from the sensed form to natural and human objects, except insofar as the imagination falls prey to whimsy, which has no place in the interpretation of art. They may seem, then, to be self-contained and closeted, like the design on a rug. But they are not closeted, for they reach a world beyond the colored canvas through the value and emotion that they express. Even a rug may do this, and it is clear that the Mondrian belongs to a world far more ordered, and the de Kooning to a world far more agitated, than any inhabited by the design of a rug. But the belonging is not through reference and representation, and formal art therefore should be distinguished from abstract art.

CHAPTER 3

The Aesthetic Object
Structure and the Concept of Form

Structure and Aesthetic Structure

A work of art is not made of bare sensation or representation, but of these as qualified by structure or unity. A musical composition, painting, or poem is not made of a single element, whether sensory or representative. Music is made of many tones which are united in the same medium of time or succession in which the single tones are intuited. A painting is made of many colors, lines, and shapes which are united in the same medium of space or coexistence in which the single elements are intuited. A poem is made of many sounds which have the same general organization in time that musical tones have.

In addition to these terms drawn from sensation, structure embraces terms supplied by representation. The figures in a medieval painting of the Crucifixion are united in a scheme of personal relationships and religious significance. The plot of a novel is a continuous and interweaving set of actions which unify motives of individual characters and unify the characters in an interacting group. Furthermore, the structures of sensation and of representation are not isolated from each other, or even parallel, but are merged in the single structure of the work of art. The organization of colors and lines in a painting blends with the organization of persons and values, so that the hue, area, and place of a color, and the chromatic relation of the color to other colors, support the role intended for the person or thing represented by the color. In poetry, rhythm is a pulsation not merely of sounds, but of meanings carried by the sounds, and rhyme and alliteration are used to support meanings that have some bearing upon each other. Finally, many of the arts have special types of structure, which are specific formulas of one kind of unity or another: heroic couplets, the Shakespearean sonnet, and the epic in poetry; or the sonata form, the concerto with solo instrument and three movements, and the mass in music. Structure is indispensable in art; and there is no controversy in aesthetics about its essential role, though there is controversy as to whether structure is the dominant value and end of art.

Structure in general, as well as in art, is a mean between two extremes. At one extreme is a mystical whole, which has no internal distinctions and thus no parts; it has oneness without plurality. At the other extreme is chaos, which is sheer plurality without relation; it has no oneness and cannot properly be said to have parts, since there is no whole of which the many are parts. Structure has the oneness of the mystical whole, and the plurality of chaos: it is a one of many or many in one. Structure thus is identical with unity, which requires plurality and relations that bind the many into one. The structure of anything consists of its parts as related into the one thing, or of its wholeness diversified into related parts.

The parts of which a structure is made may be distinguished from each other in either or both of two ways. They may differ in quality, or in position in an order or medium that abstracts from quality, such as space or time. In a painting, colored shapes are distinguished by differing positions in space. The colors may be of the same quality, such as a red that is repeated, or of different qualities, in which case the parts are distinguished in both position and quality. In music and poetry, sounds are distinguished by differing positions in time and to a slight extent in space, or by difference of tonal quality, or by both methods. A difference in position is mandatory for concrete plurality of parts. Difference in quality is optional in one respect and mandatory in another. The option is not exercised in respect of a repeated quality, since the latter is of the same kind as the original quality. But even repetition requires a difference of quality, for one part could not repeat another unless another quality intervened between the two parts. A continuous expanse of red would be taken as one expanse and as one element in a structure, unless at least a draftsman's line occurred somewhere in the expanse to divide it into parts; and the line would be discernible only by virtue of having a quality different from that of the red expanse.

The relation of parts within a whole appears to have some affinity with the relation of meaning, and in particular with syntactical meaning. A color that means referentially a rock or face may also be said to mean syntactically other colors on the canvas. Since syntactical meaning was described as a relation between signs, it may not occur in the full sense when the parts are not signs, that is, when the parts do not have referential meaning. In purely formal art, as has been indicated, the sensed object has no referent. But the mutual relations of colors that do not refer are much the same as the relations of colors that do refer. In both instances there is syntax and an element of meaning that is tied in with the syntax.

A syntax consists of a scheme of fixed, coherent relations. This is the nature of syntax in grammar, where syntax consists of fixed relations in which words may stand to each other in the whole or structure called a sentence. A work of art has such determinate relations. And the syntax of a work of art involves meaning in the semiotic sense, though different in some respects from referential meaning. There is a duality of part and part, and one part may be said to mean another. Awareness shifts from the part that means to the part that is meant, as though following a trajectory of increased essence, understanding, and appreciation. The part that means is known relatively immediately, the part that is meant is known mediately. These are traits of syntactical as well as of referential meaning. But the former differs from the latter in certain ways. The part that is meant is as real as the part that means, since they are equal members of a common whole. The part that is meant is hardly absent, except insofar as it is further from the focus of attention than the part that means. The direction of meaning is reversible, and in an ideal syntax of art, every part means every other part. Furthermore, every part is an end in itself, as well as a sign of other parts. In consequence, the shift of awareness is not one-directional but doubles back on itself, with both directions retained for maximum value. The part that was mediate becomes immediate, since awareness goes directly to it in the course of enjoyment and takes it as meaning the first part. The part that means is not subordinate to its meaning, since it has comparable intrinsic value. And transparency does not hold: every part attracts attention to its own nature. If every part that means were transparent, the work of art would have no value, since it would be made of parts that have no value.

Syntactical meaning presumably may be found in any structure, whether it is a mathematical demonstration, a chair to sit on, or a work of art, that is, a work of aesthetic art. It is, however, especially prominent in art, because of the kind and degree of unity that characterize a work of art. A work of art usually is said to have organic unity, or unity similar to that of the living body, as distinct from the mechanical unity of machines and non-living things. The distinction is not absolute or thoroughgoing, since machines have some traits of organic unity and organisms have some traits of mechanical unity. A wheel does not roll as well when separated from an automobile, and the cell that an organism produces is made in accordance with chemical laws that hold in the inanimate world. But the conception of organic unity is useful in describing the relation of part to part and of parts to whole in the aesthetic object, and it is the most basic and general aspect of aesthetic structure.

In popular terms, the conception of organic unity embraces five characteristics of art. First, a work of art has whatever parts it needs: it is complete and sufficient, without gaps. The scope of the work may be slight, as in a short story, or great, as in a novel; in either instance there are enough elements for a coherent whole. This principle does not prevent a fragment, such as a temple in ruins, from being aesthetically satisfying. And it may be observed that a particular work of art may not follow the principle strictly, as in the instance of a play with inadequate exposition or motivation. Second, a work of art has no superfluous or irrelevant parts. This becomes a principle of economy, of sincerity, and of forcefulness. But it is impossible to state a general rule of relevance, which varies with the art and the style. A Doric temper has a stricter rule than a Corinthian, a classic a stricter than a romantic. And within its premises, one work of art may conform more than another. Third, the relation of parts has maximum tightness. The syntax is intricate and close. The work has a "beginning, middle, and end": at least if it is in time. But music has a far tighter connection of parts than the novel, and a story by Chekhov may end suddenly or by drift because it has no plot and no structure of expectancies. Fourth, the parts are interdependent on each other. Each receives part of its nature from other parts or the whole. A color in painting is enhanced by other colors, and a person in a novel develops in relation to other persons and to events. Finally, the whole appears to be "greater than the sum of its parts." A chord in music has greater value than the sum of the values of the tones of the scale from which it is taken.

A somewhat more philosophical account of organic unity may be directed toward the last three points, and particularly toward the aspect of interdependence. It is misleading to say that an organic whole is greater than the sum of its parts, for the excess holds only in relation to the parts taken prior to union in the whole, and the parts thus taken are not parts of the whole. The organic whole is the sum of its united parts, for the parts increase in value by virtue of their relation to each other: this is their interdependence. The increased character or essence of each part becomes a part of that part, and the several parts thus enhanced form a sum which is the same as that of the whole. The apparent excess of whole over parts, when properly understood, becomes a consequence of the interdependence of parts.

The special tightness of connection of parts in an organic whole also derives from interdependence. Two parts have maximum tightness of connection when each enters into the nature of the other: an entry more intimate than that of a key into a lock, which does not change the nature of either the key or the lock. When one part of a work of art receives a new character by relation to another, it does so in accordance with the nature of the other as well as with its own nature. The new character thus reflects the nature of the other part, and the other spreads beyond its own boundary to enter the first part. Interdependence of parts is interpenetration of parts. This interpenetration lies somewhere between two extremes, either of which would destroy organic unity. The one extreme is that of mutually separate parts, which form a mechanical whole, such as is found in the combination of a wheel and axle. The other extreme is that of complete merging of parts, which ends with one part or term and therefore no structure. Organic unity is a unity of parts which basically are distinct, but secondarily have a partial merger. Insofar as two terms merge, the boundary between them becomes indistinct, and the definition of the parts correspondingly obscure. Organic unity therefore involves a character of fusion similar to that found in symbolic representation and in intensive magnitude. This character appears to be the special province of the imagination. It stands in contrast with the discrete analysis and external synthesis of mechanical or atomic wholes, of literal representation, and of extensive magnitude.

Because of the closeness of connection between the parts of a work of art, the structure of art has a kind of necessity. One part seems to require another, for which a substitute can hardly be found; and a change in one part requires changes in other parts if not in the entire work. A feeling of unique satisfaction arises in the awareness of the appropriateness of parts in relation to each other, and the element of uniqueness testifies to the necessity of a given part in the context provided by the other parts. At the same time, there is an element of chance or freedom in the structure, for it is not possible to predict what the unperceived parts of a work will be. Given a large part of the work of art, neither the artist nor the skilled critic can foresee what will occur in the remainder. Criticism may supply rules which indicate the limits within which the structure may be located, but no rule can determine the specific structure that will come into being. And when the unperceived part has entered perception, and the feeling of unique satisfaction has occurred, only a dogmatic imagination, and therefore a spurious imagination, would assert that only the part just supplied could fit the context. This blend of liberty and necessity is characteristic of art, and it indicates that art achieves a happier combination of vitality and order than is found in most of the affairs of men.

Types of Aesthetic Structure

The unity of parts in a work of art may be accomplished in various ways, each of which supplies a specific type of aesthetic structure. The types may combine in a given work, or one may be more evident in a given work or in one of the arts as a whole. The naming and identification of the types varies among aestheticians, and not even a detailed and illustrated description can do justice to the ingenuity and subtlety of the artistic imagination in actualizing a type of unity in an individual work of art. But a philosophical account of the specific types may shed some light on their essential nature, their relation to each other, and their relation to structure in general. Five types of unity may be considered: harmony, balance, evolution, theme, and rhythm.

Harmony is unity based on qualitative similarity. In harmony, the difference of the unified parts is entirely or mainly in position, whether in space or in time, and the similarity in nature brings together in attention the parts that are separated in position. The similarity may be total or partial. It is total in the use of the same shape and size of columns in a building, of the same color in different parts of a painting, and of the same foot in poetry. It is partial in the use of the same element in parts that have some qualitative diversity: a right angle may occur in squares, rectangles, and crossed hands; a certain hue may occur in diverse values of light and dark, and a light value may occur in different hues; a tone of a certain pitch has most consonance with its most immediate partials, its octave, fifth, and fourth, to which it stands in the simple frequency ratios of 1:2, 2:3, and 3:4: common to the tone and the partials are respectively all, one-half, and one-third of the frequency of the tone.

Similarity also is partial in the use of elements that have no identical factor, but resemble one another. The direction of the circumference of a circle changes at every point, but the change is so slight that the curve of a circle at any given point is harmonious, while the angle made by the intersection of two straight lines is not in itself harmonious due to the more evident change of direction. When a slight change in the nature of elements is repeated, gradation occurs, with the result that dissimilar elements may not be apprehended as dissimilar but as harmonious. The repetition of the curve of a circle leads presently to a direction at right angles to the initial direction, but the difference in direction is lightened for perception by the intervening gradation. The same is true of the gradation of values from white to black through the grays. Gradation is an instance of repetition, and harmony is in proportion to the completeness with which repetition takes place.

Repetition is the maximum concession of the many to the one in a structure. It gives harmony the aspect of simplicity that yields the virtue of clarity and the vice of tedium. The clear simplicity of harmony is felt emotionally as assurance and tranquillity; but when time, custom, and experience accumulate, the tranquillity becomes too readily tedium, and attention lapses or moves elsewhere. It can be seen that harmony is a mode of unity which profits least from the organic potential of art. Organic unity increases the nature of a part in relation to another part. But short of a miracle, a part does not grow in value on its own, in isolated spontaneity. If its neighbor or related part is similar to itself, it receives little added value, for the related part is itself except for the difference in space or time.

The situation of harmony is reversed in balance, or unity based on qualitative contrast. In balance, the distinction of the unified parts is double, since it involves quality as well as position. The nature of balance admits of degrees. In its simplest form, balance is symmetry, or contrast in regard to a common center of similar forms. Symmetry occurs in the relation of like wings of a building, of the left and right sides of the human body, or of two phrases of similar length and pulse in a sentence. Except for the contrasting disposition of the halves around the center, symmetry is harmony. What makes it balance is the unity in contrast, which is evident here in the fact that either part of a symmetrical relation would "fall" without the opposition of the other. When balance becomes more complex, the parts may contrast not only in disposition around the center or axis, but in their own natures. A tall, slender tower may balance a low and long building. In Duccio's *Three Marys at the Tomb,* the raised and radiant figure of the angel, with a massive peak in the background, balances the more obscure figures of the three women and their slighter background. In Rogier van der Weyden's *Annunciation* (Plate 11), the intricate design of the angel's garment is balanced by large masses of color in Mary's dress and in the bed placed behind Mary. Because of such contrasts of color and shape, balance is more intricate, and the implication of part for part is more complex.

Beyond symmetrical and nonsymmetrical contrasts around a

defined center, the concept of balance may be extended to include every relation of dissimilarity, contrast, and conflict that contains unity in the contrast. What is essential to balance around the center is not the center, but the unity of opposed forces whose opposition is defined around the center. This extended unity in contrast is a regular feature of music, where less consonant intervals are unstable and lead to more consonant intervals and to the tonic as the maximum of harmony. Here contrast is of the essence of the itinerary of music, and its stresses become productive of unity by virtue of resolution of the stress in the tones that follow. The moment of stress does not itself have unity, but it is integral to a pattern that has greater tightness and variety than would occur without it.

The enlarged conception of balance has ready application in poetry, where it indicates the special interest to be found in metaphor, ambiguity, irony, and paradox. The comparison made in metaphor, as distinct from the comparison made in describing the same term under a concept, uses a context of dissimilarity between the two terms to heighten and refine the perception of similarity. Mere similarity would yield harmony and a concept or literal icon; the presence of dissimilarity enriches the relation with balance. Ambiguity, irony, and paradox also have a relation of contrast in unity, which rises to a fine thrust in irony and has the air of contradiction in paradox. But literal contradiction does not occur in paradox, for it would strip the relation of unity and therefore of balance.

In the novel and drama, conflict of motives in character, and of characters in action, is meaningful and therefore unified, and the result is balance. The enlarged conception of balance may be found in painting whenever contrasting colors or lines are unified, and particularly when the contrast rises to conflict and tension. Balance of yellow, blue, and red in a Raphael *Madonna* is relatively simple and pleases on sight; balance of more closely related hues in the Matisse *Odalisque Rouge* is more difficult and complex. In Cézanne's *Forest of Tholenet* (Plate 12), the unity of splintered lines meeting at strong angles, and of muted, irregular patches of green, blue, lavender, and yellow, yields a work of singular massiveness and vitality.

The element of conflict in balance is the maximum concession of the one to the many in structure. It gives to balance the aspect of complexity that yields vitality, forcefulness, and strength on the one hand, and the intimation of disorder, disruption, and collapse on the other. But balance does not contain disorder, since it is a mode of unity. The ideal of balance is to bring complexity and tension to the brink of disorder, but without plunging over or even slipping. Balance is assimilated conflict, in which opposing forces join toward a common purpose, their opposition resolved but not removed. Balance is not discord. In discord, opposed forces collide and disintegrate each other; in balance, they meet and enhance each other. The enhancement means that balance makes maximum use of the organic potential of art.

The difference in nature of the parts permits each part to have adequate leverage for acting upon the other. If similar parts repeat each other and therefore effect least change in one another, dissimilar parts bring novelty to bear upon each other and therefore effect most change. When difference is multiplied by complexity of parts, the scope and intensity of change in any part is increased. Partial disintegration may abet interdependence, for it may "open" a part to another and thus increase interplay, while not going so far as to destroy the identity of the part and the unity of the relation. The stress of contrast sharpens attention and heightens it, like a catalyst, so that parts and relations have more value than they would have for a milder awareness. Difference of nature, complexity, partial disintegration, and heightening of attention give the principle of organic unity its maximum opportunity in art. The passionate pursuit of this opportunity, and the endurance of its dangers in disorder and unintelligibility, are the dominant traits of contemporary art.

Harmony and balance are the principal types of aesthetic unity, and they appear in the remaining types in conjunction with special traits appropriate to the type. The defining character of evolution is development, or unity of many parts in an order of succession that cannot be reversed without destroying the unity. Evolution involves a series of changes, from A to B and from B to C, and so on; one change is not sufficient. The changes are cumulative, each building upon its predecessor in one general direction. The process terminates at a point that dominates the process and constitutes the goal of the attention that moves with or in the changes. The process may begin with separate elements, in which case it ends with the elements unified; or it may begin

PLATE 1. *Michelangelo,* Moses *(1513–1516). Basilica di San Pietro in Vincoli, Rome. Photograph, Fratelli Alinari No. 48995, Art Reference Bureau.*

PLATE 2. *Salvador Dali*, The Persistence of Memory *(1931). Collection, The Museum of Modern Art, New York.*

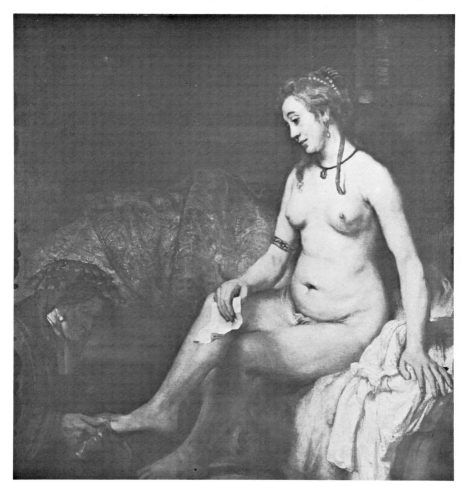

PLATE 4. *Alexander Archipenko*, Woman Combing Her Hair *(1915). Collection, The Museum of Modern Art, New York. Acquired through the Lillie P. Bliss Bequest.*

with one element and end with another and distinct element. In either instance it betrays its evolutionary nature by the impossibility of retracing the steps without losing the unity of the process. The unity of the parts consists in their common subordination to the goal that ends the process, and in the fixed order in which movement proceeds to the goal.

Evolution is most evident in the novel and in drama when plot moves to a climax and motives and characters at first hidden or separate emerge, interweave, and come to a point of decision or revelation, of conquest, defeat, or adjustment. The order of events would have no sense or interest if told in reverse; the technique of "flashbacks" does not violate this rule. Evolution appears in the progressive statement of idea and emotion in a poem, and its stages may be marked by formal divisions such as the quatrains and consummating couplet of the Shakespearean sonnet. The three stanzas of Keats's "Ode to Autumn" are successive phases of the perfection and abstraction of the idea of acceptance and repose. Evolution is inherent in musical order, since a sequence of chords has a forward tendency and the simplest melody has a finality that cannot be reversed. It is particularly apparent in the development of a theme, though it suffers a curious fate when the theme is restated at the conclusion of the movement. Evolution occurs in the visual arts when attention moves progressively from one element to another, though the elements themselves do not move. This movement usually, however, is somewhat arbitrary since there may be no single end, or the end may be approached from various starting points, or it may be approached directly by virtue of the dominance that may be involved in its being an end. It seems natural, however, for attention to move upward as to a culmination in looking at a skyscraper or a Gothic cathedral.

Thematic unity is found when an element is repeated, either completely or in a variant form, so that the element becomes the key to the work and the work receives unity from the pervasive influence of the element. When an idea or motivation dominates a novel or play by its recurrence, it becomes the theme of the work and unifies the particular decisions, actions, and persons. The role of theme is quite evident in music, where the theme is stated explicitly and at some length, then is developed or "mined" for its hidden resources, and finally may be restated to tie together the varied forms and to close in unison. Theme occurs in painting when some color, line, or shape is repeated in many places. In El Greco's *Cardinal Nino de Guevara* (Plate 13), a strong angle approximating a right angle appears in many triangular and rectangular shapes, and reinforces the volitional severity of the person portrayed. In the Persian *Youth Sleeping Under a Willow Tree* (Plate 14), long, pendant curves dominate the composition and express a relaxed and sensuous ease. In architecture, the Gothic church uses theme with exceptional scope and diversity (Plate 15). The pointed arch is a theme that recurs in windows, doorways, the low ceilings of the side aisles, and the high ribbed vaults of the bays of the nave. A somewhat more abstract theme of vertical movement links the pointed arches with the high nave, the long supporting piers, the buttresses moving upward in successive flights, and the tower. And both levels of visible theme join with and express an invisible theme: the flight of the soul from the earth to its salvation.

The last of the five types under consideration is rhythm. This type is both simple, from the directness with which it may be perceived in kinaesthetic sensation or imagery, and complex, from the possible concurrence of the other types in it. Rhythm consists of conflict brought into balance by repetition. This may readily be seen in a line of iambic verse. The weak and strong syllables of any foot, taken in merely one foot, conflict without unity and fall apart. They are discontinuous: a relation that is visible in the break of direction of the vertical and horizontal members of a step in a stair. But when the foot is repeated into a line, or the step into a stair, the conflict is assimilated, and balance in the most extended sense occurs. The repetition is a harmony of feet among each other, though not a harmony of syllables within a foot. The harmony, however, affects the individual feet, both retrospectively, as an assurance, and prospectively, as an anticipation. The result is resolution of the conflict. The resolution is a balance within the foot and indicates the organic unity of the several feet within the line.

The internal balance may be supplemented by two aspects of external balance. Insofar as adjoining feet may be experienced as contrary dispositions around the center formed by the interval between them, symmetry occurs, and a line of verse may be called symmetrical when it is a series of such symmetries. Because symmetry implies a mirror likeness of parts, a symmetrical line may become tedious, particularly when repeated. A delicate ear therefore varies the pulse, as by increasing stress in a foot, or substituting a different foot, or adding or subtracting a syllable at the end or beginning of a line. The contrast among feet thus supplied becomes a third element of balance. And beyond harmony and balance, rhythm exemplifies theme, since the recurring foot is the key to a structure and even to a style and mood. The difference in pulse of Spenser's *Four Hymns,* Milton's *Paradise Lost,* Pope's *Essay on Man,* Hopkins' sonnets, and Eliot's *Ash Wednesday* corresponds to a difference in style of thought and of sensibility, and the characteristics of the unit of pulse are a repeated index to the style. Rhythm may also illustrate evolution, as in the development of pressure in Ravel's *Bolero.*

Like evolution, rhythm is found most prominently in the temporal arts of music and poetry. But it may be found in the arts of space when it informs the movement of attention. Rhythm is of major significance in painting, where it occurs with endless variety in the nature of its unit. In the El Greco *Cardinal* (Plate 13), the angles of the robe form a rhythm as furious as the angles are sharp. In the Persian *Youth* (Plate 14), the undulating curves form a rhythm in the outline of the sleeping youth which is echoed, but changed, in the rhythm of the background mountain. Rhythm is infinitely fluent and measureless in El Greco's *Resurrection* and Van Gogh's *Starry Night.* But at the opposite pole of painting it ceases in the Mondrian *Composition* (Plate 9) noted earlier. A straight line has no discontinuity to be resolved in rhythm. It may or may not appear to move; but if it does, it lacks the propulsive force with which a unit of rhythm charges its successor.

The Concept of Form

In the account that has been made of structure, the term *form* is conspicuous for its absence. Among artists and aestheticians, the concept of form is identified with structure, and a work of art is said to "have form" insofar as it has structure. Form in this sense admits of sensation or representation or both, but it abstracts from the specific nature of parts in favor of the relations that unite them. In abstracting from the parts, this concept of form tends to view the relations with equal abstractness, as types of unity that may be found in many works of art. A second concept of form emphasizes the parts along with the relations, but restricts the parts to sensation. Here a work of art, such as a piece of "absolute" music or a formal painting, is said to "be a form"; but form is equivalent to "pure form" because of the emphasis on sensation, and the denial of representation, in the aesthetic structure. This meaning of form is central to formalist aesthetics, which will be considered later; it may be derived from the first meaning on the supposition that only in sensation can structural principles be viewed unimpeded.

There is, however, a third notion of form, which is more inclusive than the others and enables aesthetic form to be grounded in the general conception of form that occurs in the philosophic tradition. This notion embraces structure in intimate relation to parts of any kind, and adds to these certain further traits. The sum or total of the characteristics in question defines a general conception of form, by virtue of which a work of art, a mathematical demonstration, or a universal such as whiteness, two, or greater than, may be said to have form and to be a form. Form in this sense embraces the entire aesthetic object, taken as an instance of the traits now to be discussed. The third meaning of form is the one generally used in this book.

The concept of form begins with that of a character, nature, or "meaning." The character may be of any sort, subject only to the stipulation that it be capable of bearing the further aspects of form that will follow in this analysis. As bearing these aspects, the character has form and may be called a form. The character may be a quality or a relation. It may be simple or complex. It constitutes the parts that are organized into a whole, any novelty that may result from organization, and the whole made from organized parts. It may appear in a universal, such as whiteness, or in a particular, such as the white of a certain piece of paper: both of which may have the same character.

Character in an aesthetic form is supplied by sensation and representation, whether as parts prior to union or as a whole based on relations that also have a character. It is indifferent to the general conception of form whether a work of art has a representative character or is a pure form. But this indifference is not binding on aesthetics, which may legitimize or require one or the other due to conditions appropriate to aesthetic experience, but not specified in form as such.

The second aspect of form is determinateness. A character is determinate insofar as it is definite; it is definite when defined; and it is defined when it has a limit or boundary. A boundary separates one character from another, so that when the character of man or of white is predicated of an individual, it is understood that it is that character and not some other that is meant. Every form is determinate, whether it is a genus, a species, or an individual taken as a composite of characters. Only an infinite and undifferentiated whole, or mystical whole, is entirely indeterminate. But one form may be said to be more determinate than another, if it is more bounded and distinct than the other. A species is more determinate than a genus, for the differentia adds a limit to the limit established by the genus. Though color excludes sound and is thus far determinate, it is compatible with any hue and is therein indeterminate; but red excludes other hues as well as sound and is more determinate by this greater definition and distinction. Presumably an individual is more determinate than a species, since it excludes even individuals of the same species.

A work of art is a form and therefore is determinate. It is a unique individual and thus is highly determinate. A work of art cannot be substituted for another: each has a character peculiar to itself and distinct from that of any other. The words of which a poem is made may be found elsewhere, and the poem therefore is more determinate than its parts. The greater determinateness of the poem follows not merely from the summed determinateness of the words, but from the determinateness of the relations between them, and particularly from relations that are organic or internal. There are, however, qualifications to the determinateness of a work of art. Unlike an ordinary "real" or "practical" individual, such as the physical canvas of a painting, a work of art has no place or date. This aspect of art will be examined later. But it does not interfere with the determinateness of character of the work of art: on the contrary, the spatio-temporal indeterminacy of the aesthetic object provides an isolation that increases individuality. A further qualification arises from organic unity. The interpenetration of parts in organic unity makes it difficult to discern precise boundaries, and this difficulty indicates an element of indeterminateness in the parts. But the new character of the whole is quite subtly determinate, even though it cannot be traced analytically to the united parts.

The third aspect of form is unity or structure. If a form is absolutely simple in character, it has no unity of character, having no plurality to unify. But a work of art has plurality, and its form includes unity of the complex and intimate sort discussed earlier. The unity of form is the aspect of form that most readily commands attention, since many have more character and value than one, and have still more of these when united. Of the aspects of form, unity is most important, but it does not exhaust the nature of form. It has been shown that unity presupposes determinateness of parts and underlies the determinateness of a whole. And unity itself is determinate. One relation is distinct from another. Relations do not fall indiscriminately upon their terms, but are characterized by the terms they may relate and have determinate relevance to those terms.

The final aspect of form is a certain indifference to reality, by virtue of which a form may be called an essence. In the present usage, essence is not substance or essential nature. On the contrary, it is distilled in awareness and yields itself there, as though it were an appearance. But it is not appearance, if by that term is meant something opposed to reality or low in reality. Essence is character without judgment on reality, and a form is an essence. This is true alike of universals and of works of art. If a universal is judged to have or not to have reality of some sort, as in Platonic realism or in nominalism, the universal is approached as being other than merely a form. A theory of form has no comment to make on such an approach: it neither endorses it nor contradicts it. A theory of form belongs to dialectic, and problems of reality to physics; and the first can be pursued without the second.

The status of an aesthetic object as an essence can be traced through three stages. To begin with, an aesthetic object has no date or place. It is temporal or spatial or both, depending on the nature of the object or art. But it has no context in time or space to which it belongs. This may be seen in a painting. The space of the canvas and of pigments as physical objects is part of the space of the room in which the painting is hung, but the space of the painting as an aesthetic object cannot be so located. This is true not only of the space of a representative painting, but also of the space of a formal painting. And the time of a musical composition is not part of the time series in which the tones as physical or sensory elements can be dated. The work of art has a time or space of its own, which has no common boundary with parts of ordinary time and space. This isolation does not imply that art is independent of a historical culture, or that it has no effects in human life and experience.

The isolation of the aesthetic object continues in the separation of the object from the causal series in which things and events usually occur. A tree as a living thing has roots that anchor it in the ground and bring nourishment to it, and as a physical thing it provides shade as a relief from the heat of the sun. The same tree as an aesthetic object has no roots other than those that may be visible, and those that are visible have no function other than to be seen. The shade of the tree is cool only as a color of a certain hue and value: it does not invite escape from the sun, or remind us of past relief. The events of a novel do not have the connection with a larger causal context that may be found in the events of a biography. To be sure, a work of art has its own causal character, in which parts condition each other. It has motion, force, and vital pulsation, which yield a charged and active syntax. To the extent that it is modeled on a subject, as in a novel, it observes the laws of the subject, such as the laws of human motivation and conduct. Furthermore, the aesthetic experience, like every other event, has causes and effects: but these are not attended to in the experience. Even the emotion expressed in the form, though quite real and conditioned by the form, stands apart from the stream of emotion of ordinary experience.

In addition to spatio-temporal and causal disengagement, the aesthetic object is removed from the sphere of substance, and that removal is of most importance for the status as essence of the object. In the broadest sense, substance is equivalent to independence of existence of an object in relation to the knower and other objects. In this sense, any character has substance if it is thought to have reality on its own: given this condition, even an abstract universal such as two and a concrete sensory particular such as a red color are substances. But essence entails no ontological judgment. It makes no difference to art whether the content of sensation or of conception is subjective or objective. The green color of a leaf seems to be "out there," and the aesthetic consciousness is content with that seeming, since it is interested in the scheme of color and relations rather than the ontological locus of the scheme. A character, however, is not usually thought of as having reality in its own right, except when a Platonic interpretation assigns a nontemporal reality to universals. To secure independence, the concept of substance usually is tied in with the concept of a ground, which supplies to the character independence of the knower, though not of the ground. The factor of independence then shifts to the ground. Since the ground has no character, it is entirely indeterminate. For two reasons, then, the alleged substantial ground of an object is foreign to aesthetic experience: it has an ontological claim or charge, and it is indeterminate. The ontological claim is explicit in the concept of substance. The indeterminateness may be less evident, but it is logically inevitable. The green color may be grounded in the leaf, which is determinate, having a shape, size, and weight. But the last three terms are characters, which also need a ground. The result is a logical movement to an indeterminate ground quite different from the leaf that first offered itself to the color.

The notion of form as defining the aesthetic object thus sets a limit on the perceptual interpretation set forth in the analysis of sensation: for aesthetic perception, an object has as much character as a given theory of aesthetic interpretation will permit, but for no theory does it embrace substance and a judgment of existence. The theory of art as representation allows a maximum of character, and the theory of art as pure form excludes some part of that maximum range. The theory of form as determinate and unified essence, however, may be accepted by both theories.

CHAPTER 4

Emotion

The Role of Emotion in Art

An emotion, such as joy or sorrow, love or hate, may figure in human awareness in three distinct ways. It may be represented or referred to, just as a chair or centaur may be represented. It may be represented in general terms, as in a psychological or philosophical study, or in specific terms, as in the description in a novel of the subtle nuances of fear and the circumstances under which they are experienced by the persons of the novel. When an emotion is represented, it does not exist in the interpreter of the representation, or it exists only incidentally: the emotion is thought of or conceived, rather than felt or experienced. Such an emotion may be as much a part of the aesthetic object and form as a color or human face.

The second mode of awareness of an emotion is that of simple arousal. The emotion is actual, and it is felt or experienced; and the feeling and actuality are those of the ordinary, "real," and "practical" function of emotion, without modification by form. Simple arousal occurs in the ordinary course of living, when someone feels an emotion from some cause, is involved in it as his own emotion, and may act or wish to act in some way appropriate to the emotion. Simple arousal may be due to a representation, as when a bald statement in a letter leads the reader to tears. It may occur in the appreciation of a work of art, as when the reader of a mystery story is afraid of the silence in his own room or the reader of a romance falls in love with the hero. Whether this kind of awareness is appropriate to the aesthetic experience will be discussed later. Appropriate or not, the emotion thus felt is a response to a stimulus, and to an aesthetic form if the stimulus is a work of art. The form is an object, or something that stands over against attention as its goal or terminus, whereas the emotion is a more subjective element that seems to qualify attention or awareness itself. In hearing bad news, the news is an object, whereas our sorrow seems to stain our consciousness.

The last kind of awareness of an emotion is that of expression, or objective contemplation. The emotion again is actual and felt, but it sustains a striking modification by intimate relation to form, which distinguishes it from simple arousal and the experience of emotion in ordinary living. The emotion also is a subjective response to an objective form, but becomes secondarily an object by virtue of its expression in the form. The factor of contemplation will be discussed in the next chapter, and the element of expression will be set forth at length in Chapters 8 and 9. In these places, a judgment will be made on the aesthetic relevance of the three modes of emotional awareness.

Whether emotion is represented or actual, aroused or contemplated, it appears to have an important place in aesthetic experience. The lives of artists often have an emotional brightness and color, not to mention fierceness, that are less conspicuous in the lives of philosophers, scientists, businessmen, and men of other sorts; and the life of the artist is more closely interwoven with his work, as is indicated by the comparative emphasis on biographical studies in the scholarly interpretation of works of art. The process of artistic creation has an emotional charge that is due not simply to creating, but to creating a form that itself has an emotional charge. The relevance of emotion to the work of art often has been stated by the artist. At random we may note the statements of Wordsworth, that poetry "takes its origin from emotion recollected in tranquillity"[1]; of Wilfred Owen that "The Poetry is in

---

[1] William Wordsworth, "Preface to the second edition of the *Lyrical Ballads*," *Complete Poetical Works,* ed. A. J. George (Boston: Houghton Mifflin, 1932), p. 797.

the pity"[2]; and of Eliot, that a poem should furnish an "objective correlative" of an emotion.[3]

The aesthetic object or form has many evidences of special relevance to emotion. Sensation has a decided affinity with emotion, as will be detailed later, and the emotion is not merely thought of, but is experienced with the sensation. The represented content of a work of art usually consists of things, persons, events, and general ideas that have an emotional content apart from artistic representation. Nature to the poet and painter is emotionally fertile: the experience of Wordsworth with nature, as boy, youth, and man, is only a highly reflective instance of a general occurrence. The great themes of art, as of life, are erotic love, death, and deity, and these themes are perpetual foci of human emotion. In representing them, as in representing anything else, the artist is as immediate and iconic as possible, and these methods bring the emotion closer to the contemplator and tend to make them actual in the experience of contemplation. An image or narrative elicits emotion much more readily than an abstract concept, and the artist deals with the former rather than with the latter. This is true also of symbol and metaphor, which do not particularly satisfy the intellect, but reach the sensibility through the associations of the symbol, the concreteness of symbol and figure, and the subtle shock and expansion due to unexpected comparison. The unity of art reflects the structure of emotion. The interpenetration of organic unity is like that of emotion, which drifts, permeates, and has no fixed boundaries. Emotion thrives on contrast, and conflict of elements in a form is ultimately emotional. Rhythm has marked emotional import. At one end of its scale, it builds up a physical emotion through movement of the body. At the other end, it frees emotion from the abstraction of concepts, while containing it in the regular recurrence of the unit.

Despite these indications of the emotional import of art, it is not uncommon to hear arguments against the use of emotion in the aesthetic experience, and particularly against the experience of emotion by the appreciator as a response to the aesthetic object. There are many reasons for the rejection of emotion in art,

[2] Wilfred Owen, *Poems* (New York: Huebsch, 1921), Preface, p. ix.
[3] T. S. Eliot, "Hamlet and His Problems," *The Sacred Wood* (London: Methuen, 7th ed., 1950), p. 100.

or in aesthetics, and some of them arise from legitimate concerns although they do not thereby reach legitimate conclusions.

The behaviorist or physicalist regards emotion as too mental and inward a term. He prefers to speak of events with spatial coordinates, which may be investigated publicly and even may be measured. The events may be responses of the physical organism, or the work of art taken as an external and "objective" thing. The behaviorist represents the interest of scientific method in the study of art. By a perverse paradox he goes beyond a description of what the aesthetic phenomenon is, to a prescription of what it ought to be. Such prescription is not authorized by science. And the description that can be made in physical and behavioral terms is meager, if not foreign to art.

The color of a painting, which presumably can be seen by many people, is a quality that cannot be measured. Its identity in the experience of many percipients cannot in principle be verified. Beyond the object, the neuromuscular response of the appreciator of the work of art is largely unknown to him, to the artist, or to the critic. It is of interest for the description of aesthetic experience only insofar as it can be correlated with a peculiarly conscious event, a sensation, emotion, or idea: and it is these that are of aesthetic importance. A work of art comes from a complex and subtle inwardness, which is made objective or "outward" in the aesthetic form. The objectification modifies but does not negate the inwardness. The emotion objectified by the form finds in the form a vehicle by which it may, to a surprising extent, be shared by many persons. Art and science both pursue intersubjectivity or shared awareness, and art need not borrow from science in pursuing this common end.

The ethical voluntarist regards emotion as an inferior condition of consciousness, characterized by passivity and other forms of weakness. In the conduct of life he prefers volition to feeling; from art he wants a strengthening of will, and he is not reluctant to dispense with art altogether because it is not sufficiently muscular. The position of the voluntarist assumes a false dichotomy of will and emotion. Willing and striving have an emotional character, of confidence and anxiety, of achievement and frustration. Their goal, which is part of their reason for being, is nothing if not enjoyed, which implies emotion. What the voluntarist really values is an emotion of power. This is not to deny emotion as such, but to limit it. Limitation on positive and socially compatible emotion, however, is an ethical impoverishment, and it may be a cause of mental discontent and illness. What is more desirable is power in an emotion, particularly if the power is not egocentric. Such power, in a contemplative rather than practical form, is precisely the characteristic of emotion in art, as the expressional interpretation of art makes clear.

The intellectualist emphasizes ideas in art, and the deliberate analysis of structural features of forms. Ideas do indeed have a large place in art, but they are not alternatives to emotion, since they enter into the aesthetic form to which the emotion is a response. The selection of ideas in art, and their handling in art, is such as to unite them with emotion rather than to set up an antagonism. To make ideas the exclusive goal of art is to invite unfavorable competition with philosophy and science, which have greater resources for specifically intellectual activity because of their command of methods of analysis, abstraction, generalization, and inference. It is scarcely necessary to point out that in the systematic analysis of structures, an individual aesthetic form dissolves into abstract forms or formulas. A knowledge of these formulas is necessary for the artist, and useful to the appreciator in the initial stage of the apprehension of the work of art. But in the final and finished awareness of the work as an individual aesthetic form, the knowledge of formulas must be superseded by an organic intuition, or it must melt into the intuition without explicit remainder.

The moralist is not opposed to emotion as such, but wishes to censor certain kinds of emotion in art. He may object to the representation of emotions and situations of pride, lust, cruelty, or pity, because of fear that the appreciator will be led to experience these emotions during and after the moment of aesthetic enjoyment. The moralist errs in not understanding the difference in nature and function of emotion in ordinary life and in art: a difference that depends on the unique distance, disinterest, and expressed or objective character of emotion in art.

The formalist opposes formal beauty and perfection of form to emotion, and seeks to eliminate emotion from the aesthetic experience. It is likely, however, that his real aim is to eliminate from art emotion as it occurs in ordinary life. But no art of consequence merely duplicates the emotion of ordinary life in its

content: and no art repeats it in its form, as the expressional
theory shows. The attenuation or elimination of representational
forms does not imply the disappearance of emotion as such. It
means merely a shift toward kinds of emotion that are abstract,
having no specific context from ordinary life, or formal, having an
object solely in the sensory form.

Apart from any special theory or bias, the discerning critic
objects to sentimentality in art, and when his discernment wavers
he may identify sentimentality with emotion in general. But the
two terms are distinct, as they must be if human life, and art,
are not to be somewhat of a farce. Granting the distinction, it
does not lie in the specific nature or color of an emotion, for
every emotion may be sentimental under certain conditions, and
no emotion need meet those conditions. The condition is not one
of weakness in the person involved, or of demonstration and ex-
ternalization of the emotion, or of demonstration of weakness.
Lessing wisely observed that, in Homer's view, only the civilized
Greek could at once be brave and yet weep.[4]

The condition is not one of delicacy as opposed to vigor, for
delicacy may have qualities of discrimination and penetration that
indicate an alert sense of value. It is not triviality, which would
be overlooked or passed by rather than rejected. The condition
evidently is one of unreality or falsity. This character is more
easily felt by the critic than defined. The emotion plainly is real,
since it is experienced. It is not a proposition or assertion, which
is the proper subject of truth and falsehood. But a sentimental
emotion does involve a disproportion between the substance and
the appearance of what is felt: the appearance, whether in the
recesses of consciousness, or in verbal demonstration, exaggerates
the substance. When the exaggeration is done for extrinsic
reasons, it is hypocrisy; when it is done for intrinsic self-enjoyment,
it is sentimentality. It is difficult to show in general terms what is
substantial and what is not in emotion. But the discrimination
required for artistic form is inimical to sentimentality, and sentimentality is unable to stand up against the distance of objective
expression.

All of the replies to the six arguments against emotion in art

---

[4] Gotthold E. Lessing, *Laokoon*, in *Sämtliche Schriften*, Vol. IX, ed. K. Lachmann (Stuttgart: Göschen, 1893), Pt. I, Sec. 1, p. 9.

obtain some of their meaning and support from an expressional theory of art. This is proper and inevitable, for the expressional theory alone makes emotion fundamental (but by no means exclusive) in aesthetic experience, and alone undertakes an explicit and systematic account of the place of emotion in art. But the replies to the objections may be accepted in spirit, and in various details, by other theories of art, though these theories are not equipped to undertake as full a justification of emotion in art. The role of emotion in relation to a given theory of art will be set forth in Part II.

The replies also derive meaning and support from an analysis of the nature of emotion. It is not hard to show that emotion has a relation to experience and to value that explains its commanding place in human life and in art, which is both a mirror and creator of life. Emotion is steeped in experience and bears the characters and colors of experience. It does not arise in a vacuum. It is securely lodged in experience that transcends emotion, and it is differentiated by the causes and contents of experience. The factors out of which experience arises are the self and its world, and emotion testifies to the nature of both of these. It testifies either directly and concretely, when an emotion is associated with a specific circumstance of the world and a specific problem and action of the self, or indirectly and abstractly, when it is a distillate from one or many circumstances and actions, which may have disappeared from attention but live on, subtly and intimately, in the tissue of the emotion. Emotion is not, however, an impassive mirror of experience. What it particularly discerns in an experience is its value or disvalue: its value in joy and love, its disvalue in sorrow and anger. When value and its negative are apprehended immediately, the awareness is an emotion. Values may be apprehended mediately in thought, as an object of sign function in the referential mode. Mediate awareness of values is necessary to understanding and control of values, and there is no quarrel between the two approaches. But a value is fully real only when realized, and it is realized only in immediate experience, that is, in emotion. The value of a friend, or the evil of death, are realized only in the emotions of love or of despair: not at the symbolic remove of thought, however profound and specific.

The relation of emotion to thought often is misunderstood as

one of antagonism. But thinking, like every other activity, is
enhanced by emotion in the form of an accompanying pleasure.
It has a goal, the value of which is realized in emotion. Emotion
for its part is enhanced by thought. The experience out of which
emotion arises is ordered and diversified by thought, which
supplies meaning and structure. Without thought, experience
lacks scope and emotion is narrow and often shallow. It is therefore true that thought without emotion is merely technical and
instrumental, and emotion without thought is blind and often
inane. Art is the most systematic realization of the interdependence
of thought and emotion, for it expends great thought on the
production and discernment of form, and form lives in its relation to emotion. The vitality of form is most evident from the
standpoint of an expressional theory, which will be set forth later.
But the relation of emotion to thought, experience, and value is
evident in general terms in the constitution of emotion, as will be
apparent immediately.

The Nature of Emotion

Emotion is susceptible of five characteristics: an object, a feeling
of pleasure or pain, a further feeling which may be called an
"inward texture," sensations derived from bodily events, and an
attitude or "set."

An emotion usually has an object, which may be present in
sensory feeling, intuition, or perception, or may be represented in
memory, imagination, or conception. The object may draw upon
a minimum or a maximum of experience and thought: it may
be a red color that alarms an infant, an animal's tracks that
excite the hunter, or the vision of a dead universe that desolates
the philosopher. In addition to its "descriptive" characters, the
object has the prescriptive character of value or disvalue. The
tracks are not simply indicators of an animal of a certain kind
located at a certain place, but of the good of food and the trial
of skill, and of the evil of physical hurt and death.

The ascription of normative character to the object implies no
theory of the objectivity or independent reality of the value.
Whether the value is discovered in the object by experience or
reason, or is conferred on the object by desire, will, or emotion,
it appears to our experience and thought as an attribute of the

object. This character survives even when the descriptive characters are absent, as is the case when the emotion is said to have no object. Emotions may have no object in the descriptive sense. What are sometimes called moods, and pathological states of sensibility, appear to have no discernible object. But emotion in the aesthetic experience always has an object, which is the aesthetic form. It is sometimes said that in listening to music we feel without knowing why we feel. But there is a conjoint object and cause, which is the organized tones: the object of our emotion is the tones.

As indicated in the preceding section, a value may be known mediately or immediately. When it is known mediately it is known through the mechanism of signs, concepts, and judgments: a mechanism that involves no more emotion than the awareness of the descriptive characters that the value may qualify. Thus we may judge, as intellectual beings, the evil of a murderer with no more emotion than we judge his height or age. But when the value is known immediately, the awareness involves pleasure or pain, and every feeling of pleasure or pain is an immediate awareness of value or disvalue. This statement also may be interpreted with maximum flexibility. That pleasure is the immediate awareness of value does not mean that pleasure is value or the source of value: the intent is epistemic rather than ontological.

Pleasure and pain are the necessary and sufficient characters of emotion, as the term is used here. Other experiences may or may not have them, but an emotion has one or the other, and sometimes both. The primary division of emotions is that of emotions based on pleasure, such as joy, love, and hope, and emotions based on pain, such as sorrow, hatred, and despair. An emotion may involve both: hatred is pain in another person's happiness and pleasure in his misery. In this instance, pleasure and pain are distinct in nature, but intermixed because of the concomitance of their causes or objects. In other instances, the line between pleasure and pain becomes subtle and elusive, and it is difficult to discern the one without the other in the same nature. This will be noted further in a later place,[5] for the highest art seems in some respect to transcend the ordinary distinction of pleasure and pain.

The transcendence may be evidence of the qualitative differenti-

[5] Below, Chap. 11, "Tragedy as Power."

ation of pleasures and pains; for if pleasures were all alike, and pains were identical in an opposite kind, it should be easy to separate them in nature or character. Pleasures and pains are to some extent diverse in quality, and the diversity is correlated with the diversity of objects. The pleasure of one wine is different in nature from that of another, and the variation of the pleasure is not reducible to the variation of the object or taste. The aesthetic object has a varied, subtle, and highly controlled spectrum of characters, and the pleasures and pains that respond to it are also varied, subtle, and highly controlled.

If there should be any error in the ascription of qualitative diversity to pleasures and pains, it would arise from confusion of pleasure and pain with the third characteristic of emotion, the "inward texture," in which diversity is paramount. As emotion becomes complex, it achieves an aspect of depth and inwardness that contrasts with the more superficial, or objective, aspect of the object, and that is less evident in pleasure and pain. The depth and inwardness are attributes of the self, and they mark the specific contribution of the self to the emotion that begins with the awareness of an object, moves forward with approval or disapproval by the self in pleasure or pain, and is completed in the realization of self in the inward texture.

The self has a fund of sheer inwardness which is indefinitely varied, fluent, and elusive. The particular character of this inwardness undoubtedly arises in part from the objects of experience: directly from the object presented or represented for the emotion, and indirectly from an indefinite context of objects of past experience. The indefinite context is sifted in memory until the outlines of events and persons are blurred and the lines of association are hopelessly confused: only the savor of value remains, individuated by the context, but unable to restore the context. The savor contributes to the inward texture. But the specific character of the inwardness arises also from the concrete individuality of the self, apart from the influence of the world of objects. The self is not simply a transcript of the world, able only to organize contents taken from the world. It is itself a part of the world, endowed with specific characters like any other part, and more richly endowed than those parts that are only inanimate or subhuman. The inward texture of emotion is the most concrete actualization of the self, and it may be said to be the primary mode in which the self experiences itself. In the inward texture, the self is most deeply and subtly aware of itself and evaluates itself in that awareness. It appears to dilate and brood upon its evaluation and to seize itself in the act of evaluation. That seizure is appropriate, for the self is the source of value and the only object of unconditioned value.

The inward character of emotion appears to be the same as the "feeling" (*Gefühl*) that was described with fine accuracy by Volkelt in his analysis of emotion. Volkelt emphasizes the sheer immanence of feeling: the feeling is contained and complete within the self. "Joy is a particular way in which the self has and experiences itself in its selfhood, is inward to itself. In contrast to objectivity, it is its immanent condition (*Zuständlichkeit*) to which the self is immediately inward."[6] The feeling is organic rather than atomic: "This immediate inwardness (*Selbstinnesein*) implies that the self has itself in its undivided wholeness, in its unanalyzable unity."[7] The inwardness is not reducible to any other aspect of experience: "The undivided inwardness of our *Zuständlichkeit* is a unique mode of consciousness. . . ."[8] It is opposed not only to objectivity, but also to tension toward activity. Granting that hope, love, and indignation, for example, have a character of striving, there is something that lies below the tension, striving, and transcendence:

> Even in these emotions there lies at the bottom of the self a "condition" (*Zustand*), in which the self is contained simply. One must consider: each emotion exhibits a specific quality. In this quality the self "stands," the self "rests," the self is "filled." This momentary quality is the "*Zustand*," in which the self is simply contained without that tension of transcendence (*Darüberhinaus*).[9]

The theory of inward character of emotions needs to be protected against misinterpretation. The negation of striving is not a denial of activity, as though the heart of an emotion were inert: on the contrary, the inward texture is a concentrate and plenum of the activity of awareness, as is indicated by the diverse

[6] Johannes Volkelt, *Versuch über Fühlen und Wollen* (Munich: Beck, 1930), p. 12.
[7] Volkelt, pp. 12–13.
[8] Volkelt, p. 15.
[9] Volkelt, p. 14.

color of the emotion, the activity of evaluation, and the alert focusing of awareness. The inward character is not divorced from the world and its experiences, for the "savor of value" from objects is integrated with the contribution of the self, and no fixed line can be drawn between the self and its world. The inward character is not egocentric, for what is important is its tapping the deepest resources of the self, rather than its being located within the privacy and possession of "my" consciousness. And it may be brought out of that privacy into a social light. This is done by art, which is the mode of experience that perfects the inward character of emotion and makes it communicable. Without lessening the uniqueness of the self in distinction from its environment, art fashions an impersonal and public self, which is the locus of the emotion experienced by the appreciator of the work of art. The sequel will clarify this function of art.[10]

The fourth aspect of emotion is quite distinct from the third and leads to an interpretation of emotion that contradicts, or threatens to contradict, the theory of inward texture. An emotion may have a marked bodily character. In strong anger, the sympathetic nervous system and the adrenal glands are active; the stomach is inhibited and the heart works harder; circulatory and muscular changes in the face may lead to pallor and scowling, and the whole body may be propelled in attack.[11] These events illustrate the biological function of emotion in summoning the resources of the body in an emergency situation. Sensation of such bodily events appears to be at an opposite pole from the inward texture: the one is outward, "physical," directed beyond itself, and characteristically violent; the other is inward, "psychical," self-contained, and characteristically subtle. Nevertheless they may coexist, perhaps in an inverse relation to each other, such that an emotion distinguished in the one aspect is slight in the other. Difficulty arises, however, when psychological theory asserts that sensations derived from the bodily changes are the sole conscious content of emotion, apart from the consciousness of the object that sets off the changes. Such an assertion was made by William James and by Carl Lange; it appears to ignore,

[10] Below, Chap. 5, "Disinterest."
[11] Compare R. S. Woodworth, *Psychology* (New York: Holt, Rinehart & Winston, 4th ed., 1940), pp. 426–431.

deny, or strangely convert the inward texture of emotion: but the issue is mixed.

In his *Principles of Psychology,* James wrote:

> Our natural way of thinking about these coarser emotions is that the mental perception of some fact excites the mental affection called the emotion, and that this latter state of mind gives rise to the bodily expression. My theory, on the contrary, is that the bodily changes follow directly the perception of the exciting fact, and that our feeling of the same changes as they occur *is* the emotion.[12]

> The more rational statement is that we feel sorry because we cry, angry because we strike, afraid because we tremble, and not that we cry, strike, or tremble, because we are sorry, angry, or fearful, as the case may be.[13]

> If we fancy some strong emotion, and then try to abstract from our consciousness of it all the feelings of its bodily symptoms, we find we have nothing left behind, no "mind-stuff" out of which the emotion can be constituted, and that a cold and neutral state of intellectual perception is all that remains.[14]

> Where an ideal emotion seems to precede the bodily symptoms, it is often nothing but an anticipation of the symptoms themselves."[15]

James then went on to include in his theory certain ingredients of the "subtler emotions," or "moral, intellectual, and aesthetic feelings."[16]

James misrepresents ordinary experience and his own theory in saying that "we feel sorry because we cry," and the like. Common experience shows that a person may weep in joy as well as in sorrow; the shedding of tears and the derived sensations do not distinguish the one emotion from the other, and therefore do not enter very deeply into the nature of either emotion. The

---

[12] William James, *The Principles of Psychology,* Vol. II (New York: Holt, Rinehart & Winston, 1890), p. 449.

[13] James, p. 450.

[14] James, p. 451.

[15] James, p. 458.

[16] James, pp. 468–470.

theory that James is setting forth contemplates not so much peripheral bodily changes and sensations of them, as internal, visceral changes and their derived sensations. A more accurate statement of the theory is that we feel sorry because our visceral organs or (less politely) our belly is behaving in a certain way. Presumably the theory regards the tears as a physical effect of the visceral condition, and the feeling of grief as an effect in consciousness and epiphenomenon of the visceral condition.

Certain difficulties arise regarding the visceral condition and sensation. The organic states in anger and in fear of a kinetic type are said by investigators to be similar.[17] A man running very hard in a track meet may have an organic state similar to that of a man running from danger.[18] Laboratory and clinical observation show that emotion, or at least its peripheral bodily expression, may occur despite visceral anesthesia. James notes the case of a boy who was "entirely anaesthetic, inside and out, with the exception of one eye and one ear," but who "had shown shame . . . and grief."[19] In obedience to his theory James observes: "It always remains possible that, just as he satisfied his natural appetites and necessities in cold blood, with no inward feeling, so his emotional expressions may have been accompanied by a quite cold heart."[20] So strained a view should have more than a theory to commend it.

We may also inquire about the nature of the "mind-stuff" that is denied, and the nature of the "feelings of . . . bodily symptoms" that are affirmed of emotion. James does not deny that emotion includes a state or process of consciousness: the word *feeling* means at least that much. In denying to emotion the nature of "mind-stuff," he should be understood to mean that the conscious state is not a substance, or an attribute of a spiritual substance, but has a ground or cause in a physical thing or event, such as a nerve fiber active in a certain way. Such a view of consciousness is compatible with the most introspective theory of self and inward texture of emotion: the theory does not state the ultimate nature and dependencies, if any, of consciousness. But the denial by James of "mind-stuff" in the emotion is not simply the assertion of a correlated neural state. It is also the assertion that the

---

[17] Woodworth, p. 428.
[18] Woodworth, p. 437.
[19] James, Vol. II, pp. 455–456.
[20] James, Vol. II, p. 456.

neural state is caused by some visceral change, as of the action of the stomach or heart, and that the conscious quality or content correlated with the neural state has an object in the visceral state, on which it is a report: the sensation of trembling is a report on the organic state of trembling. This is the purport of the "feelings of bodily symptoms," which are implied by James to be the alternative to "mind-stuff," the intellectual perception excepted.

There is, however, an alternative, which lies between bodily feelings and discarnate spiritual substance. The alternative consists of conscious states or feelings that may well depend on neural states, but have no special connection with the visceral condition or environment and make no report on it. This alternative is acceptable to the theory of the inward character of emotion. Like the theory held by James, it is not strictly a theory of the nature of consciousness, but a theory, and alleged description, of the contents or objects revealed to the conscious process. For James, emotion is a feeling of bodily states and nothing else; for the theory of inward texture, emotion also, and most profoundly, is a feeling of qualities that cannot significantly be described as bodily.

The gap between the two accounts is narrowed somewhat by James's view of the organism as a "sounding-board." "The various permutations and combinations of which these organic activities are susceptible make it abstractly possible that no shade of emotion, however slight, should be without a bodily reverberation as unique, when taken in its totality, as is the mental mood itself."[21] If the metaphor from sound is appropriate, it contains a tacit admission of priority of the "shade of emotion" to the "bodily reverberation," since a sound has a nature and existence prior to its reverberation. Furthermore, the organism as a sounding-board is much more diffuse in its activity than a particular organ, or even the body trembling as a whole. Given such diffuseness, organic sensation loses the local character of sensation, and the report on bodily activity becomes extremely vague: we cannot say that our heart hurts, or that our breathing is calm, but only that our body is astir. At this point the line becomes obscure that divides feelings of bodily states from feelings that have no bodily reference.

[21] James, Vol. II, p. 450.

It is indubitable that the self is intimately related to the body, and a poet may affirm the relation with conviction and ardor. But when the self celebrates the body, it need not limit itself to a report on the body. In erotic love, as distinct from erotic sensuality, the self lives partly, and most meaningfully, in an awareness that has no bodily report: the awareness of the inward character of emotion. And the self may feel complex emotion without any relevant bodily sensation. The melancholy of passage and evanescence is different from that of mere denial; the melancholy of the passage of the year in autumn is different from that of the passage of the day at twilight; and the melancholy of a ruined field in autumn is different from the melancholy of a single weed that stands in the sun, faded, brittle, but exquisitely shaped. No organic state is visible in these experiences, and if it were, it would distinguish them as clumsily as an axe would separate the petals of a flower. The emotions are distinguished initially by the differences of their objects. But the heart of each experience is a character that eludes the organic state and passes beyond the object.

The aesthetic experience emphasizes the inward texture of emotion and has less place for sensations of bodily changes. William James found an important place for bodily sensations in the "secondary emotions" of art: "A glow, a pang in the breast, a shudder . . . may be felt the moment the beauty excites us."[22] A reviewer of Housman wrote that Housman "knows the very essence of that strange imperious stuff which sends a quiver along our nerves, chills our blood and makes the skin roughen as though a cold breeze had suddenly blown upon us."[23] Nothing may be said against such bodily celebration of a poem: it signifies full submission to the meaning of the poem, as of lovers to each other in ecstasy. But the meaning of the poem is not found in the quiver and chill, however sharp; it is found in the inward texture of the same emotion, to which the bodily sensation is a witness.

Bodily sensation is particularly relevant to the final aspect of emotion, which is a "set" or attitude tending toward action of

[22] James, Vol. II, p. 470.
[23] Sterling North, Review of *The Name and Nature of Poetry*, by A. E. Housman, *Chicago Daily News*, June 21, 1933, p. 16.

some kind. Emotional awareness is not simply contemplative, registering the character of an object, a pleasure, a texture, or a bodily condition; it is also practical, containing an impulse to do something about the character. The maximum of practicality is found in the tendency of the aroused organic state, where it exists, to lead to external physical action in regard to the object: to flee from the object in fear, to embrace it in love, or to destroy it in anger. The energy for the external action is supplied by the organic state, and the sensation of the state furnishes a conscious incitement to the action. This pronouncedly practical nature of the organic state and sensation indicates that the latter are mainly or entirely means rather than ends, being of value because of the action they cause rather than of value for themselves. The instrumental role is a further argument against organic sensation as essential to emotion, since emotion indubitably occurs in aesthetic appreciation, but is an object of contemplation rather than a cause or set toward external action. Apart from such action, however, set occurs in emotion as a tendency to prolong or to shorten the experience of the emotion itself. Pleasure endorses itself and seeks its maintenance; pain rejects itself and cries out for respite. This phase of emotional set is compatible with the emotion as an end, for the maintenance is of the experience as an end in itself, and the respite is from an intrinsic evil.

Emotion and Sensation

The emotion experienced by the appreciator of a work of art arises from two sources. The one more readily noticed is representation, as when a painting of a mountain arouses emotions of awe, adventure, or curiosity, or a painting of the Crucifixion arouses emotions of sorrow, sympathy, and penance. When emotion is based on representation, it tends to have several characteristics. It may not be universal, due to variations in the experience and evaluation of the represented object among individuals, cultures, and times. It may be specific or may at least readily receive the name of a specific emotion, due to the specificity of the object. And it may fall apart from the work of art, due to trains of association that start with the object as represented but end elsewhere.

The situation of emotion is somewhat different when the source is sensation. Apart from any representation of things, persons, events, or abstract ideas, a red color may be felt as stirring, an acute angle as agitated, and a melody as somber, charming, or wild. The emotion based on sensation is more universal, due to the universality of its cause in human perception. It is less specific, or is less readily named, though it varies subtly with variations in the sensation. It maintains an integral relevance to the work of art, since it is based on no specific associations but is founded on the present sensed content, and is founded on that content with its present structure. Emotion derived from sensation requires the utmost support from the determinate structure of the work of art: a single color or tone does not have the emotional potential of a single person or event.

The relation of emotion to represented objects is not of distinctive interest to the aesthetician. Approximations to the emotions and objects occur constantly in the ordinary course of life, and the relations between them draw in varying degrees on instinctual needs and learned associations. But the relation of emotion to sensation is of special interest to the aesthetician, for the sensation that elicits the emotion is especially the property of the aesthetic experience, and the connection between the two is a challenge to general theory, psychological and metaphysical.

An attempt to establish a connection between emotion and sensation was made by William James, in the theory that an emotion essentially is a mass of organic sensation. The criticism of the theory made in the preceding section was not directed toward any general thesis of the relation of sensation and emotion, but to the special thesis that emotion is a sensation, or other experience, of bodily changes. James appears to have made an important exception to his theory, or to have broadened and diluted it by extending it from organic sensation to sensation in general, in a brief statement about "aesthetic emotion, pure and simple." He states that

> The pleasure given us by certain lines and masses, and combinations of colors and sounds, is an absolutely sensational experience, an optical or auricular feeling that is primary, and not due to the repercussion backwards of other sensations elsewhere consecutively aroused.[24]

[24] James, Vol. II, p. 468.

This emotion is not to be confused with the "secondary emotions" mentioned earlier, which are posterior to it and are identified with organic rather than visual or auditory sensations. But James did not develop his view of the emotion derived from color and sound as "an absolutely sensational experience." We may conjecture that here, too, sensation is taken as the explanatory term and emotion as the term to be explained. But no concepts are introduced to refine upon the notions of sensation and emotion and to clarify their relation. For a general theory of the relation we may turn to Charles Hartshorne, whose *Philosophy and Psychology of Sensation* puts a subtle introspective and metaphysical capacity to work on the single problem of the relation of sensation and emotion.

Hartshorne uses the terms *feeling* and *affection* rather than *emotion,* but all three terms appear to have important common denominators in the character of value and in closeness of relation to the self. Feeling is said to resemble emotion "in certain respects," but not to embrace or require the "marked consciousness of intrabodily activities" connoted by emotion.[25] " 'Affection'— pleasantness–unpleasantness" is stated initially as "one among a number of dimensions of feeling,"[26] but appears in practice to be used interchangeably with *feeling.* The analysis of sensation and feeling is part of an idealistic ontology in which feeling is the basic constituent of reality; sociality, or " 'feeling of feeling' " is the basic relation; and sensation is assimilated through its foundations in feeling and sociality.

We may begin with Hartshorne's denial of any relation of learned association between a sensation, such as a certain color, and a feeling, such as joy, which is experienced on the occasion of the sensation. The relation is not a "purely personal" one which "reduces art creation to a pure gamble."[27] The relation is not cultural, uniform within a culture but varying among cultures. The use of white in Chinese funerals

> is no proof whatsoever that the Chinese feeling for white is different from ours (do we not call white a "pure" color, see in it a certain detachment from the passions and the joys of life?) but suggests rather that the Chinese do not share our conviction that

[25] Charles Hartshorne, *The Philosophy and Psychology of Sensation* (Chicago: University of Chicago Press, 1934), p. 7.
[26] Hartshorne, p. 7.
[27] Hartshorne, p. 169.

the symbols connected with a funeral should be such as to express
solely the sheer negativity, destructiveness, and despair of death,
which our black does for us (and would, I believe, also do for the
Chinese).[28]

The relation is not one of conditioning from a uniform natural
environment, as from sky, leaves, and blood. Such a relation would
imply "rather drastic differences between city dwellers and country
folk" and would be subject to "personal and eccentric associations."[29]

The three denials have some force, but are not entirely convincing. The argument regarding cultures opens the probability
that the use of different colors in a similar circumstance, such as
a funeral, reflects not a difference of feeling toward the colors,
but a difference of feeling toward the circumstance. The probability requires, however, anthropological confirmation: and the
mere relevance of an empirical inquiry is disturbing to a non-
associative theory, which envisages a necessary connection between
sensation and feeling to which exceptions are impossible. Apart
from necessity, uniformity of connection is not open at present to
scientific establishment, due to the number and variety of persons
that must be sampled, the inadequate definition of the characters
involved, and the privacy of the experience in which the connection is to occur. A learned association may be entirely uniform if
the terms are sufficiently simple and common. It therefore is impossible to refute an associationist theory on the basis of uniformity of connection or to establish the thesis of uniformity if it were
sufficient for refutation. The experience and hope of the artist, to
which Hartshorne appeals more than once, indicates a postulate
rather than a fact, and a postulate limited in scope. The artist
wishes for, but cannot forecast, an audience that shares his appre-
ciations, and he works with some innocence as to whether the
product will be shared by some men or by all men, and whether
the sharing is due to a common association or to innate principles.

If the connection between sensation and feeling is not learned,
it must be innate, and this is Hartshorne's view. A physiological
theory of innateness asserts that "the mechanism which produces

[28] Hartshorne, p. 170.
[29] Hartshorne, p. 173.

the sensations in question is innately integrated with a mechanism which produces the feelings."[30] The main objection to this theory is that "such innate integrations appear rather exceptional in the makeup of the human mind, which is characterized by a remarkable freedom in its responses from any such predetermined patterns."[31] It may be asked, however, whether Hartshorne's own view permits any greater latitude of affective response to sensation, since it seals the one within the other. The theory held by Hartshorne asserts an immediate qualitative identity, partial if not total, between the sensation and the emotion. The feeling tone of a sensation is intrinsic to the sensation and fundamental to it. The gaiety of yellow "is the yellowness of the yellow," and "the sense datum green . . . is the coolness itself."[32]

The relation of sensation and feeling is further stated in the theory of "the affective continuum, according to which the dimensions of sensory quality are identically dimensions of affective quality."[33] There are four principal dimensions of feeling, each of which admits of continuous variation between opposite poles and is independent in variation of the others. The dimensions are "self–other, active–passive, positive–negative, faint–intense."[34] The dimension of self and other involves distinctions in space and in time: in space, for instance, the "zero of perceived depth is one's self, the maximum or infinite of depth likewise the infinite of social independence."[35] Activity and passivity involve "the exertion and the sufferance of power or influence,"[36] presumably by the self or subject of the feeling. The distinction of positive and negative is found in pleasure and pain, love and hate. Intensity is "the degree . . . with which a factor is present."[37] These dimensions are found initially in feeling, and are confirmed in sensation. The sequence apparently indicates the priority of feeling over sensation: feeling is not a charge upon an already determinate sensation, but a matrix upon which sensation is determined.

The dimension of self–other, with its distinction of depth in

[30] Hartshorne, pp. 173–174.
[31] Hartshorne, p. 174.
[32] Hartshorne, p. 7.
[33] Hartshorne, p. 126.
[34] Hartshorne, p. 196.
[35] Hartshorne, p. 197.
[36] Hartshorne, p. 195.
[37] Hartshorne, p. 195.

"space," or of distance of some character from the self, affords a general distinction between feeling and sensation. Feelings are subjective or self-oriented, near, and diffuse; sensations are objective or self-opposed, far, and localized. The distinction thus found between feeling and sensation is not absolute, however, but relative, consisting of degrees on a line of continuous variation. On a line of increasing distance Hartshorne places successively "sorrow, grief, unpleasantness, pain, sour or bitter in taste or smell, sad sounds, blackness, etc."[38] For pleasant experience there is a related succession: "joy, pleasure, sweet tastes, fragrance, sweet sounds, joyful colors."[39] The position of a sweet taste illustrates the graduated nature of the spatial distinction. Sweetness has an aspect of value judgment, which places it near the subjective pole along with pleasure and joy; but it is more neutral in regard to value than these feelings, since it may be disliked: thus it is further from the self than they are.

In addition to the positional distinction of feeling and sensation, which is entirely credible in theory and confirmable in immediate experience, Hartshorne asserts a consequent qualitative differentiation, which is far less evident. Taking pleasantness and warmth, he appears to claim the generation of determinate sense qualities by a mere shift of position.

> What is the quality of sweetness if not a pleasantness sharply localized on the tongue instead of vaguely suffused over a larger area of consciousness?[40]

> When I conceive of the warmth as out there where a color ordinarily is, I find that my conception is unmistakably that of the sort of color that would be called "warm," namely, a reddish or orange glow.[41]

It is difficult to agree to these assertions. Sweetness is pleasant, though not as solidly or invariably pleasant as a feeling of pleasure; but it has a character of its own which is not exhausted in the character of pleasure, however specific the pleasure. Pleasure

---

[38] Hartshorne, pp. 205–206.
[39] Hartshorne, p. 206.
[40] Hartshorne, p. 204.
[41] Hartshorne, p. 204.

is comparably localized in sex sensation, but it is not there tantamount to sweetness; and the difference between the two pleasures or sensations is not in the report on different organs. A blind man would not spatialize bodily warmth as a red color or any other color. What is left to the assertion is the attribution of a feeling of warmth to the color, but not the constitution of the color, as red or as color, out of the feeling, or out of the bodily sensation of warmth to which the feeling is an analogue. In general, space has no magic by which to differentiate characters through mere difference in position. It would need intrinsic characters of its own to do so, and such characters, rather than those of feeling, would account for the qualities of sensation.

The role of the other three dimensions in Hartshorne's theory may be seen in his analysis of color, where the spatial dimension is constant at a relatively objective position. The analysis lists four primary colors: scarlet and sea-green, the one active, the other passive, and both neutral in regard to joy–sorrow; and buttercup yellow and violet, the first joyous, the second sorrowful, and both neutral in regard to activity–passivity. Joy and sorrow are the positive–negative dimension; activity and passivity are identified with warmth and coolness. In addition, white and black are respectively intense and faint. Apart from the chromatic determination of the primaries, which is a difficult matter on a purely visual level, certain questions arise regarding the relation of the sensory to the affective elements, which are regarded as dominant in the sensory and as furnishing the order of the hues.

We may ask to what extent the affective dimension of joy–sorrow describes the chromatic contrast of yellow and violet. Joy may be taken as an abstract characterization of yellow, to which the hue adds a specifically chromatic determination; or it may be taken as a concrete characterization, as though it were the heart or ground of the determination. When the gaiety of yellow is said to be "the yellowness of the yellow," and the two are said to be "identical in that the 'yellowness' is the unanalyzed and but denotatively identified x of which the 'gaiety' is the essential description,"[42] the affective term appears to be taken as a concrete characterization. But here, as in the preceding instances, there is a gap between the affective and sensory qualities. The gaiety of

[42] Hartshorne, p. 7.

yellow, however determinate it be as gaiety of yellow, resembles the somewhat different gaiety of a conversation more than it resembles the visual character of yellow, though a conversation is not particularly a visual experience. Yellow and violet are truly opposed in affective tone, but they resemble each other more than either resembles a conversation, whether gay or funereal. If gaiety serves for the description or analysis of yellow, it is because it has a nature that occurs apart from yellow and therefore cannot penetrate the heart of yellow. The truth seems to be that each is a distinctive and unique character, related to the other in some important and intimate way, but not identical with the other. And the difference fits into a division of general type, for the gaiety loses its nature when separated from value and pleasure, but the yellow does not.

Hartshorne observes that persons skilled in matching colors depend on their awareness of affective tone. But it cannot be alleged that persons with "sterilized sensa," to use Collingwood's phrase, are as unperceptive of the hue as they are of the absent feeling. The color remains: it is not seen as another hue or as gray. The expert matcher may be registering not a more exact hue, but a shade of feeling correlated but not identical with the hue, and more eloquent than the hue.

Similar remarks may be made about the identification of the scarlet and sea-green contrast with the active–passive dimension. In addition, the neutrality of this contrast in regard to pleasure–pain seems to strip the colors involved of the heart of affection. Perhaps Hartshorne wavers in this matter, since he speaks in one place of the "quiet cheerfulness" of green.[43] Such a description accords with experience, and it restores or enhances affective character; but it raises a question of the effectiveness of the joy–sorrow dimension in characterizing hues, since positive affection then must account for hues as diverse as yellow and green. The active-passive dimension may well indicate abstract characters belonging to red and to green. But it is not clear that activity and passivity belong originally or peculiarly to affection; they may therefore belong to sensation without implication of the presence of feeling in sensation. The same is true of intensity–faintness in the white-black contrast. A more systematic analysis of the nature and mu-

---

[43] Hartshorne, p. 254.

PLATE 5. *Jacques Lipchitz,* Figure *(1926–1930). Collection, The Museum of Modern Art, New York. Van Gogh Purchase Fund.*

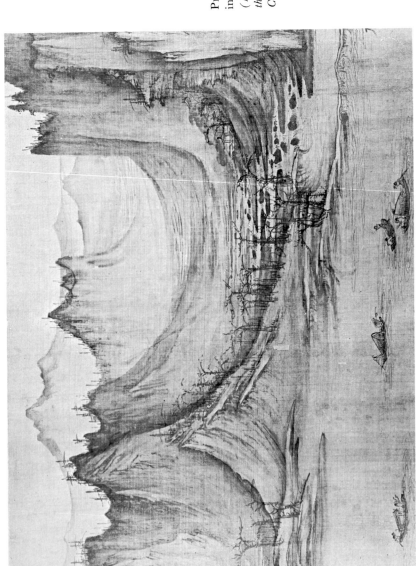

PLATE 7. *Claude Monet, Bordighera (1884). Courtesy of the Art Institute of Chicago.*

PLATE 8. *Paul Klee*, Landscape with Yellow Birds *(1923). Owned by Herr Richard Doetsch-Benziger, Basel. Permission SPADEM 1968 by French Reproduction Rights, Inc.*

tual relations of this pair of dimensions is required. They may overlap, or have a common denominator in strength. They may be so general as to apply to all sensation, in which case the neutrality of yellow and violet in regard to activity–passivity would be an anomaly. They may appear as nonaffective ingredients of pleasure–pain, violating the independence of dimensions essential to Hartshorne's color scheme.

In summary of this evaluation of an intriguing theory, it appears that the characters comprised in the dimensional analysis of feeling have a complex and undetermined relation to sensation. None of them is a concrete characterization of a sensation. Activity–passivity and intensity–faintness are abstract characters and constituents of sensations. Pleasure–pain are not intrinsic to sensation, whether concretely or abstractly, but arise in consciousness on the occasion of sensation: they are correlates rather than components of sensation. Although a uniform association and evaluation, as of red with blood and danger, may yield a uniform connection, the sheer diversity of colors in the spectrum, and of feelings regularly and subtly correlated with them, suggests a more intimate connection than association can readily supply. Blood, sunshine, leaves, and sky do not yield as elaborate a tissue of feelings as those elicited by the nuances of sensation, of red, yellow, green, and blue. Some innate connection between sensation and feeling, apart from experience of things and events, seems to be required. If the connection is not of identity, total or partial, it must be one of cause and effect. A color is a cause, or partial cause, of a feeling, or their neural causes are similarly related; and the partiality of the cause answers to variation in the existence, intensity, and character of the feeling.

One element of the relation of feeling and sensation has been left out of this discussion: the objectification or embodiment of the feeling in the sensation, which gives the feeling the appearance of being intrinsic to the sensation. But the appearance of such a relation may not be the reality of the relation, and aesthetic experience is not concerned to decide between the alternatives. If the feeling is intrinsic to the sensation, it will doubtless appear to be lodged with the sensation, or embodied in it. If it is correlated by association or by a more direct causal relation, it may be experienced as lodged in the sensation or in the self, depending on the attitude of the percipient. The objective or object-centered aspect of the feeling does not settle the question of the actual relation of feeling and sensation. It is, however, of great importance to aesthetic experience, where it takes the general shape of the embodiment of feeling in form, whether sensory or nonsensory. In that guise it will be discussed further, in the theory of expression.

CHAPTER 5

Contemplation

The Aesthetic Attitude

The aspect of contemplation in aesthetic experience rounds out the basic nature of the experience. Contemplation embraces the awareness to which the other factors of the experience appear and the disposition or attitude of the self that governs the awareness. It is the most subjective element of the experience, for contemplation as an act of awareness has its seat at the heart of the percipient, at a point more inward than even the emotion experienced by the percipient on the occasion of the form. The movement inward from object to emotion continues and terminates in contemplation. But the awareness has an attitude which, without contradiction of what has just been said, makes contemplation highly objective.

In the aesthetic experience, the natural object or work of art is engaged for its own sake rather than as an instrument of our practical action, and the emotion is contemplated for its own characters rather than taken as an incitement to action or as a constituent of the self. Contemplation of a tree implies that we enjoy the tree in the mere àct of looking at it, apart from its timber, its fruit, or its shade. And contemplation of the pleasure or other emotion occasioned by the tree implies that the emotion is otherwise related to the self than the emotion of joy on the successful completion of some plan of action.

The spirit of aesthetic contemplation has been set forth in two well-known passages in the literature of aesthetics. In his essay on "psychical distance," Bullough described the contemplation of a fog at sea:

> Abstract from the experience of the sea fog, for the moment, its danger and practical unpleasantness . . . direct the attention to the features "objectively" constituting the phenomenon—the veil surrounding you with an opaqueness as of transparent milk, blurring the outline of things and distorting their shapes into weird grotesqueness . . . note the curious creamy smoothness of the water, hypocritically denying as it were any suggestion of danger; and, above all, the strange solitude and remoteness from the world, as it can be found only on the highest mountain tops: and the experience may acquire, in its uncanny mingling of repose and terror, a flavor of such concentrated poignancy and delight as to contrast sharply with the blind and distempered anxiety of its other aspects.[1]

Noteworthy in this description are the abstraction from "danger and practical unpleasantness," which in another situation might be a similar removal from success and practical pleasantness; the emphasis on the object, of which the blurring and grotesqueness should be taken as incidental, or as dramatic indicators of the removal from ordinary reality; and the "mingling of repose and terror" which testifies to the distance of the emotion from the self.

A more complex, metaphysical, and debatable description of aesthetic contemplation was made by Schopenhauer, who wished to show in contemplation the denial of the will on the part of the subject or percipient, and the denial of relation and individuation on the part of both the object and the subject:

> If one . . . surrenders the whole power of his spirit to the intuition, sinks into the intuition, and lets his entire consciousness be filled by the peaceful contemplation of the directly present natural object, such as a landscape, a tree, a rock, or a building; while he . . . wholly loses himself in this object, that is, forgets his individ-

---

[1]Edward Bullough, " 'Psychical Distance' as a Factor in Art and an Aesthetic Principle," *British Journal of Psychology*, Vol. V, June, 1912, pp. 88–89.

uality, his will, and remains only as a pure subject, as a clear mirror of the object; so that it is as though the object alone were there, without anyone that perceives it, and he can no longer separate the person that intuits from the intuition, but both have become one, since the entire consciousness is filled and occupied by a single intuitive image; if in such degree the object has passed out of all relation to something outside itself, and the subject out of all relation to the will: then, what is so known is no longer the individual thing as such, but it is the Idea, the eternal form, the immediate objectivity of the will on this level; and thereby the person engaged in the intuition is no longer an individual: for the individual has lost himself in such intuition: but he is a pure, will-less, painless, timeless subject of knowledge.[2]

The attitude with which these quotations are concerned is complex and hard to unravel. It may perhaps be analyzed in two phases of interest or desire: intrinsic interest and disinterest. In aesthetic contemplation, the object, emotion, and awareness are valued intrinsically, as ends, rather than extrinsically, as means. But this condition is found also outside of the aesthetic experience. The special character of aesthetic contemplation lies in the disinterest with which the intrinsically interesting item is approached. The disinterest in turn admits of two phases: an attitude of detachment, or disengagement of the experience from the self, and the parallel attitude of objectivity, or absorption in the object. Even these phases are not unique in the aesthetic experience. But when they are concerned not simply with a literal or customary object, such as a sensum, thing, or concept, but with an experienced emotion, they define aesthetic contemplation proper. In aesthetic experience, not only an object, thing, or truth is contemplated disinterestedly: the experience reveals its special virtue in the disinterested contemplation of emotion.

The concept of contemplation applies primarily to the appreciator of the work of art or of natural objects. The words "appreciator" and "contemplator" have been used interchangeably for that reason. The concept does not apply as directly to the artist, for he does not merely look or listen, but goes through a process

---

[2]Arthur Schopenhauer, *Die Welt als Wille und Vorstellung*, Vol. I (Leipzig: F. A. Brockhaus, 1891), Bk. III, Sec. 34, pp. 210–211. *The World as Will and Idea*, Vol. I, 231.

of making which is partly extrinsic in its value, and experiences an emotion of creation that drives passionately toward the completed work of art as its goal. This will be evident presently. But intrinsic interest and disinterest are present to some degree in the creative act, for the artist makes an object for aesthetic contemplation and has a similar though fragmented attitude toward the object as it develops under his hands. Apart from the creative act, the artist more than any other man is saturated with the spirit of contemplation: this is his attitude toward the experience, reality, and values on which he draws during creation. While not forgetting the requirement of originality, we may agree with Schopenhauer that genius has "the most complete objectivity, that is, objective direction of the spirit, as opposed to the subjective direction towards one's own person, the will."[3]

Intrinsic Interest

Aesthetic contemplation is an activity of intrinsic interest and value, and the interest may be approached through the activity. It is well to stress that contemplation is active, for a hurried, extroverted, or muscular view of life is apt to condemn contemplation as inert, idle, and worthless. But contemplation is active, and it is active in a high degree. Activity is defined by two characters: by change of some sort and by freedom in change. Change implies a cause, and freedom implies that the cause lies within the changing thing. Whatever changes has some freedom, for it changes in accordance with its nature, which therefore is a cause or partial cause of the change. And whatever is free has some limit to its freedom, insofar as its changes are effects or causes of changes elsewhere.

Without stating at this point a theory of aesthetic freedom, it is clear that contemplation is a complex of activity, and perhaps a silent whirlpool. Contemplation is awareness or consciousness in a certain mode, and consciousness is inherently connected, or charged, with time and change. The atom of classical physics changed only externally, from one place to another, and made that modest change only because of changes in external forces.

[3]Schopenhauer, Sec. 36, p. 218. *The World as Will and Idea*, Vol. I, 240.

But consciousness is vibrant and literally alive. It is a stream that presses forward at every moment of its time, and does so of its own internal tendency. Contemplation is attentive, and attention shifts or renews itself from moment to moment, refreshing awareness and keeping it alive. Contemplation is highly concentrated and alert in its attention, undistracted by irrelevant stimuli and searching the nature of every relevant stimulus. This may be seen in the aesthetic contemplation of a single color, which exhausts the color in a demanding awareness. Contemplation, however, pursues relations and meanings, which are not thrust upon awareness but must be pursued by an alert intelligence. The object thus contemplated is evaluated in emotion, which has been shown to be an immediate and vivid judgment of value and thus of the position of the contemplator in regard to the object. The emotion, though held at a distance, is susceptible of a pure intensity. In all of these ways contemplation is not merely active, but exceptionally active, though it contracts no muscle and moves no body.

Activity is of two kinds. It is immanent if it is complete in its own nature and self-contained. It is transitive if it is completed in another activity or in some thing. Every activity is both immanent, since it has a nature of its own, and transitive, since it has effects: the distinction becomes arbitrary, because of the indeterminateness of the concept of completeness. An activity, however, may be said to be complete in itself if it satisfies an interest within its own nature and boundaries, and to be completed in something else if the interest is satisfied only by what lies beyond the activity. This is to say that an immanent activity may be defined as the object of an intrinsic interest, and a transitive activity as the object of an extrinsic interest.

Aesthetic appreciation is an immanent activity of intrinsic interest and value. It has a well-defined nature of its own, given by the aesthetic form, the experienced emotion, and the time during which the awareness occurs. It also has effects at later times, which are less determinate but of undeniable reality and variable importance. These effects may vary from a condition of tranquil sensibility to a desire for action of some kind suggested by the aesthetic object. Some of these effects would indicate imperfect contemplation. But though the experience may cause these effects, it is not a means to them, since it is not engaged in for their sake.

Aesthetic appreciation is of intrinsic value, for it is engaged in for no value other than its own. We enjoy the work of art as an end and are motivated to look or to listen solely for the experience contained in that act. Contemplation is a self-contained activity, internally diverse and alive, but bounded and made complete by an interest fulfilled within its borders.

The condition of the artist is more complex, as regards interest, than that of the appreciator. Artistic creation is an activity of making which is directed toward the work of art and terminates in that object. The nature of the object is not clearly known until the object is finished, but it is adumbrated during the creative process by concept, image, and emotion; by rules of technique; and by the nature of the medium with which the artist works. Whether clearly or obscurely anticipated, the work of art is intended as the end and goal of the creative act, which is felt as satisfied and brought to rest in the work of art. The artist works for the sake of an object and relevant emotion, which he and others may contemplate. To this extent, the activity of art is transitive and of extrinsic value. Furthermore, the artist experiences during the creative process an emotion of a rather generic sort, distinct from the emotion that is appropriate to the specific object being made. That emotion literally is an inspiration to make something, a pleasant and restless urge to create, which becomes painful when blocked by uncertainties and blind alleys in the creative process. The inspiration and urgency indicate a transitive aspect and an extrinsic value in the emotion, in comparison with the intrinsic value of the object and emotion that are to be achieved through the creative process. This is a further evidence of extrinsic interest in the activity of art.

At the same time, the activity has value in itself. Creation has pleasure in the anticipation and excited approach to the object, or to some part of the object that is about to dawn. More profoundly, creation has pleasure in the sheer power of the creative act: a power and pleasure that are accorded to genius, leaving all other men stranded. For these reasons the artist may spend little time with the finished work, but may go on to the creation of a second work, and then another, as though creating were of greater consequence than what is created.

Systems of philosophy have a watershed in their respective preferences for creation and creature, and the Bergsonian preference for creation finds authority in the behavior of the artist. In meta-physics, a creative compromise may be found by considering the creature as a creator. This synthesis is not possible for the artist, since the work of art cannot itself create. But another synthesis is possible. The work of art develops during the creative process, and it is contemplated with the keen eye of the person who is responsible for the growth. The contemplation is limited by crea-tive and critical factors that are dominant, but these factors can-not occur without awareness of intrinsic interest in the object. The contemplation is fragmented, because of the incomplete-ness of the object and the succession of trials and revisions. But it is there, and expands as creation prospers, until it can take over when creation is over and the work can be experienced as a whole. The work of art thus does not stand aloof from the creative process, and the intrinsic value of the one is an aspect of intrinsic value in the other. The activity of art is both extrinsic and in-trinsic in value, in contrast to the exclusively intrinsic value of the activity of aesthetic appreciation.

The complexity of artistic creation gives it a significant relation to work or labor and to play, without causing art to be identified with either of these. Ducasse proposed that art, in a generic sense similar to that defined in Chapter 1 of this book, be divided into three species according to the locus of the intrinsic value govern-ing the art. The species are "ectotelic" art, or useful art, which finds its value in a result external to the activity; "endotelic" art, or art characterized by "objectification of self," which finds its value in a result contained in the activity though distinct from it; and "autotelic" art, or play, which uses the intended result merely to support the activity, which in turn is the locus of value.[4] If we imagine a carpenter, sculptor, and child making their re-spective objects, and distinguish between the activity of making, the object made as the direct result of the activity, and any ob-jective beyond the direct result as the indirect result, it appears to be Ducasse's view that the carpenter values the indirect result, the sculptor objectification of feeling in the direct result during the activity, and the child the activity.

Accepting in essence Ducasse's distinction between work and

---

[4] Curt J. Ducasse, *The Philosophy of Art* (New York: Dial Press, 1929), pp. 99–113.

(aesthetic) art, we may qualify it by observing that the two are similar in having an aspect of extrinsic value, but dissimilar in the location and weight of that value. The activity of the artist is for the sake of the direct result, which completes the situation with its intrinsic value. The activity of the carpenter is superficially for the sake of the direct result, but really for the sake of the indirect result, in relation to which the direct result has only extrinsic value. The relation of means and end occurs twice in work and once in art, and the difference is fundamental. Furthermore, the extrinsic value of the activity of art is accompanied by an aspect of intrinsic value, as indicated earlier in the discussion of the pleasure and power of the creative act, whereas the activity of work, if taken purely as work, has no intrinsic value and may often be experienced as drudgery or boredom. These distinctions hold even though no concrete case may exemplify them absolutely. To some extent the artist labors, and the laborer may enjoy his activity in its own right and by transfer from the value of the final result.

The distinction made by Ducasse between art and play is substantially correct, but it is subject to certain qualifications which indicate, as Ducasse apparently agrees, that the difference between the two activities is not solely a matter of the locus of intrinsic value. If any activity is engaged in for its own sake, it is play, which usually is said to be done "for the fun of it." Ducasse's view that the end or result of play is trumped up for the sake of the activity is illustrated when a child contentedly destroys the sand castle it has made and goes on to make another. But it is hard to draw the line between the pretense that the result is of value, and a momentary but genuine belief in the value of the result. Nor is it easy to distinguish between the result in its own right, and the result as an instance and symbol of ability to produce results in some specified manner of acting: the one may be dismissed, but the other may be valued; and the value may indicate an aspect of the general subordination of activity to results. In addition, an activity and its product have some degree of interdependence of nature, which causes interdependence of value; and the choice of one product rather than another within the scope of the activity reflects a value set on the product.

From the side of art, the intrinsic value of the act of creating is a point of similarity to play. From the standpoint of the locus of value, it is easy to establish a clear distinction between work on the one hand, and art and play on the other; but it is less easy to distinguish between art and play. Except for the speculative theory of the utility of play as preparation for adult responsibilities, which makes no difference to the experienced structure and values of play, play resembles art and differs from work in having no objective beyond the result that completes the activity. But there is no sharp and fixed distinction between art and play in regard to the comparative value of activity and result. Undoubtedly the result has greater value for the artist than for the player, and the activity has greater value for the player than for the artist. And probably the artist values his result more than his activity, and the player does the reverse. But this probability indicates a dominant rather than an exclusive interest.

Despite the similarity of art and play with regard to the target of interest, and the spontaneity of both in contrast to the comparatively compulsory nature of work, art differs from play in certain important respects. Art has a character of seriousness that play does not have. This belongs to art irrespective of its subject matter and tone: it belongs to comedy as well as to tragedy. It is difficult to define the quality of seriousness that distinguishes art from play. It is not a difference in the estimation of their activities by artist and player, for a man playing tennis, or a girl playing with a doll, may set a high value on the play and be absorbed in it. It is rather a difference in scope and reality. Art draws upon an indefinitely large tissue of experience and meaning, which it absorbs and formulates; but play separates itself from life. This is shown in the function of much play as relaxation and escape, and in the contrast between genuine art and entertainment art. Art pleases inherently but entertains incidentally, and when it becomes essentially entertainment it passes into play. Art meets, formulates, and perhaps resolves problems of life, which play tends to ignore or to bypass. And when play takes on scope, as it perhaps does when a girl imitates adult concerns in playing with her doll, it does so without the reality implied by art. Imagination is involved in both instances; but in play it takes the place of reality or intervenes between player and reality, whereas in art it probes into reality.

The scope of art means that art draws more fully on the self than play. The escape of play often is an escape from self. But the self contains a multiplicity of evaluations, which are emotions when immediate. Art engages the diversity and subtlety of emotion far more than does play: compare a dancer with a tennis player. The emotion of play is experienced without the disinterest of the emotion common to the artist and appreciator. Play draws on limited parts of the self and its emotion, but does so with the self-appropriation of ordinary experience. Art draws on an indefinite amount of the self and its emotion, but contemplates them disinterestedly. The distinction between art and play may be found more readily on the ground of disinterest than of intrinsic interest.

Disinterest

The disinterest of aesthetic contemplation is not a lack of interest. Such lack would mean boredom, cessation of activity, and sleep, and it would contradict the intrinsic interest of the experience. Disinterest is intrinsic interest in a certain condition. The analysis of that condition is more difficult and hazardous than the analysis of intrinsic interest. But the condition appears to be made of reciprocal moments: a detachment of interest from the self, and an attachment of interest to objects. We may begin with the second.

Contemplation is characterized by a riveting of attention and interest upon objects, to a degree and even of a kind not found in other experience. The objective direction of contemplation is emphasized in the quotation of Bullough, which speaks of directing "the attention to the features 'objectively' constituting the phenomenon" and vividly describes an object of contemplation.[5] It is indicated in the statement of Schopenhauer that one "wholly loses himself in this object . . . and remains only as . . . a clear mirror of the object; so that it is as though the object alone were there."[6] Contemplation is steeped in the characters of the object: the scope and perfection of the aesthetic form draw and sustain attention, and attention seeks these as the fulfillment of its own bent. This moment of contemplation is associated with the intrinsic rather than extrinsic value of the object. A means can be looked at conceptually and schematically, as an instance of a class, since the

[5]Above, "The Aesthetic Attitude."
[6]Above, "The Aesthetic Attitude."

utility of the thing is associated with selected aspects of the thing and the aspects can be identified as present without total examination of the thing. A means is meant to be passed through. But an end is a point of rest and invites attention for its own nature, as a unique individual. A person intent on eating an apple is content to recognize the thing as an apple, or as an apple of a certain variety. But the aesthetic contemplation of the apple probes deeply into the color and shape of the apple without disturbing it. The utility of the apple can be identified by a generic shape and color; aesthetic contemplation can be satisfied only by a highly specific shape and color, in which it loses itself.

The objectivity of contemplation extends from the obvious object, or form, to the emotion experienced on the occasion of the form. The emotion is not only valued in itself, as in friendship and love, but it is experienced in disinterested fashion, unlike the latter. The disinterest means an objective attitude toward the emotion, which in turn means that the emotion is looked upon as having a position comparable to that of usual objects, in which it engages an outwardly directed attention. The "psychical distance" of Bullough is a distance essentially of emotion. Trees and colors ordinarily are experienced as objects, as objective, and as in some sense distanced from the self; the accomplishment of aesthetic contemplation is to do the same for emotion, which ordinarily clings to the self as its response and property. The objectivity of emotion becomes a cue to the expressional interpretation of art, which supposes that emotion achieves objectivity not by hanging in mid-air, as it were, but by embodiment in the form. The objectivity of emotion is the summit of contemplative objectivity, and by its distance leads to the question of detachment from self, which is so closely associated with emotion. The concepts of objectivity and of detachment neither affirm nor deny the independence of the object, emotion, or interest in relation to the percipient, the self, or awareness: an apparent rather than an ontological relation is intended.

Detachment may be characterized initially as nonattention to the self or percipient. This aspect of detachment is the obverse of the objectivity of contemplation. In looking at the aesthetic object we do not attend to our self. The self is a cause of the experience, and the object is valued by the self; but the object is not considered in its relation to the self. This aspect of detachment is not confined to aesthetic experience, just as the objective direction of attention is not so confined. A man seeking food for himself may for some time be absorbed in thought of the food rather than of himself and his hunger. This is a forgetfulness of self, which ceases when hunger reasserts itself or food is absorbed into the body. But the nonattention to self in contemplation is not forgetfulness: it occurs on principle and steadily. It is not a simple ignoring of the self, for the emotion of the self remains at the center of attention, though felt objectively. It is better described as a new orientation and location of the self.

The new orientation sometimes is described as one in which the self is not possessive, having no wish to control, own, monopolize, or consume the object. The aesthetic contemplation of an apple does not lead to a desire to eat the apple, and the same contemplation of a nude does not lead to a desire for sexual gratification. To this extent it is true that we do not wish to possess the apple or the body. But no one wishes to possess an object in which he has no interest, and in the moment of contemplation, the aspects of food and of sexual gratification are not objects of interest. The intrinsic interest of the activity of contemplation makes the activity self-sufficient and complete, so that it does not tend to pass over into some other activity. The lack of possessiveness of aesthetic contemplation is not a peculiarity of aesthetic experience and interest, but of any experience in relation to an absent interest. Where contemplation has an interest, it has some aspect of possessiveness. The experience is possessed by the self that has it, and the self does not part with it until interest lapses or some necessity intervenes. A person enjoying a still life is as possessive of his enjoyment as an eater of his food. He does not consume the painting and loses nothing by allowing others to look at it. But if it is necessary to control the object to have experience of it, the contemplator will wish to do so. It is true, however, that the wish to possess does not occur as part of contemplation, and the fact of possession is not noted in that activity.

Detachment is construed by Schopenhauer as separation of the percipient and his experience from the will, as the passage quoted above emphasizes.[7] Central to that passage are the statements that "the subject [has passed] out of all relation to the will," and

---

[7]Above, "The Aesthetic Attitude."

that the individual contemplating has become "a pure, will-less, painless, timeless subject of knowledge." For this reason Schopenhauer regarded art as an image of salvation, differing from salvation only by the transitoriness of the release from the will and its painful striving. The fact that contemplation awakens no desire for some further action and object gives color to this view. But will is not confined to extrinsic interest and transitive activity. It is the source of all activity in Schopenhauer's voluntaristic idealism, and for any psychology it must be granted to be the source of interest and evaluation, which are ordered but not created by reason.

The intrinsic interest of contemplation and the active character of contemplation imply an exercise of will. In contemplation, the will is satisfied by the mere act of looking or listening, and the will is the motor of the act. There is no obvious striving in the act, for the object is steadily present and the will is steadily gratified. But an interruption would disappoint the will and initiate striving for recovery. There is a subtle striving in the tendency of the act to project itself forward in time. The present moment is much closer to nonexistence than to everlastingness, and the will strives not only to increase what it has, but to perpetuate it. The emotion contemplated in the experience is specifically a content of will, having its own pleasure or pain and its own set or tendency. Aesthetic contemplation may be said, in respect of this emotion, to be an act of the will contemplating itself. This is the most general level of the synthesis in art of Dionysian content and Apollonian form.

More apposite in the quotation from Schopenhauer is the statement that "the person engaged in the intuition is no longer an individual: for the individual has lost himself in such intuition." The loss of individuality may furnish the key to the status of the self in the condition of detachment. The detachment is of the experience from the self. But the experience contains an emotion that is a response and manifest of the self. The self acts fundamentally by evaluation, and the emotion is an immediate evaluation by, and perhaps to some extent of, the self. The detachment of the experience from the self thus is a detachment of self from self. To avoid contradiction, the separation must involve a sifting and relocation of self, which may be analyzed in three stages.

The first stage is detachment from the "practical" self, which is concerned with transitive activity. The self as seeking or avoiding, or disposed to seek or avoid, objects beyond the immediate experience of contemplation drops from relevance and attention. This is the element of nonpossessiveness and will-lessness in contemplation, and the purport of the opening injunction by Bullough to "abstract from the experience of the sea fog, for the moment, its danger and practical unpleasantness." The second stage is detachment from the "personal" self. The intrinsic interest of the object and emotion is not regarded as peculiarly mine as distinct from yours, or as reflecting my life history and immediate situation more than yours. The distinction of selves and of individualities collapses, and a general self takes over. This aspect of detachment becomes a basis for the expectation of communication and of likeness of judgment upon the experience. The third stage is detachment from the "subjective" self. The emotion that is contemplated is apprehended at a distance from the center established by the subject of awareness, and the center drops out of the awareness. At the distanced position, the impersonal self unfolds in the impersonal emotion, as though it were a set of essences endowed by some miracle with consciousness: a consciousness comparable not to a spotlight shining upon an object, but to an illumination from within. In this way music, painting, and poetry are contemplated. The contemplation, like every experience, is by a self that is practical, personal, and subjective; but it is of a self that is distilled out of these attributes and framed at a distance.

PART II

The Interpretation
of Art

CHAPTER 6

Art as Representation

The Representational Thesis

The analysis of art was concerned with five important aspects of aesthetic experience: sensation, representation, and structure, which define the aesthetic object; emotion as felt by the appreciator, which is a response to the object; and contemplation, which defines the attitude of the appreciator to the object and the emotion. The analysis of art takes note of the high frequency with which these characters occur in aesthetic experience, but it does not offer a judgment of their comparative generality, function, and value. It is content to describe and clarify the nature of the five aspects, both for the intrinsic interest of the aspects and as an aid to the subsequent interpretation of art. It falls to the interpretation of art to construct a hypothesis as to the essential nature of art. Such a hypothesis attempts to explain, unify, and evaluate the characters of art rather than merely to describe them. The hypothesis selects one of the characters and ideally makes three claims for it: that it is necessary to art; that it defines the characteristic value and purpose of art; and that it governs the value and scope of the other characters.

Three hypotheses will be considered in this Part: that art is representation; that art is form, meaning here "pure" form or sensory design; and that art is expression of emotion. These hypotheses thus single out respectively representation, sensation, and emotion as the key to art. The other two aspects of art, structure and contemplation, are of less value as subjects for hypotheses, at least in the context of the three already stated. They are not rivals to the trio, as each member of that group is to the others, but may be accepted without debate by each of the three hypotheses. Their role in art is so general and simple that they may be said to cover everything and to touch nothing. As touching nothing, they are not keystones to some fertile and systematic development of concepts about art. They furnish no specific guidance, whether good or bad, to the artist or the appreciator. And the three hypotheses admitted to litigation have a systematic completeness suggested by the three directions of function of a sign.

Starting with the sensed object, art as representation stresses the referential relation of that object to objects not sensed or presented; art as form stresses the syntactical relation of parts of the sensed object to each other; and art as expression stresses the pragmatic relation of the sensed and represented objects to the appreciator or artist. This comparison is made heuristically, as an analogy instructive for organization, and not substantively, as an indication that a work of art is a sign. Such an indication would be part of the representational theory, and therefore in-appropriate to this introductory theory of the relation of the three theories. It would contradict the expressional theory that will be favored and emphasized in this Part and in the remainder of this book. We may begin the interpretation of art with the theory of representation, which is in some sense the most simple and direct; continue with the theory of form, which is a sophisti-cated negation of the representational theory; and end with the theory of expression, which is the most catholic of the theories and admits of the most complex development.

The theory of art as representation regards representation as essential to art and as the basic source of value in art. It regards the sensed content of art as subordinate to the represented content: a color and shape on canvas are not of primary interest in themselves, but as signs and imagined constituents of a face, a tree, or some other object not presented. It grants the importance of structure, but makes structure doubly a means: structure organizes the sensed content for the purpose of representation, and it organizes the represented content for the better discernment of that content. It admits emotion as an object of representation, though it thinks more characteristically of things, persons, actions, and ideas as objects of representation. It may admit emotion felt by the appreciator, but has no account of the aesthetic status of that emotion, other than to regard it as the effect of the represented object. And it may stress contemplation or in effect deny it, depending not on the theory as such, but on the special theory of representation that may be advanced.

The heart of the representational theory is its orientation toward a world, experience, and value that may be found essentially or completely outside of art, and to which art is subordinate. As a photograph or map testifies to a person or place beyond its own border, so representational theory finds in art primarily a witness to a world beyond art. As shown in an earlier chapter, representation may be endlessly flexible and varied in its relation to its world: it may use arbitrary or natural signs; it may be passive or active; it may be literal or symbolic; and it may be concrete or abstract. But whatever the interpretation, the representation has a foundation and target in objects beyond the interpretation and the work of art, for interpretation always starts with something given to it, and usually modifies it only in the interest of a better view of the same object. In contrast, the formalist theory emphasizes the orientation of the work of art toward itself, as an object self-sufficient and distinct from the world. The expressional theory may draw either upon the world as its subject or upon the peculiar resources of the artistic medium; in either case it emphasizes our emotion about the object rather than the object, and it holds that the emotion is present in the condition of embodiment rather than merely referred to, or experienced in some unspecified condition.

For a statement of a representational aesthetic we may turn to Plato. This first of philosophers has an ontological and speculative interest which gives a maximum opportunity to representational theory and its preoccupation with the world beyond art. He is distinguished for his aesthetic sensitivity, as indicated by his praise of beauty and by his uncommon command of prose cadence, metaphor, and myth. But despite these propitious traits, Plato divorces art from beauty, makes representation the purveyor of practical or transitive interest, and proposes a drastic censorship of art.

Plato: The Imitation of the Particular

The aesthetic of Plato appears to fall into two main parts. One is concerned with art and imitation; the other with beauty, order, and love. The aesthetic of art and imitation may be approached in three phases: an ontological phase, concerned with the kind or grade of reality possessed by the work of art; an epistemological phase, devoted to the kind or grade of knowledge of the represented object that is furnished by art; and an ethical phase, concerned with the impact of art on the life and morality of the appreciator. To these three topics may be added a fourth on the contrasting treatment of beauty.

The philosophy of artistic imitation is stated in the Tenth Book of the *Republic,* and it begins with an ontological discussion of three beds, which are made respectively by God, the carpenter, and the painter.[1] The first bed is an idea or universal, which (drawing on other Platonic discussions) may be described as single, eternal or changeless, absolute or unconditioned, perfect, archetypal, and known through mind or reason. The second bed is a particular thing, which is one of many instances, temporal or changing, relative or conditioned, imperfect, ectypal, and known through the use of the body and the senses. In the spirit of this dualism, which is the most commonly known phase of Plato's metaphysic of thought and sensation, the particular is regarded as inferior in reality and value to the universal, but it is not stripped of either. That condition, or an approximation to it, is assigned to the work of art, on the ground that the latter is an imitation of "that which the others make," that is, of the particular.[2] This is specifically asserted of painting and of poetry. These arts are described as "third in the descent from nature" and as "thrice removed from the king and from the truth."[3] We may

---

[1] Plato, *Republic,* in *The Dialogues of Plato,* trans. B. Jowett, 2 vols. (New York: Random House, 1937), 597.

[2] Plato, 597.

[3] Plato, 597.

say that the first result of the representational theory for Plato is to assess art by the categories of reality relevant to the world represented by art, and to find art in consequence hopelessly inadequate. The painter makes an imitation or image, which is lacking in reality of its own.

Without criticizing in this metaphysical aside the ontology of the greatest of metaphysicians, we may observe that the ontological verdict given by Plato is not to the point. He was entirely right in claiming the unsubstantial nature of the work of art; but this claim is of no consequence to aesthetics, for the work of art has no intrinsic requirement in regard to reality. As stated in an earlier chapter, the work of art is an essence, which is contemplated in abstraction from any judgment about the status in reality of the characters contemplated.[4] A representational aesthetic may assent to this view of the aesthetic object, for the use of a sensory content to refer to something does not add any ontological weight to the sign, and artistic representation does not presuppose the reality of its object. But such an aesthetic is under standing temptation to assess the work of art in ontological terms, due to the emphasis that it places on a world beyond art and to which art is subordinate. This world is the object of ontological judgments by the practical man and the scientist, and the habit spreads to art because of the identification of art with its world through the theory of representation. Plato is a clear example of the spread of the habit.

The epistemological phase, which is concerned with the grade of knowledge of the represented object, or the world, that is furnished by art, cannot be disposed of so summarily. A work of art may have a saving innocence in regard to its own nature and reality; but insofar as it represents, it stands under contract to its object and may be judged by the significance of the object and the adequacy with which it conveys that object to the appreciator. Here Plato's judgment again is negative: art represents not the universal, which alone yields knowledge, but the particular, which yields only true opinion; and the representation is inadequate even to the particular, and therefore falls below true opinion.[5] The painter represents the particular bed not as it is,

---

[4] Above, Chap. 3, "The Concept of Form."
[5] Plato, 598.

but as it appears from a given point of view. Furthermore, the
artist is ignorant of the nature of many of the things he represents.
The painter represents the reins of a horse, but knows less about
them than the maker, who in turn knows less than the user:
"He will no more have true opinion than he will have knowledge
about the goodness or badness of his imitations."[6]

The artist does not have the kind of interest in the nature of
things that Plato supposes. The painter is not concerned with the
reins as having a certain physicochemical constitution, size, and
shape which in turn are to be correlated with certain techniques
of use and ensuing results. The painter is not interested in the
internal constitution; he cares for the size and shape not merely
as indicators of use, but as visual attributes of a thing in space;
and the use of the reins concerns him not for the practical control
of the horse, but for the interplay of the actions of horse and
rider: an interplay, and a set of visual attributes, into which he
may have far greater insight than the maker of the reins, the user,
or any other person.

The allegation that the painter represents the object from a
point of view is substantially correct, but it does not justify the
derogation of art. A Picasso head in simultaneous profile and front
view does not yield deeper knowledge of the subject than an ordinary head, despite the double access to the subject. A novelist
may represent a person in many times and situations, but does
not thereby achieve greater insight into a personality than a
single portrait by Rembrandt. If the difficulty is not merely with
the limitation of a single appearance, but with the contradiction
of multiple appearance, the contradiction is removed if the
appearances are not naïvely construed as intrinsic properties of
the thing, but as properties of the thing relative to a context
which includes a point of view. An appearance always is of
something, is related to that thing according to a law, and sheds
light on the thing when interpreted according to the law. If the
aim of representation is to convey the characters of some particular
thing, representation of an appearance may do so insofar as the
characters appear.

But the artist may be more interested in the appearance of the
thing than in the thing, and he may go so far as to reduce the

6 Plato, 602.

thing to its appearance. This reduction does not entail super-
ficiality, but challenges the imagination of the artist to probe the
presented essence for its most elusive and difficult values. If it
seems strange that a sheer image should be probed, as though it
had an ulterior nature, the answer is that though the image is
no longer the appearance of a thing, it has an autonomous nature
which the imagination searches on behalf of the sensibility of the
percipient. When this happens, the question is not whether the
work of art conveys the nature of an external thing, but whether
it conveys the nature of the spirit that creates or contemplates.

The relation of things and appearances is more complex in the
aesthetic domain than Plato supposed. The artist communicates
either the particular thing, or an image which is an insubstantial
but autonomous particular of greater interest than the thing from
which it was freed. In either case we may consider the ground
secured from which the further question may be raised, whether
art is limited to the particular or may represent the universal.
Plato's denial that art achieves the universal is the crux of his
criticism of art, for it strips art of intelligibility. Without awareness of the universal, the work of art is a local and blind stimulus,
unable, for example, to convey the essential nature of the persons
in a play, to show the causes and effects of their actions, or to
establish a common audience for the play.

The theory that art represents only the particular has its basis
in the fact that the particular is the initial and nominal object
of attention in the aesthetic experience. A person in a play has
a proper name, has a number of specific attributes, is related to
other persons similarly equipped, wears the costume of some
period, and acts at specific times and in specific ways. A painted
tree has a specific size, shape, and color and stands at certain
distances and directions from other trees that are represented.
It must therefore be granted that artistic representation includes
the particular and does not yield the abstract universal. But it
may still represent a concrete universal, which is a universal
identified with the particular but not limited to it. This may be
seen in the person of Shakespeare's Othello. Unlike a genuine
particular, Othello has only the characters with which he is
endowed by the artist. The characters are selected for their
mutual relevance, so that nothing essential is left out and nothing
superfluous included. The characters are developed and clarified in

actions which have a similar relevance, and which come to a halt
when the development has reached its essential point. The interplay of characters and actions constitutes a chain of causes and
effects, which makes it possible for us to understand what happens:
the man is complete and his behavior is grounded. Through the
twin virtues of the essential and the causal, the love, jealousy,
credulity, and remorse of Othello are made universal rather than
blindly particular. Othello therefore is a concrete universal, in
which the universal supplies breadth and connection and the
particular supplies vividness.

The ethical phase of Plato's aesthetic shared with the epistemological a common criticism of the alleged irrationality of imitation.
As the painter imitates the confusion of visual appearance, so the
poet imitates the confusion of human passion. Reason bids a man
in adversity to discipline his sorrow, but another principle "in-
clines us to recollection of our troubles and to lamentation."[7] This
rebellious and irrational principle offers more material for poetic
imitation than does the "wise and calm temperament," which is
not easy to imitate and not readily understood or recognized by
the multitude at the theater. Our "natural hunger and desire to
relieve our sorrow by weeping and lamentation . . . is satisfied
and delighted by the poets"; we do not consider that "the feeling
of sorrow which has gathered strength at the sight of the mis-
fortunes of others is with difficulty repressed in our own."[8] This
description of tragic poetry applies also to comedy, with the
substitution of buffoonery for pity in the spectator's life. In general,
"poetry feeds and waters the passions instead of drying them up;
she lets them rule, although they ought to be controlled."[9] The
result is the need for strict censorship of poetry: "we must remain
firm in our conviction that hymns to the gods and praises of
famous men are the only poetry which ought to be admitted into
our State."[10] Thus the most celebrated statement of the representational theory of art leads to a proposal for the attrition of
art.

This proposal follows from two antecedents, one formal, the other
material. The formal premise is that artistic representation has the

[7] Plato, 604.
[8] Plato, 606.
[9] Plato, 606.
[10] Plato, 607.

same effect on the viewer that the represented content would have in an actual experience: sorrow, for example, has the same constitution and effect in art that it has in a real calamity. The material premise is that art is disposed to represent states which are impassioned, irrational, and bad. The conclusion is that art is disposed to double, through representation, the evil of existence: and censorship is the reply to this conclusion.

The material premise must be granted, both as a description of artistic practice and as a prescription to it. There are at least three reasons for the preoccupation of art, or of literary art, with states of passion. One is that human nature is itself so occupied, and art can avoid them only by denying or ignoring reality. The reality consists both of the external world of society and of the internal world of the artist and appreciator: to deny or ignore it is to commit impiety toward our world, and to dry up the springs of artistic creation. Another reason is that the states of passion reveal men in the ardent pursuit of values. The anger of Clytemnestra at the death of her daughter, the pride and contrition of Oedipus, the madness of Lear, the chill scorn of Hedda Gabler, and the boastful love of an American salesman reflect the depth of human need and have the dignity of great commitment. In comparison, hymns and praises, though salubrious, are trivial. And art uses such subjects as corollaries to the structural principle of balance, which is richer aesthetically than harmony by the presence of conflict.

If art is to be rescued from the censor and consequent collapse, it must be by negation of the formal premise. This premise is the practical expression of the representational theory, since it identifies art with its subject and thus evaluates art by its subject. But there are two ways in which the premise may be limited or denied completely. The first is to insist on the universal in art, with its contribution of understanding and insight to the viewer. The universal transforms artistic representation from a mere stimulus, blindly repeating the experience and passion of the persons represented on the stage, to a lucid understanding which gratifies the intelligence and provides a leaven for the viewer's sympathetic reenactment of the experience. This method is compatible with a representational theory of art, since it involves no more than what representation may accomplish by taking for its object the universal. It was not available to Plato without revision of his particular theory, and that accounts in part for the severity of his censure of art.

The universal is not, however, sufficient, for it does not entail any fundamental difference in the spectator's sensibility. Only a contemplative attitude toward the experienced emotion can secure a general difference between the passion of the protagonist and the emotion of the spectator: the one is personally interested, the other is disinterested. Contemplation guarantees the harmony, sanity, and control of the aesthetic experience when confronted with the sea of represented passion. Its presence is the basis for denying completely the formal premise and for forestalling the censor. But a representational theory cannot appeal to contemplation for the delivery of art, since representation has no essential place for contemplation.

The only disinterest that representation may sponsor is one based on the unreality of the represented object and its separateness from the actual life of the spectator. But this is a disinterest constituted by feebleness of interest, and it differs only in degree and not in kind or principle from ordinary interest. It is threatened by the vividness of the representation and by the very great relevance of the theme of the representation to the spectator's life. Representation may be accompanied by genuine disinterest, but does not of its own nature entail it. The representational theory provides for the representation of objects, including emotions, and it may admit emotion experienced by the appreciator. But it has no account to give of the latter emotion and cannot claim that it will be experienced disinterestedly. Plato's aesthetics shows the weakness of representational theory in accounting for contemplation, and the tendency of the theory to afflict art with a narrow moralism.

His aesthetics also shows the inadequacy of the theory of representation to deal with beauty, since Plato states a virtual bifurcation of art and beauty. Where art makes a passing and highly relative image of a deficient reality, beauty is an eternal and absolute idea.[11] Where art is irrational, because of appearance and destructive passion, beauty is rational, because of its order, grace, and symmetry. Where art and artists are contrasted with a

[11] Plato, *Phaedrus*, 250, *Symposium*, 210–211, in *The Dialogues of Plato*, trans. B. Jowett, 2 vols. (New York: Random House, 1937).

productive and useful life, beauty educates the soul for its life and presides over birth and creation.[12] Works of art are sometimes said to have beauty, as in the praise of music and visual arts for their grace and harmony; but beauty is not mentioned in the criticism of imitative art. Beauty is more often identified in places removed from art: in pure colors, simple geometrical forms, the human face, laws and institutions, concepts and systems, and foremost in the Idea of Beauty, of which these are reflections.

It is not surprising that a representational theory should leave beauty to another domain, for representation and beauty are logically independent of each other. Representation may occur without beauty in the subject matter or in the work of art, and beauty may occur without representation. The beauty of nature does not involve representation in the literal sense, and representation has no mechanism for creating beauty. If a work of art has beauty, it has it either by representing an object that has beauty beforehand, or by using a method distinct from that of representation, though available for use in the process of interpretation. For Plato, beauty is founded on structure, and more particularly on the unity than the variety of structure. It is related to harmony, grace, and simplicity in Book III of *The Republic*,[13] and to measure and symmetry in the *Philebus*.[14] These are syntactical rather than referential characters. They define what is ultimately real for Plato, whether it be the transcendent Ideas of the *Phaedrus* and *Symposium*, or the immanent Mixture of the *Philebus*. And when they are referred to sense, they are found rather in abstract designs than in concrete things:

> I do not mean by beauty of form such beauty as that of animals or pictures, which the many would suppose to be my meaning; but, says the argument, understand me to mean straight lines and circles, and the plane or solid figures which are formed out of them by turning-lathes and rulers and measurers of angles; for these I affirm to be not only relatively beautiful, like other things, but they are eternally and absolutely beautiful.[15]

---

[12] Plato, *Republic*, 401–402; Plato, *Symposium*, 206.

[13] Plato, *Republic*, 400–401.

[14] Plato, *Philebus*, in *The Dialogues of Plato*, trans. B. Jowett, 2 vols. (New York: Random House, 1937), 64–65.

[15] Plato, *Philebus*, 51.

Thus Plato's representational theory is supplemented by a formalist theory in order to complete the aesthetic domain, and aesthetics is left without the unity so highly praised in philosophy by Plato.

Evaluation of Art as Representation

The merit of the representational theory of art consists in its assertion of the value that representation may have in the experience of art. The weakness of the theory lies in the further assertions that representation is essential to art, that it defines the characteristic value and function of art, and that it explains, organizes, or sheds light on the other traits of art. We may begin with a view of the merits and conclude with an analysis of the limitations.

1. Representation occurs naturally, quickly, and rather spontaneously for both artist and contemplator. The question, "What does it mean?" occurs before any other for the typical appreciator of many of the arts. The appreciator is oriented toward a world more massive and continuous than art, and looks for suggestions of the one in the framework of the other. This tendency needs only a slight iconicity to make itself known. As Bernheimer pointed out in his defense of representation, a horizontal line will suggest the horizon, a slanting line the slope of a hill, and spheres and cubes in represented space will suggest familiar things of real space.[16] What occurs naturally may be a resource in art. At the same time, art is not simply naïve, but has disciplines of its own, in relation to which the natural movement of attention may be a temptation and distraction. The trained percipient may look at a line with no awareness but that of the present line, its motion and force, and the emotion of these.

2. Representation draws on the intrinsic interest of a given subject and thus enlarges the scope of art beyond the intrinsic interest of the sensory vehicle. The interest of objects outside of art is made available to art; and it seems gratuitous sacrifice to dismiss it from art, particularly when the artist may provide an interpretation that the subject may not yield to the untutored

---

[16] Richard Bernheimer, "In Defense of Representation," *Art: A Bryn Mawr Symposium* (Bryn Mawr, Pa.: Bryn Mawr College, 1940), p. 24.

eye in nature or reality. But interest in the subject may distract attention from the sensory vehicle and from the organization of both sense and representation. It may lead attention from art to something else, as in the case of the hunter who values a painting simply as a reminder of the hunt. And it may involve insincerity, as when painter or beholder may rely on the representation of an emotional subject rather than on the more integral treatment of the same emotion through line and color. Rodin's *Prodigal Son,* with face almost averted but with a body formed of fluent, contorted lines, has a more bare necessity than the representation of a face in tears.

3. Representation enhances communication between artist and appreciator, due to the preceding reasons. Communication is vital to art, for the impersonal self contemplated in the aesthetic experience embraces in principle every self, and the artist can do no more than to submit his work as a hypothesis to be verified, whether now or in the future, by an experience similar to his and more authoritative. The contemporary schism between artist and society has more than one cause, but it has been attended by an emphasis on pure form, abstract representation, and private or indeterminate allusion that baffles the beholder. It is difficult to say whether the schism is cause or effect of the drift from identifiable subject matter: probably it is both. But communication does not rest exclusively with subject. A housewife who takes no interest in either Rembrandt or Mondrian may appreciate instantly the design of a spoon or the color of a drape, and a person accustomed to the formal absoluteness of Mozart may wonder what Strauss is doing in *Thus Spake Zarathustra,* or Debussy in *The Sea.* Stress on abstract and formal art, or on indeterminate imagery and allusion, may be the occasion for a new education of public taste, which occurs in almost every generation. Evidences of contemporary art may now be found even in American advertising.

4. The final advantage of representation, which may also be said to summarize the others, is that representation binds art generally to life and the world, by virtue of its subjects and the light it sheds on them. Art is doubly a part of life. It is a life in its own terms, as every artist knows; and it draws upon and influences the life that flows beyond its own borders. Representation is concerned with the latter, and it consents less readily to an

ivory-tower attitude than does its negative. But representation has
no monopoly on this virtue, though it may have a monopoly on
the determinateness or specificity with which the world is engaged
in art. Without representing anything, music expresses the depth
and subtlety of human experience, and a building may express a
religious or secular value. Expression engages the world as much
as does representation, though in a different way.

With these virtues of representation in mind, we may proceed
to the weaknesses of the theory which not only sets a value on
representation, but makes it the end and key to art. From the
examination of the theory in Plato several limitations appeared:
to which may be added others.

1. The representational theory tends toward an ontological
assessment of the work of art, which contradicts the ontological
neutrality of the aesthetic object as an essence. In Plato, the
representation of an appearance of the particular leads to the
condemnation of the work of art as a shadow reality. In Schopenhauer, the representation of the universal, or *Idee*, which is the
immediate objectivity of the will, leads to the praise of the work
of art for its reality.[17] It is not necessary that representational
theory should have this ontological bias; but where it appears, it
is due to preoccupation with subject and to evaluation of art by
categories derived from subject matter.

2. Representation inevitably has a degree of inadequacy in its
communication of its subject. Representation is a referential use
of signs, and like all instances of that use it suffers from the
defects of distance, mediation, and substitution in the relation
of sign to referent. As stated in an earlier chapter, reference is
compatible with the nonexistence of the referent; it implies some
aspect of absence as regards the referent; and it confesses the
subordinate and surrogate status of the sign in relation to the
referent.[18] A sign necessarily is less complete than its referent:
if it were identical in kind, it would supersede rather than signify
its object. A map is less complete than a country, and a photograph is less than a human face. This was evident to Plato in

[17] Arthur Schopenhauer, *Die Welt als Wille und Vorstellung*, Vol. I (Leipzig: F.
A. Brockhaus, 1891), Bk. III, Sec. 36, p. 217. Arthur Schopenhauer, *The World
as Will and Idea*, trans. R. B. Haldane and J. Kemp, Vol. I (London: Routledge,
1957), p. 239.
[18] Above, Chap. 2, "Representation and Meaning."

the hierarchy of imitations and the descent from model to copy. Where abstract and relational knowledge are desired, or a guide to transitive action is wished for, the sign may be preferable to the referent because of its schematic clarity and the ease with which it may be manipulated, as in a map. But where a qualitative appreciation of the individual is desired, the sign is the lesser choice. Mysticism demands that no sign, image, or concept intervene between the mystic and God. A similar demand is appropriate to art, though the subject often makes it impossible to gratify the wish and representation is the best compromise. The distance of representation is not an argument against the use of representation, but it is an argument against representational theory, which makes representation the essential function and source of value in art and thus accepts at the heart of art a curious imperfection.

3. The representational theory has an inadequate account of the place of emotion in art. Representation may as readily be of an emotion as of any other kind of object, as when a novelist describes both a chair and the disordered emotion of the occupant of the chair. Here an idea of an emotion is part of the aesthetic form, and the emotion that may pertain to the appreciator is not in view. Representational theory takes no general position in regard to the aesthetic relevance of the appreciator's emotion: it may admit it, as Plato did, or it may ignore or deny it. But the basic interest of representation is in the object represented rather than in the response to it. Where an emotion is felt by the appreciator, it can hardly be said to be represented, since it is real, present, and of primary rather than substitute standing. The theory that the appreciator responds not by feeling but by conceiving emotion, of which the aesthetic form as a whole is a sign or representation, will be discussed at length, and contravened, in the analysis of the structure of embodiment that will be made in a later chapter.[19] If the emotional value of the work of art is not represented, it is left unaccounted for by the representational theory: worse still, it is left exposed and stranded, and subject to misunderstanding and abuse.

4. The representational theory is unable to give an account of contemplative interest or disinterest, except quantitatively as a

[19] Below, Chap. 9, "Form as the Sign of Emotion."

weakened interest. This was evident in Plato, and it has a bearing on the misunderstanding and abuse of emotion just mentioned.

5. The representational theory is unable to give an account of beauty, as was shown in the discussion of the differential treatment of beauty and imitation in Plato.

6. The representational theory does not take seriously the problem of control, which engages every creative act of the artist, including the act of representing when that occurs. All representation begins with selection of subject, but the subject does not select itself: an interest of the artist does that. Once selected, the subject provides no law to the artist, who may represent it passively or with a high degree of interpretation. In the process of interpretation, the subject may be modified extensively by the artist, and only the literal-minded would cry out that the subject is being misrepresented or, more significantly, that the artist is in error. Representation clearly is controlled not by the subject matter or object, but by the artist's interest, and a similar interest in the appreciator underlies communication. The interest discovers or creates a value, however, and the value is apprehended immediately in emotion. The artist's emotion thus controls the representation. The representational theory has no particular place for this emotion, however, but speaks on the contrary as though the represented object had some sacred right of its own. Since the object is governed interpretively by an emotion, it would be more appropriate to say that what is ultimately represented is not the object, such as a face or tree, but an emotion concerning it. But the concept of representation does not provide the mechanism for dealing with emotion, as was indicated in Number 3 of this series.

7. The representational theory exposes art to moralism, or the evaluation of art by its subject matter and the allied emotion experienced by the beholder. The moralistic attitude is influenced in Plato partly by the denial of the universal, but fundamentally by inability to account for contemplation as distinct from personal interest. As a result of moralism, the subject of art either is restricted to one that is innocuous, like "hymns to the gods and praises of famous men"; or it is made the occasion for a moral judgment within the work of art, as when the artist takes pains to show or to state that evil is punished.

8. The representational theory exposes art to the charge that it

is a vicarious experience, that is, a substitute engaged in because of deprivation of original or firsthand experience of the objects and actions and values represented. According to this charge, the artist and his audience are starved for some gratification afforded in some real and substantial way in nature and society, and afforded in an unreal and phantasmal fashion by art. Depending on the charity of the psychoanalyst, or of the "man of action," the gratification given by art is said to be mildly beneficial, or harmless, or damaging. A representational theory is required for this view of art, for only such a theory establishes a general contrast between a subject in nature and a representation in art. When the theory states, as it must, that representation is the end and characteristic achievement of art, it plays into the hands of the theory of vicarious experience, for the latter theory may reasonably contend that only a person deprived of gratification in reality would be content with an image that furnishes no new dimension of gratification, but only the echo of a value whose true character is to be found elsewhere.

Against this theory, representation must be viewed as part of a form that does not merely repeat a situation and value to be found outside of art, but provides them for a mode and perfection of experiencing to be found only in the aesthetic experience. What the artist and appreciator look toward is not the shadow or even the recovery of some event and emotion, but the formulation of these for disinterested contemplation. When thus formulated and contemplated, the experience has an order of value distinct from any to be had outside of art. That is why the experience of love may be engaged in poetry not only by a Keats, who was bereft in love and confronted by early death, but by a Byron jaded by excess of women, by a Shelley dreaming beyond expired raptures, and by a Goethe whose many-sided life appears to have included a complete eros.

9. By its failure to put its finger on what is unique in art, the representational theory is a poor guardian of the autonomy of art. The mad devotion of the artist and the milder madness of the appreciator are based on the perception that art is something new in the world, which no other activity can duplicate or approach. Because of this unique value, art is self-governing and autonomous. But the representational theory imposes upon art one degree or another of heteronomy, and of subservience to

nonaesthetic criteria, as may be seen in Numbers 1 to 4, 7, and 8 of this series, and particularly in the inadequacies regarding emotion, contemplation, moralism, and vicariousness. The autonomy of art is represented in the theory mainly by the interpretation of the subject made by the artist. That is of great importance. But it is not sufficient, since it does not include or lead to other aspects of aesthetic autonomy. Art is neither secluded nor irresponsible: it embraces the whole of life and has a sensitive conscience. But the uniqueness of its method and end require that it be judged by principles peculiar to it and not to something else.

10. The final criticism of the representational theory is perhaps the most elementary: that it cannot be applied generally among the arts, since music, architecture, and certain minor arts have no representative content. Either the theory leads to pluralism in aesthetics, or it must be strained into the view that these arts do indeed represent. Pluralism should not be embraced at the first hypothesis, but only when the field has been surveyed and no alternative remains. The theory may be strained in at least two ways. It may be said that a rug represents unity. But it is incorrect to say that the rug represents something that it presents, and presents quite completely. If it is replied that the unity that is represented is an abstract universal, it should be countered that such an idea is not an object of aesthetic awareness. On the contrary, the rug borrows nothing from such an idea, for what is contemplated is a visual unity which satisfies in the act of vision, and is neither excelled nor approximated in an invisible idea. Furthermore, representation in the sense of the relation of particular to universal is neutral to the representational theory and its opposite, the formalist theory; it therefore is no issue between them.

The other way of straining the theory of representation is to hold that music represents emotion, and in general that it represents human inwardness and temperament. But arguments will be given in the discussion of expression to show that the emotion of "pure" music, or of any other formal art, is not related to the form by representation, but by expression.

If the criticisms made in this section are valid, representation may be admitted to art, but the theory of art as representation must be rejected. Representation is important in art, but it is not universal to art, or essential to art, or the end of art. It may be considered as a means to some other end. The end may be stated provisionally as the experience of adequate emotion. Representation is part of a method for achieving that end: but it is subordinate to a more complex method, which may be defined through the conception of expression. Before considering the theory of expression, we must examine the formalist theory, which is diametrically opposed to the representational theory and claims, like its two rivals, to be an adequate hypothesis about the fundamental nature of art.

CHAPTER 7

Art as Form*

The Formalist Thesis

The theory of art as form identifies art with "pure" form, which
may be defined as structured sensation or sensory design. It regards
pure form as both necessary and sufficient to art, and as supply-
ing the characteristic and unique value of art. It rejects representation as being at best incidental to art and at worst damaging
to art. It has a variable attitude toward emotion as experienced
by appreciator or creator: in some presentations it permits emotion, in others it disavows emotion heatedly, depending apparently on the independence or dependence of the emotion on
situations that belong to "real life" and that may be depicted
in representative art. When it permits emotion, it has no particular account of the status and nature of the emotion, other than
to insist that the emotion be germane to the sensory design and
to nothing else. It stresses contemplation, which it grounds in
the separation of the sensory design from the things and situations, and consequent uses, incitations, and temptations, of
ordinary experience. The contemplation extends to any emotion

* The first three sections of this chapter, here slightly revised, were read with
omissions at the annual meeting of the American Society for Aesthetics in Cin-
cinnati, October, 1959, and were published as "Formalism in Painting and
Music: A Critique," *Bucknell Review,* Vol. IX, May, 1960, 159–175.

that may be present, and it entails a general supposition of the disinterested status of the emotion.

The terms *structured sensation* and *sensory design* leave some doubt as to the comparative role and importance of sensation and structure in pure form and in formalist theory. When expounding the theory, it is customary to emphasize structure and, in structure, the aspect of unity. There can be no doubt about the importance of structure to formalism and, for that matter, to any aesthetic theory and to every work of art. But structure is essential to representative art, as in the plot of a novel, and we must ultimately hold that the emotion of both creator and appreciator is structured by the work of art. Structure, therefore, is not the monopoly, or the distinguishing characteristic, of pure form or sensory design. It has perhaps a more essential role in pure form than in representative form, for a single color or sound has less interest than a single face or tree, and the artist has more freedom and responsibility in ordering sensory elements than in organizing things from nature. But music is nothing without tones, and painting is nothing without colors; and the differences between the two arts are governed fundamentally by the difference of sensory elements.

The structures available to a given art are not conceived in the abstract, but grow out of the natures and potentialities of the given sensory elements; and these elements profit from the structures as ends from means. Tones in music do not exemplify relations, but relations are of tones and enhance the value of tones. A work of art as an individual has an individual structure, which has no meaning apart from the specific sensory elements that are present in the work. Thus there is no ground for giving precedence to structure over sensation: on the contrary, there is reason to do the opposite. This is especially true in identifying formalism: for the theory is distinguished not by its special praise of structure, but by its resolute rejection of representation and by its judgment that the sensed object is self-contained and of unique value. We may say, then, that a pure form is sensation profiting from the maximum contribution of structure, and that formalism is a theory of the value to be found in organized sensation.

Formalism varies from art to art in its emphasis, purity, and rigor. Its maximum demand may be found in music. Not satisfied with the proscription of program music, which is only a small part of the literature of instrumental music, formalism goes on to the rejection of all or almost all emotion. Its aim is to eliminate any emotion related to events of nonmusical life; but its net is so tight that no emotion remains to music, except for the direct pleasure of patterned tone. Formalism is less confining in painting and sculpture, though still quite resolute. Its main concern is to eliminate any reference to things in space, and to psychical states conveyed through such things: for example, a human face and the personality of a harlot or saint. Having less attention to bestow on emotion, it is content to ban any emotion related to the proscribed subject matter, without going so far as to attack emotion as such.

Formalism is most flexible and modest in poetry. The most enthusiastic formalist must grant that the tonal value of words is far inferior to that of music, and that poetic rhythm depends at least partly on the meaning, and consequent stress, of words. For both reasons formalism in poetry seldom goes so far as to dismiss from awareness the meaning, and therefore the representative content, of words. It is satisfied to hold a second line of defense, at which words are interpreted not abstractly for their conceptual value and their statement of general truths, but concretely for their imagistic value, their indeterminate allusiveness, their subtle and dark magic. It is only by courtesy that this important program for poetry can be called formalist.

We may therefore limit the examination of formalism to painting and to music. For a vivid statement of formalism in painting we may consider Clive Bell, critic of painting, and author of *Art*, which was written about seven years after the death of Cézanne, whom he greatly admired. For a systematic view of formalism in music we may turn to Eduard Hanslick, critic of music, author of *The Beautiful in Music*, and antagonist of the "opium" of Wagner.

Formalism in Painting: Bell

The basic concept in Bell's aesthetics is that of "significant form." According to Bell, every work of art produces an emotion which varies specifically with each work of art, but has a generic identity as an "aesthetic emotion." The aesthetic emotion is not described, but it is referred to an equally generic quality of the objects that provoke it. That quality is significant form, which is the source of the aesthetic emotion. Significant form is referred by Bell to color and line. "These relations and combinations of lines and colors, these aesthetically moving forms, I call 'Significant Form'; and 'Significant Form' is the one quality common to all works of visual art."[1] We may analyze the theory of significant form under three headings: the reciprocal denial of representation and affirmation of sensory design; the relation of form to emotion in the creative act; and the relation of form to reality.

Of representation Bell says: "The representative element in a work of art may or may not be harmful; always it is irrelevant. For, to appreciate a work of art we need bring with us nothing from life, no knowledge of its ideas and affairs, no familiarity with its emotions."[2] This implies the elimination of any reference in a painting to rocks or trees, to human bodies, personalities, or events. But an exception is made for three-dimensional space.

> Pictures which would be insignificant if we saw them as flat patterns are profoundly moving because, in fact, we see them as related planes. If the representation of three-dimensional space is to be called "representation," then I agree that there is one kind of representation which is not irrelevant.[3]

There are, however, some "magnificent designs" which are viewed in flat space only. Finally, Bell grants that there is a "representative or descriptive element in many great works of art."[4] This means that "a realistic form may be as significant, in its place as part of the design, as an abstract."[5] But the interpretation of the form as a representation is irrelevant; in effect, reference must be neutralized. "But if a representative form has value, it is as form, not as representation."[6]

[1] Clive Bell, *Art* (New York: Frederick A. Stokes, n.d.), p. 8.
[2] Bell, p. 25.
[3] Bell, p. 27.
[4] Bell, p. 28.
[5] Bell, p. 25.
[6] Bell, p. 25.

The thesis that the appreciation of art requires no knowledge of the ideas, affairs, and emotions of life is the heart of formalist aesthetics. It must be denied as a misinterpretation of two indubitable facts. One is that the experience of artistic representation is never the same as the experience of a related object in nature or human affairs. The other is that the formal art of a rug or bowl, or of a painting by Mondrian, has no direct connection with life. But the uniqueness of art in relation to subject matter is a result of interpretation, improved structure, contemplative distance, and emotional objectification, none of which contradicts representation. And the most formal design appeals to an interest that arises in generic fashion out of the mainstream of human experience. A person who had no prior feeling about the value of order would be cold to the subtle unities of formal art. An emotion about order, which is an emotion from a life of orders and disorders, informs the appreciation of the formal design.

If this is true of art without representation, it is the more true of the great bulk of art, which offers direct and concrete clues to experience that precedes and overflows art. We expect of the major artist an insight into human life, partial or total, generic or specific, that arises from imaginative observation and acute reflection. This may be found in a face by Rembrandt or by Picasso. If the apparent subject is nonhuman, as in a landscape or still life by Cézanne, we may find in it also the evidence of a human sensibility that matures in the total course of experience, not apart from it. The difference between the artist as a young man and the artist in his prime is not primarily one of training and technique and scholarship, or of sensory acuity or sensory practice, or even of experience of specific events and situations: it is one of depth of total perception, of a wisdom that does not issue in precepts, of an obscure balance of hunger and strength. This difference is strangely ignored by the formalist.

The exception made for representation of the third dimension of space is necessary. It is surprising that Bell should entertain some reservation as to whether the treatment of the third dimension is representation: clearly it is not presentation. And an exception is always a flaw in theoretical statement, which raises questions about the ultimate purport of the statement. The admission of deep space is an admission that the sensory design

on canvas is not sufficient: that the painting refers to a world of
space beyond the work of art, and to objects which at least
have the property of being extended and arranged in that space.
The denial of any further representation is a denial of the consideration of the spatial object as a physical thing having weight
and solidity, as a biological thing having the life and special
properties of the human body, or as a spiritual thing having the
characteristics of an old man, a person in weariness or sorrow,
or a lover in pursuit or frustration. What is denied, then, is any
interpretation of the intuited sensum beyond the most elementary
of the stages sketched in Chapter 2, the second section. It is not
a denial of representation as such, but of representation of certain
subjects.

To rectify the theoretical statement, it would be helpful to
make use of Ducasse's distinction between designs and dramatic
entities. A design is defined by quantitative relations such as
those of space, time, pitch, volume, hue, and saturation. A
dramatic entity is defined by causal and teleological relations.[7]
A table as a set of relations in visual space is a design; the
same table as a material thing made from a tree by a carpenter,
and useful for eating or writing, is a dramatic entity. A design
is a presentation or a representation, depending on the omission
or use of the third dimension; a dramatic entity always involves
representation or reference. It is therefore possible to restate Bell's
formalism as an admission of designs and a rejection of dramatic
entities. The restatement requires no exception, and it sheds light
on what is at issue in Bell's aesthetics. The issue is not representation as such, but the distinction between the world in
its visual and spatial character and the world as having further
characters of various sorts.

This distinction sheds some light on the contention that art
may use realistic forms, but must divest them of reference. The
demand seems at first sight to be both illogical, trimming the
facts to suit the theory so that the history of art cannot be used
against it, and impertinent, informing the artist what it is that
he has valued in his painting. If the painter has made an icon of
a tree or face, it would seem that he has tacitly taken an interest

[7] Curt J. Ducasse, *The Philosophy of Art* (New York: Dial, 1929), pp. 204, 207.

in these things in choosing them rather than some other object as his subject, and that any suggestion to the contrary is presumptuous. But the distinction between the object as design and as dramatic entity leads to a similar distinction in the definition of the artist's interest. It is entirely credible that the painter should choose and view his subject without any dramatic character. With great perception Bell speaks of the "sudden vision of landscape as pure form," with no interpretation of the objects as "fields and cottages."[8] In Bell's view, the artist works entirely with such vision, which is a high vision indeed. One may forgive the formalist for his excesses when he speaks so finely of artistic intuition at its subtlest reach. But certain arguments appear, which limit the scope of formalism at this point.

To some extent, the formalist is attacking a straw man. The ordinary recognition of a painted tree is not of a thing defined by certain biophysical properties and human uses, but of a thing that has a certain type or range of shape, size, and color. For this recognition, the dramatic characters serve mainly as a label for fixing in mind the design characters, which in turn are viewed as familiar objects in nature. If this approach to the painting is deficient, it is not because of the reference to nature, which is admitted in Bell's sanction of the third dimension; nor is it because of emphasis on the dramatic characters, which does not occur. It is because of the tendency to look upon the design as a type rather than as an individual: a tendency which appears both in the demand for familiarity and in the use of a dramatic type as an identifying label.

The pure discernment of individual design is the goal of painting as vision or sight; but its subtle perfection is no argument against the use of painting and vision for the representation of dramatic characters. Though we may be interested in a landscape entirely for its design, we may have a further interest in the human body or face and its dramatic character, which includes the whole range of psychological or spiritual traits of humanity. The interest of a cardinal to El Greco (Plate 13), or of an absinthe drinker to Picasso, is not simply in a visual and spatial object, but also in a human personality and situation. The evi-

[8] Bell, p. 53.

dence for this statement is twofold. The acuteness with which
the spiritual traits are represented makes it unreasonable to suppose that they are accidental or incidental. And the mind of the
painter is an organ for more than seeing: like the mind of every
other artist, and human being, it is interested in man and his
values. A visual form provides a mode of access to this subject
that neither sounds nor words can provide: the painter inevitably
and properly exploits his opportunity. In so doing, he needs no
reminder from the formalist that in conveying his subject he
must, as painter, press every opportunity of visual awareness
and thus of visual design. Design and dramatic entity need not
conflict: they may be organically united in an experience of the
most complex aesthetic value.

Despite the vigor and incisiveness of his statement, there are
two respects in which Bell opens the door to the alternative
hypotheses about art. One involves his analysis of the creative
act. In looking at an object, such as a tree or a chair, the painter
may see it as a pure form, or visual design, and feel an emotion
for it as pure form. He now has a desire to express what he has
felt. In making his design on canvas, the artist may use forms
derived from those perceived prior to creation. But he "will not
be bound by his vision. He will be bound by his emotion."[9]
This is a true account of the artist's motivation and procedure.
But the desire to express what the artist has felt and the control
of the created form by the emotion are central to an expressional
theory of art. They are compatible with the use of pure forms or
designs, but incompatible with a formalist theory, which makes
such forms the basic and characteristic value of art. If the emotion controls the form, the emotion takes precedence over the
form. Bell unwittingly confesses the inadequacy of his formalism
in appealing to the terms of expressional theory for the description of artistic creation.

The second exit from formalism provided by Bell's statement
concerns his "metaphysical hypothesis." The emotion felt for a
pure form is felt for that form as an end. The artist "did not
feel emotion for a chair as a means to physical well-being . . . nor
as the place where someone sat saying things unforgettable . . .

[9] Bell, p. 58.

he sees objects, not as means shrouded in associations, but as pure forms."[10] The individual form thus stripped of its instrumentalities and associations is a thing-in-itself, an ultimate reality. Again, Bell speaks of the form as not of itself the ultimately real, but as a revelation or manifestation of reality. He conjectures that the ultimately real is approached by the artist through pure form, by the mystic apart from form.[11] The value of pure form now is seen as the value of reality, and the emotion of pure form is fundamentally an emotion about reality. A hierarchy emerges: the ultimately real, emotion felt for that reality, and pure form as the expressor of the emotion. The phrase *significant form* now begins to display meaning, for the pure form of the artist's creation is significant of ultimate reality, from which it acquires its deepest interest.

We need not linger with this metaphysic, which will concern us in Chapter 13, the second section. It is sufficient here to note that representation in the most fundamental sense has taken over Bell's aesthetics. Having rejected representation of the concrete things and events of nature and society, he has ended with representation of nature in its most essential terms. We saw earlier that Bell's formalism, true to the instinct for visual form, does not reject representation as such, but permits any representation of things in nature that is uncontaminated by dramatic characters. Although this permission is a departure from sensory presentation and the letter of formalism, it is within the spirit of formalism, since it uses vision on canvas to serve vision in nature, and merges the two in the single-minded pursuit of visual form and design. But the metaphysical hypothesis departs from the spirit of formalism, for it makes the value of form to consist in its relation, as constituent or manifestation, to a reality which lies at least partly beyond vision. This reality is the most dramatic of all characters and beings, since its causality and its relation to our purpose are limited by no determination. Here, again, Bell's formalism deserts itself. But though the infidelity is harmful to his theory, it is not harmful to art, which may profit from a vision that goes beyond sight.

[10] Bell, p. 52.
[11] Bell, pp. 54, 82.

Formalism in Music: Hanslick

The formalism of Hanslick is directed primarily against any relevance of music to emotion, whether the emotion be merely represented, or experienced by listener or composer. Of representation in general, as distinct from that of emotion, he has less to say. He rejects the representation of concrete things and events, but grants the appropriateness of a highly abstract kind of representation of events, which does not, however, extend to emotion. Although distinguishing initially between the excitation of emotion as the aim and the representation of emotion as the subject matter of music, he discusses interchangeably excitation and representation, and appears to use representation and expression as synonyms. This looseness will appear in the exposition, but it will not impair the spirit and main contentions of the theory. Hanslick's argument is primarily an opposition of two approaches to music: one emotional and disparaged, the other aesthetic and praised. We may begin with the one and conclude with the other.

The emotional hearing of music, or an exaggerated species of it, is considered at length by Hanslick. The emotional listener is in a passive state, in which he is influenced by the physiological affinities of sound and motion rather than by the artistic form, to which he does not attend. "They are, as it were, in a state of waking dreaminess and lost in a sounding nullity, their mind is constantly on the rack of suspense and expectancy."[12] Alexander the Great became furious on hearing the flute, and calm under the influence of song. As wine loosens the tongue, so music loosens the feet and heart. "To be the slave of unreasoning, undirected, and purposeless feelings, ignited by a power which is out of all relation to our will and intellect, is not worthy of the human mind."[13]

Though this kind of listening does indeed occur, it is not sanctioned by the perceptive nonformalist any more than by the

---

[12] Eduard Hanslick, *The Beautiful in Music* (London: Novello, 1891), p. 124.
[13] Hanslick, p. 129.

formalist, and the denunciation of it is no advancement of the formalist argument. What is required is a consideration, and from the formalist standpoint a criticism, of the emotion that both the composer and the aesthetically initiated listener may find in music. Whether in the spontaneous and ephemeral experience of a Grieg piano piece, or in the reflective and enduring experience of a late Beethoven sonata, music deals with emotion with the utmost resources of the imagination or forming intelligence, and it is not so much under the control of the will as it is delivered to an impersonal will. Sullivan's perceptive interpretation[14] of what is at once Beethoven's spiritual development and his art is scarcely approached, and still less disturbed, by Hanslick's indictment of the "pathological" listener. In general, Hanslick appears to be unaware that emotion may be contemplated and made an object of understanding, rather than be referred to the viscera and to transitive activity.

Hanslick states that there is no causal connection between a given composition and the feelings that may be experienced, for the feeling varies with the "experience and impressibility" of the hearer. The emotional relativity is also historical:

> The placidity and moral sunshine of Haydn's symphonies were placed in contrast with the violent bursts of passion, the internal strife, the bitter and acute grief embodied in Mozart's music. Twenty or thirty years later, precisely the same comparison was made between Beethoven and Mozart.[15]

There is some justice to this relativistic thesis, since the connection between the music and the emotion depends on the listener as well as on the music. But listeners vary most in the imagery and informal programs that they bring to the tonal pattern. Since, as Hanslick is the first to insist, the former are not germane to the musical experience, it is only fair to discount their emotional effects in assessing the emotional import of music. If the patterned tone itself is considered, uniformity is greatly increased. As we have seen, the theory advanced by Hartshorne is so confident of the relation between a sensum and a feeling that it

[14] J. W. N. Sullivan, *Beethoven: His Spiritual Development* (New York: Knopf, 1927).
[15] Hanslick, p. 25.

PLATE 10. *Willem de Kooning.* Excavation *(1950). Courtesy of the Art Institute of Chicago.*

PLATE 11. *Rogier van der Weyden,* The Annunciation *(15th century). The Metro-politan Museum of Art, Gift of J. Pierpont Morgan, 1917.*

PLATE 12. *Paul Cézanne*, Forest of Tholonet *(1904). Private collection. Permission SPADEM 1968 by French Reproduction Rights, Inc.*

regards it as one of identity, which admits of no variation.[16] Pepper affirms a similar constancy in the relation to sensation of the emotional states that he refers to as "sensory fusions" and moods.[17]

The similarity of emotional response requires, of course, similarity of sensation, and specifically of the intuition of the structured tone of the composition. Hanslick assumes the stability to the trained ear of that intuition. But variations in the interpretation of a composition by conductors and instrumental soloists are, among other things, variations in the objective form, as in volume and tempo. The form is inseparable from its structure, and an important consideration in structure is the distinction between harmony and balance. The complex balance, or near discord, of one generation becomes almost a harmony to the next generation, which has devised new forms of strife to take the place of those become tame with custom. The difference of emotional response to Haydn, Mozart, and Beethoven may therefore be to some extent a difference of formal perception: the emotion corresponding to the perceived balance or harmony, and changing with the change in perception. The relativity of emotion thus is far less than Hanslick claims, and the form that is so highly praised is itself not free from variation.

The last argument against emotion that we may consider is the statement that emotion cannot be the subject matter of musical representation or expression. Neither a definite nor an indefinite feeling can be negotiated by music. A definite feeling, such as sorrow at a broken love, requires ideas of persons, circumstances, and events, and the musical pattern cannot of itself represent such ideas.[18] An indefinite feeling is incompatible with the nature of aesthetic form, which always is individual and determinate.[19]

We may agree with the argument against the treatment of definite feeling: if music represents or expresses emotion, it is in some sense indefinite or abstract. But the argument against

---

[16] Charles Hartshorne, *The Philosophy and Psychology of Sensation* (Chicago: University of Chicago Press, 1934), p. 7.

[17] Stephen C. Pepper, *Principles of Art Appreciation* (New York: Harcourt, 1949), p. 127.

[18] Hanslick, pp. 34–35.

[19] Hanslick, p. 54.

indefinite feeling rests on confusion about the meaning of "indefinite feeling." The emotional content of music is extrinsically indefinite in three related senses: it cannot be described in words; it cannot be subsumed under a general concept that relates it significantly to some other instance of emotion, whether found in music or elsewhere; and it cannot be related to specific events and situations of life. But this does not mean that the emotion has no intrinsically definite or determinate nature: it means rather that its determinateness affords no footing for effective comparison, which is determinate comparison. Hanslick is entirely correct in asserting the definiteness of musical form and the anomaly that would result from the expression of indefinite emotion by definite form. But the emotion is itself determinate and secures its determinateness from the musical form. It is because of the absolute involvement of the emotion with its tonal form that the emotion resists comparison with anything else.

The discussion of emotion in relation to music is a negative preparation for the positive theory, which has to do with the aesthetic hearing of music. Properly experienced, music has a "self-subsistent and specifically musical beauty," which is "extremely difficult to define."[20] Music consists of musical ideas: that is what is expressed in melody, harmony, and rhythm. But a musical idea is an end in itself and is not subordinate to concepts, images, and emotions. Music is comparable to an arabesque and to a kaleidoscope: the main difference between music and a kaleidoscope is that music is the "direct product of a creative mind, whereas the optic one is but a cleverly constructed mechanical toy."[21] It is apprehended by the imagination in a "voluntary and pure act of contemplation which alone is the true and artistic method of listening."[22]

We must agree that music has a "specifically musical beauty." But the discussion of musical ideas, of the imagination, and of contemplation is left in too rudimentary a state to give an adequate distinction between the "cleverly constructed mechanical toy" and the musical composition. Both have sensory elements unmarred by representation, and both have structure of varying

[20] Hanslick, p. 70.
[21] Hanslick, p. 68.
[22] Hanslick, p. 134.

degrees of complexity and unity. If music can achieve greater complexity or unity or both, that is a difference of degree, not of kind. The structural superiority of music may yield a more varied and intricate pleasure, but it would not of itself provide the meaning and depth that distinguish art from its mechanical analogues. For that distinction, emotion is required. And Hanslick does not rest his case with structure. He notes that an insipid theme may be symmetrical and inquires after the content that impresses us as being symmetrical.[23]

Confronted with the threat of triviality, formalism often seeks to escape by invoking the prestige and intrinsic value of intellect. This motive appears in Hanslick, though in a modified form.

> The most important factor in the mental process which accompanies the act of listening to music, and which converts it into a source of pleasure, is frequently overlooked. We here refer to the intellectual satisfaction which the listener derives from continually following and anticipating the composer's intentions—now, to see his expectations fulfilled, and now, to find himself agreeably mistaken.[24]

It is difficult to find any difference between this activity and a game of chess. In speaking elsewhere of feeling and the composer, Hanslick is willing to speak of a theme as sad or noble, but not as expressing the sad or noble feelings of the composer[25]: one wonders why the intentions of the composer are of more relevance than his feelings, since both lead attention from the objective form to a private and limited biography. The function of intelligence in art goes far beyond the comparison of expectations and outcomes. That is true even of intelligence in the form of intellect, which is intelligence directed toward the universal and abstract and guided by logical analysis. But a purely intellectual activity cannot distinguish art from science and philosophy, and leaves art in a condition of pale competition with them. Hanslick on the whole does not fall into intellectualism: his stress is on the imaginative mode of intelligence, which is directed toward the particular and concrete, is guided by intuition, and

[23] Hanslick, p. 90.
[24] Hanslick, p. 135.
[25] Hanslick, p. 103.

has a special affinity with emotion that Hanslick curiously neglects. Hanslick states that the described intellectual activity takes
place unconsciously, which must mean that it is not an explicit
analysis. In making a formal analysis of Beethoven's *Prometheus
Overture*, designed to show that no feeling is represented, he grants
that such analysis destroys the beauty of the composition.[26] He
affirms that musical beauty is entirely independent of mathematics, and that no mathematical calculation ever enters into a
composition.[27] He finds musical beauty equally in romantic and
classical styles, and says that "the finely-chased salt-cellars and
silver candlesticks, so to speak, of venerable Sebastian Bach, are
but small provinces within the kingdom of musical beauty."[28]
Except for the limited image of Bach, these are refreshing statements from any musical theorist, and especially from a formalist.
It is interesting that he chooses sheer designs to express his opinion
of the limited scope of Bach.

If the beauty and basic value of music are not found in either
structured sound or intellection, we may wonder what is left to
the formalist. The answer appears to be found in a conception
of specifically musical meaning.

> The forms created by sound are not empty; not the envelope
> enclosing a vacuum, but a well, replete with the living creation
> of inventive genius. Music, then, as compared with the arabesque,
> is a picture, yet a picture the subject of which we cannot define in
> words, or include in any category of thought. In music there is
> both meaning and logical sequence, but in a musical sense; it is
> a language we speak and understand, but which we are unable
> to translate.[29]

The text continues with allusions to "logic in music," "the primordial law of 'harmonic progression,'" and the connection
of musical elements by "certain natural affinities."[30] If this is
meaning, it is only syntactical, and therefore can only clarify
our understanding of the form: it does not state what fills the
otherwise empty form and distinguishes it from an arabesque,

[26] Hanslick, pp. 41–42.
[27] Hanslick, pp. 91–93.
[28] Hanslick, p. 90.
[29] Hanslick, pp. 70–71.
[30] Hanslick, p. 71.

which also has a syntax. A nonsyntactical meaning is required to make sense of the initial quotation about meaning; a well is filled not with the bricks of which it is arranged, but by water. A subsequent statement comes much closer to the required meaning.

> The error is due to the extremely narrow conception of the beautiful in music, leading people to regard the artistically constructed form and the soul infused into it, as two independent and unrelated existences. All compositions are accordingly divided into full and empty "champagne bottles"; musical "champagne," however, has the peculiarity of developing with the bottle.[31]

The "soul infused into" the form, or more accurately, the champagne that develops with the bottle, is not identified in the context; but some clues to its nature are given in the passages quoted. It can in some sense be spoken and understood: that is, it can be formed, expressed, and grasped by the intelligence. It is inseparable from the form of which it is the meaning, since it is not infused into the form as though already complete, but develops with the form. It cannot be defined in words or concepts, or translated into another form: which is to take seriously the inseparability of the meaning from the form and the consequent inability of nonartistic life, or of another form, to duplicate the meaning.

It seems certain that these clues and requirements are the essence of what concerns Hanslick in his formalist aesthetics. The requirements are both sound and discerning. But they do not forbid emotion in music: on the contrary, they virtually clamor for it. It is difficult to conceive what the "soul" or "meaning" of music may be, if not emotion: no other candidate suggests itself, since the structured sensation is what must be filled, and the representation of things, actions, and situations is forbidden and could not in any case "fill" the form. The emotion need not be one borrowed from life, as though music were to repeat the sorrow of death or the ecstasy of love. No art repeats the emotion of life. If it represents some situation of life, it may retain the material of the associated emotion, but transforms the emo-

---

[31] Hanslick, p. 74.

tion formally, as will be shown in Chapter 8, the fourth section. Since music does not represent, it does not deal with such concrete or "definite" emotion. But it may, and does, deal with an abstract or "indefinite" emotion, which doubtless occurs in some degree or shape in life, but slips subtly through the concrete characters of love and hate, courage and fear, and can be identified only in patterned tone.

Although Hanslick rejected the notion of an indefinite emotion as the subject or content of music, a notion of which he makes significant use points toward such emotion. Hanslick states that a "certain class of ideas" can be "adequately expressed by means which unquestionably belong to the sphere of music proper."[32] The class is made of ideas

> associated with audible changes of strength, motion, and ratio: the ideas of intensity waxing and diminishing; of motion hastening and lingering; of ingeniously complex and simple progression, etc. The aesthetic expression of music may be described by terms such as graceful, gentle, violent, vigorous, elegant, fresh; all these ideas being expressible by corresponding modifications of sound.[33]

Hanslick unerringly distinguishes between the actual gentleness of an adagio, and the hypothetical notions of "gentleness and concord in the abstract" and, at still further remove, of "the placid resignation of a mind at peace with itself."[34] He thinks that music by its force and motion may "reproduce the motion accompanying psychical action."[35] An emotion involves such psychical motion, and it might be supposed that Hanslick would therefore relate music to emotion. But he disavows such a relation on the ground that the "motion is only one of the concomitants of feeling, not the feeling itself."[36] Music can reproduce the motion of love, but this "may occur in any other feeling just as well as in love, and in no case is it the distinctive feature."[37]

The argument discerns that the subject or content of music is something mobile and abstract. But it errs both in denying

[32] Hanslick, p. 35.
[33] Hanslick, pp. 35–36.
[34] Hanslick, p. 36.
[35] Hanslick, p. 37.
[36] Hanslick, p. 37.
[37] Hanslick, p. 38.

that psychical motion is emotive, and in assuming that psychical motion is inherently abstract. Since the motion is psychical, it is essentially qualitative, unlike the motion of physical things in physical space, which is essentially quantitative. Its quality is not that of the tonal motion, which expresses or represents it but by hypothesis does not constitute it. The domain of quality that remains is that of emotion. The infinite qualitative variety of psychical motion, entailed by the like variety of musical form, can be found only in the domain of the inward textures of emotion. Moreover, the terms used by Hanslick to describe the aesthetic expression of music, and thus psychical motion, are terms of evaluation. To speak of something as graceful or gentle, violent or elegant, is to assign a value. In an art as incomparably direct as music, the awareness of value can be no less immediate, and thus constitutes an emotion. And emotion moves: the subtle pulsation of inward textures is motion at its greatest fluency. In that pulsation change, and nisus toward change, are interwoven with quality: motion and quality are respectively the dynamical and intelligible aspects of a single life.

Because of this close relation, psychical motion is no more abstract than the emotional quality with which it is identified. Since music does not represent the contexts and causes of natural emotion, but produces emotion by tonal structures which are not governed by those contexts, emotion and motion in music are abstract in relation to their counterparts in life. But the emotion conveyed in music is never abstract in the sense of a genus, or formal in the sense of a skeleton. At every instant it is full, or highly determinate. The terms that Hanslick uses to describe aesthetic expression thus are clumsy. If grace or violence is involved, it is different for every composition: the grace with which an emotion moves is inseparable from the emotional texture that moves.

If the foregoing analysis is correct, Hanslick's formalism may be said to dissolve at its own instigation. It denies an emotional content to music, but the content it permits beyond pure form turns out to be emotion. It affirms the musical idea as an end in itself, but the idea has a meaning which is distinguishable from sensory design. The meaning is surrounded with requirements designed to make it specifically musical, but the requirements can be met by emotion which has some affinity with the sensibility of nonmusical life. Hanslick's real interest is not in showing the sovereign value of the sensory design, or in ruling out emotion, but in showing the uniqueness of the meaning or emotion when compared with the experiences of life and the unique ability of the musical form to produce and communicate the meaning. This interest does indeed oppose the representational theory, which supposes that art in its essence refers to something which may be found, literally, substantially, or in its elements, in an existence prior to art. But it is not served by formalism: it calls rather for an expressional theory, as the sequel will attempt to show.

Evaluation of Formalism

The strength of the theory of art as form consists in its recognition of the value that pure form may have in the experience of art and, for that matter, in aesthetic experience outside of art. The weakness of the theory lies in the further assertions that pure form is essential to art, that it defines the characteristic value and function of art, and that it accounts for the other traits of the experience of art. The merits and limitations of the formalist theory may be considered together in a statement that partly ties together and partly extends the observations of the earlier sections of this chapter.

1. Formalism provides an education in sensory awareness that no other theory is likely to undertake. When colors and sounds are subordinated to the interpretation of perceptual objects and their dramatic characters, sensation tends to be stifled and awareness sustains a heavy loss in variety and vitality. Formalism counters that tendency. But sensory design may be a sufficient form in one work of art without dominating the form in another work of art. The enhanced intuition of color and line may be the basis of a sensitive representation of a dramatic character, and of the firm and integral expression of emotion related to such representation. The vivid red color and sharp angles of the El Greco *Cardinal* (Plate 13), and the subdued hues and gentle curves of the Persian *Youth* (Plate 14), convey the nature of stern power and of sleeping ease with perceptive clarity and unerring emotion.

2. Formalism provides a similar growth of sensitivity to struc-

ture. But it sometimes falls into the error which identifies
aesthetic experience with discursive analysis of structures. Analysis
considers a structure as an instance of a type, thereby destroying
the individuality of the form. It separates the parts of a structure, thus destroying the organic unity of the structure. Properly
used, analysis is the propaedeutic of intuition, which alone grasps
the structure as an organic individual. But whether structure is
intuited or analyzed, formalism is unable to give any final account
of its value, whether it be the value of unity in general or the
comparative value of a particular structure. The value of unity
may be alleged as an a priori precept of reason: but human response is quite capable of ignoring abstract reason. The value of
particular structures may be referred to rules and the dogmas of
a tradition, with the result that art eventually is imprisoned. It
seems much better to say that artistic unity is valued because it
expresses an emotion about unity. The emotion derives at least
partly from reason, since it would not exist in a consciousness
that was reasonless: but it is more than bare reason. Similarly,
one structure is better than another because it more adequately
serves the formulation of emotion. The forms of emotion shift
from generation to generation, and methods of structure thus are
permitted and required to change also.

3. It is hardly necessary to repeat that formalism by a strange
abnegation dispenses with the catholic values of representation,
and that a general rejection of representation is pointless if design
is integrated with dramatic character. In addition, formalism is
capable of ambiguity in its account of representation, as we have
seen in Bell's provision for deep space and ultimate reality, and
in Hanslick's admission of a musical meaning. Bell's provision
for realistic forms that do not represent, but are sheer designs,
introduces some perplexity into the decisions as to whether a
work of art does or does not represent, and whether it represents
concretely or abstractly. A photograph of a girl would ordinarily
be called a concrete representation, and a Brancusi statue of the
same girl would be called an abstract representation. But if the
sensed objects do not represent, there is no reason to speak of
them as either concrete or abstract, since there is no original,
model, or standard in relation to which they give a full or partial
view. Taken as formal art, they would better be described as
complex and simple designs. But if the photograph is viewed

as a representation of a girl who in turn is viewed as a design, it may be called visually concrete, since it reproduces the entire visual subject, and dramatically abstract, since it omits the dramatic character of a living body, a sex, youth, and a personality of a certain kind. On the other hand, the Brancusi viewed as an interpretation of such characters may be called visually abstract, since it omits many visual features of the girl, and dramatically concrete in comparison with the photograph. The discussion of concrete and abstract representation in an earlier chapter was free, fortunately, from such complexities, since it assumed some correlation between visual and dramatic characters whenever representation occurred, and thus some correlation between visual and dramatic concreteness and abstractness. Perhaps the assumption is necessary to sanity in the discussion of artistic representation.

4. Formalism frequently is obtuse in its view of emotion. This was evident in Hanslick's theory, which assumes that an emotion either can be identified as love, courage, and the like, or is not an emotion. But emotion has an infinite spectrum of quality, only part of which is isolated for ordinary attention and named; and the part that is named receives labels that are clumsy indeed, since the labels are more appropriate to objects and sets than to the subtle inwardness and variety of emotional textures. Hanslick appears to be unaware of the close connection between sensory quality and emotion: a connection asserted by psychologists who have no axe to grind in aesthetics. Further, the emotion of ordinary life is left aside by those formalists who, like Bell, escape the charge of emotional obtuseness. The formalist is content to let the emotion of life drift blindly and in wild eddies, or to consign it to the psychiatrist, although art is able to understand, ennoble, and even to heal the emotional life of man. Formalism has no account to offer of the condition and position of whatever emotion it may admit to art. The emotion is granted to be occasioned by the form and to be appropriate to the form. But there ought to be a further stipulation that the emotion is identified with the form and in that position in consciousness leads a distinctive kind of existence. What is called for is a theory of embodiment of emotion in form.

5. Formalism provides for contemplation, due to the detachment of the form from life situations, urges, and utilities. A nude seen

as a design, whether in art or in the flesh, has no sexual character and cannot tempt those who are susceptible. Since such persons
would not be likely to see such an object as a design, formalism
can be more certain of contemplation if the design is not realistic.
This is to say that formalism can provide for contemplation where
no problem is involved. It is a far greater achievement to secure
contemplation of dramatic characters. That can be done, however,
only if the emotion occasioned by the characters has the "distinctive kind of existence" mentioned in the preceding paragraph.

6. Formalism explains beauty as a property or effect of sensory
design. Sensory quality provides stimulus and charm, and structure
provides order, implicit intelligibility, and quiet control. The fusion of these values is beauty. No complaint can be made of this
description of beauty, except that it does not go far enough. The
quality and order of a sensory design can be intuited without any
experience of beauty. But if the intuition includes the emotion
which sensory quality and order are able to elicit, the experience
is one of beauty. A certain radiance belongs to beauty, and it is
supplied only by emotion. Without emotion, sensory design is a
formula but not an experience of beauty.

7. Formalism does not consider sufficiently the problem of control. A sensory design is not an end and self-governing; it has its
final value and law elsewhere, in emotion. If beauty is an exposition of emotion, and structures are chosen for their emotional
appropriateness, and sensory qualities live only in their emotional
charge, it is reasonable to say that the form serves the emotion
and that the emotion is the end. If another design could express
exactly the same emotion, it would be indifferent as to which design
is sensed. Since a given emotion can be produced only by a given
form, there is no question of competition between form and emotion, or of a claim of independence of the emotion. But the emotion clearly controls the form. Bell was shown to realize this: but
to do so outside of formalism, since formalism by definition makes
the form the essential fact of art.

8. Formalism sometimes falls into intellectualism. Hanslick,
however, does not commit himself to this doctrine, and Bell appears not to have approached it. Apart from misplaced pride,
intellectualism rests on two mistaken beliefs. One is that structure as aesthetic is discerned in an act of analysis. The other is
that emotion is necessarily blind and meaningless. We have seen

that analysis yields to intuition in the consummate experience of aesthetic structure. And emotion embodied in a work of art is neither blind nor meaningless, as the expressional theory shows.

9. By its negatives on representation and emotion, formalism incurs the danger of esotericism. Formalism aids art by its sharpening of perception and its definition of standards, but it damages art when it pursues the select and remote for their own sake. Pure forms are not esoteric, except when surrounded by the artificial discipline of a special theory. The greatest beauty is incredibly remote, but it comes immediately and not by pursuit of its remoteness.

10. Formalism at times appears to have no organ of spirituality. This certainly is not true of Bell, whose theory joins with a profoundly religious, or total, impulse. But it surely is true of Hanslick. How else can one explain the denial of a transartistic ground for an art commanded by Bach and Beethoven? Granting that there is more to the "kingdom of musical beauty" than the "finely-chased salt-cellars and silver candlesticks" of Bach, there is more also to Bach: but if Hanslick is aware of it, it does not move him to a good phrase. We may agree with Hanslick that the symphonies of Beethoven do not reveal a republican philosophy or the affliction of deafness. But the symphonies, and particularly the chamber works, reveal something deeper and more complex than the impetuousness and unsatisfied longing mentioned by Hanslick. No image, biographical fact, or concept can illuminate the emotion of the last piano sonata. It needs none. But the emotion is not simply one of structured sound, however great the tonal talent. It arises from a sensibility great in its native power, its informing intelligence, and its discovery of human life and inhuman fate.

11. Formalism has the great virtue of taking seriously the autonomy of art. The sensory design exists only in art, and any admissible emotion exists only in relation to the sensory design. But the autonomy of art secured by formalism is at a price, since it removes art from life. It is necessary to find for art a formula that balances two great demands: that art be steeped in life, and that it have a nature and value not duplicated in life. The representational theory is impressed by the one requirement, the formalist theory by the other; for a synthesis, the expressional theory is needed.

12. The final criticism that must be made of formalism is that this theory, like the representational, cannot be applied generally among the arts. If poetry cannot seriously be alleged to be sensory design, still less can the drama and the novel. To have a representational aesthetics for literature, and a formalist aesthetics for music and the visual arts, is to fall into a pluralism whose necessity has not yet been demonstrated.

We may conclude that pure form or sensory design is adequate form and important in art, but that formalism must be rejected. Pure form is not the universal condition of aesthetic form, and when it occurs it is not the end and characteristic value of art. The end of all form, pure and representative, is the experience of adequate emotion. We may now turn to the theory that accepts this end and attempts seriously to clarify it: the theory of art as expression.

CHAPTER 8

Art as Expression

The Elements and Transitive Expression*

Thesis and Problems

The expressional theory of this book holds that the expression of emotion is the essence of art and the source of value in art. The theory thus emphasizes emotion among the basic aesthetic factors. In so doing it stipulates that expressed emotion differs from ordinary emotion in several ways: it is adequate; it is contemplated; and it is fused with the aesthetic form as the condition for adequacy and contemplation. The theory therefore gives secondary emphasis to contemplation among the basic ingredients of aesthetic experience: it does not accept emotion in the consummate experience unless it is contemplated, and it regards expression as the condition under which contemplation is secured.

Like the other hypotheses about the essence of art, the expressional theory takes form very seriously. It has a special motive toward form, since it regards form as that through and in which expression takes place: form is the means, indispensable and preserved and immanent, for the expression of emotion. In this means the theory can accept sensory design, or representation, or the mixture of the two as sufficient for expression, subject to the universal requirement that the elements from sensation or represen-

* Parts of this chapter are taken from "The Structure of Transitive Expression," *Revue internationale de Philosophie*, 1958, Fasc. 2, pp. 174–195.

tation are adequately structured. But the theory goes one step further with structure than do other theories: it holds that the ultimate locus of structure is in emotion, which achieves that state through the structure of the aesthetic object. Granting expression, the theory asserts that beauty occurs as the joyful fruition of expression: it traces the rise of beauty in expression and the elusive qualities that define this high value.

Expression occurs for both the creator and appreciator of the work of art. It may be illustrated, and its range emphasized, in five quite diverse works of art. For each of these it is certain or probable that the artist approached creation with an ordinary emotion, which he transformed into adequacy and for contemplation through the creation of appropriate form. The appreciator may or may not approach the work of art with such an emotion; but he can, like the artist, contemplate an adequate emotion in the distanced form of the work of art.

Goethe's early novel, *The Sorrows of Werther,* represents concretely the situation of a young man who loved an affianced woman and, in despair, killed himself. The artist had had a similar love less than two years before writing the novel, and even gave Werther his own birthday; he expressed and resolved his emotion of unhappy love in the writing of the book. The *Guernica* of Picasso (Plate 16) represents abstractly and symbolically the bombing of the Spanish city of that name. Picasso began the mural two days after the bombing, and expressed in the severe black and white, the kinetic lines, and the harsh angles of the painting his feeling of the suffering of the victims of violent, mechanized injustice. Wordsworth's "Intimations of Immortality" represents the loss in maturity of a "celestial light" beheld in nature by the child. The sonnets of Shakespeare, as in Numbers 60, 64, and 65, represent the loss of beauty, love, individual lives, and natural forms in universal change. In both poets the theme of destructive change was based on long experience and profound meditation, and emotion elicited by the experience and thought was expressed in sounds and rhythms, images and metaphors, to which emotion is readily married. And Mozart's *String Quintet in G minor,* K. 516, represents nothing at all. If it has meaning other than syntactical, the meaning must lie in emotion. The quintet was finished shortly before the death of Mozart's father, and it has been suggested that the quintet expresses filial love. But the

Adagio movement and the Adagio section of the last movement express an emotion of the utmost generality, which cannot be specified as love of a parent, or fear of death or acceptance of it, or even as sorrow or joy. The emotion appears to embrace what is momentous in every significant occasion, whether pleasant or painful, and therefore to occupy so fine a line between joy and sorrow as to combine both of these in one sovereign emotion.

The vividness, range, and unity of examples such as these have helped to foster the theory of art as expression in approximately the last hundred years. Despite this assistance, and the dominance of the theory in the first half of this century, the expressional theory has suffered from contradiction and ambiguity in basic concepts, and from failure to develop in the theory the systematic structures and elusive qualities of the experience of expression.

Schopenhauer regarded music as the image of the Will and the other arts as the presentation of *Ideen* or dynamic universals; in both instances he regarded the relation as similar to or founded on the relation between nature and the Will, which he thought of as one of objectification. Nietzsche emphasized the roles of personality and historical culture in art, and concealed an expressional aesthetic in the specialized thesis that genuine tragedy is a fusion of Dionysian content and Apollonian form. The aesthetics of Santayana set forth what amounts to a dual theory of expression, since on the one hand beauty is pleasure regarded as the quality of an object, and on the other hand an object is expressive only to the extent that it suggests a value derived from another object. Croce identified expression with beauty. Under the apparent influence of Kant and Schopenhauer, he also identified it with intuition: under which notion he modified the concept of expression to include the imaginal forming of all individual objects, and to exclude the construction of perceptual objects or physical things.

Ducasse vigorously opposed several of the Crocean theses and replaced them with the view that art is one of several types of self-objectification, whose special content is feeling as distinguished from thought and from will. Caso was in part a follower of Croce, but he used the term *empathy* for the perception of subjective items as properties of external objects, and *expression* for the making of objects especially suited for such perception. Bell combined an enthusiastic formalism with elements of an expressional theory, suggesting that nonrepresentational forms may express an emotion felt for ultimate reality. Greene contrasted formal beauty and expressive value, but regarded the expressed content of art as an interpretation of objective reality. One hundred and thirty-four years after the publication of *The World as Will and Idea*, but closer to it in spirit, Susanne Langer proposed a theory of art as expressive semblance, in which symbols mediate the conception of the forms of feeling or sentience, and actual feeling carefully refrains from making an appearance.[1]

Such divergence of expert opinion reduces the common denominator of historical concepts of aesthetic expression. It reflects in part the nature of philosophy, whose subject matter and methods do not admit of exact and public formulation. It arises also from diversity of interest and application among individual thinkers, which contributes to the wealth of philosophy. But it also reflects failure to analyze the structures of expressive activity and to locate in them qualities that thus become more meaningful and secure. It is not sufficient, for example, to think of expression as a relation of form and emotion, by virtue of which emotion or the self is clarified and made free and beauty is brought into being. It is necessary, among other matters, to consider how emotion is related to the expressing form, how clarity and freedom arise among other changes in emotion, and how beauty enters the expressive act.

The appropriate analysis may well start with a consideration of the unstudied range of meaning of the word *expression*. In the simplest context, the term can be applied to the act of squeezing water out of a sponge: the water literally is expressed from the sponge. An angry animal is said to express its emotion by growling and snapping. Concepts are expressed in words and sentences. And in the most complex context, emotion is expressed in a work of art. But although these instances cover a good deal of ground, they admit nevertheless of a sizeable generic meaning and of a cumulative order of meanings.

In all four samples expression involves four characteristics: (1)

---

[1] Arthur Schopenhauer, *The World as Will and Idea* (1819); Friedrich Nietzsche, *The Birth of Tragedy* (1872); George Santayana, *The Sense of Beauty* (1896); Benedetto Croce, *Aesthetic* (1902); Curt J. Ducasse, *The Philosophy of Art* (1929); Antonio Caso, *Principios de Estética* (1925); Clive Bell, *Art* (1913); Theodore M. Greene, *The Arts and the Art of Criticism* (1940); Susanne K. Langer, *Feeling and Form* (1953).

A material of some kind exists prior to and independent of the act of expression. The water, anger, idea, and emotion exist and may be identified before they are expressed, though undoubtedly with different degrees of completeness. (2) The material changes from an inward to an outward condition. The change corresponds to the difference between the initial state, of impression, and the final state, of expression. It occurs in a physical and literal space, as in the first instance, or in a nonphysical and possibly analogical space, as in at least the third and fourth instances. (3) The change is not instantaneous, but is a process, or connected sequence of changes. And (4), the outward condition has a content which has some similarity of nature to the material expressed. Expression is neither destruction nor total transformation, but contains identifiable continuity in the natures of the initial material and final content.

To these shared traits the third and fourth instances add certain restricting characteristics. (5) The process of expression is one of development or growth, so that the material of expression may appropriately be called the matter of expression. When thought and emotion are expressed, they undergo changes which increase the amount of character they contain, or improve the way in which they are apprehended. The one change is material or contentual, the other formal or structural. (6) The development is mediated by the construction or simple apprehension of a form, which is transparent to the content expressed and has a similarly outward locus. Construction occurs for the creating thinker or artist; simple apprehension for the reader or appreciator. The outwardness of the expressed content depends on that of the form, and the development of the matter into final content is inseparable from the creation or apprehension of the form. The content is not something that can be poured into or extracted from the form, like water and a bottle; it is internally related to the form. And (7) the content is not dissipated after the outward condition and developed state are reached, but is in some way preserved by the form. This is to say that expression of thought and emotion is not discharge, which would contradict development or at least make it pointless.

These specialized traits do not exhaust the characters available to expression in its most complex mode; for of art it should also be said that (8) the content expressed has a peculiar intimacy of relation to the form, so that the content is incorporated in or fused with the form. Emotion in art is not only inseparable from form in its origin, but indistinguishable from it in the living intuition of art.

These statements have been made in fairly popular terms, and they describe only the bare skeleton of aesthetic expression. To implement them, it is useful and perhaps necessary to distinguish two phases of expression: transitive expression and embodiment. On the supposition, presently to be justified, that the matter and content of aesthetic expression are emotion, transitive expression may be defined as the passage of emotion from a primitive to a developed and adequate state through the mediation of form, and embodiment may be defined as the perception of developed or otherwise adequate emotion as incorporated in form. Transitive expression is described primarily by the first six of the preceding statements, and embodiment by the last two statements.

The nature of expression as distinctly outward activity is present in both phases. It is clearly evident in the transitive phase, where the outward condition of emotion is emphasized by contrast with the preceding inward state and the mediating change. It is also present in embodiment apart from any connection with preceding development, since embodied emotion has an outward condition even on the supposition that its entire history is contained in that state.

Beyond their common ground in expressive activity, the two phases are significantly different in function and problems. Transitive expression is a passage; it is justified by its terminal point in embodiment, which may continue or be repeated after transit or development has ended. Embodiment is the perfect or consummatory phase of expression, comparable to a moving equilibrium, and sufficiently valuable in itself. The problem in transitive expression is the relation between two stages of emotion; the problem in embodiment is the relation between emotion and the form in which it moves. These problems partly overlap; but the differences in the respective terms and relations collect around two different centers, the distinction of which is therefore an aid to subsequent analysis. It is possible that embodiment may exist without transitive expression. Embodiment occurs in the contemplation of a work of art by the artist who made it and by the recipient who merely beholds what another person has made.

Transitive expression is prominent in the history of the one case, but less prominent and sometimes doubtful in the history of the other. Embodiment occurs as well in natural beauty as in art, as Santayana's formula of objectified pleasure indicates;[2] but the existence of transitive expression is not obvious in that sphere. An expressional aesthetic can be certain of embodiment as a general feature of aesthetic experience, but it cannot be as certain of transitive expression. The division into the two phases thus provides elasticity for the theory: the minimum required for the theory is embodiment, and the maximum it may hope for is this and transitive expression. The difference between the minimum and maximum is worth noting: in philosophy, as in diplomacy, it is well to say no more than one needs to say.

Granting the division of aesthetic expression into transitive expression and embodiment, the items that must be accounted for within the frame of an expressional aesthetic are four in number: (1) the role of emotion in expression as a whole, (2) the role and nature of form in expression as a whole, (3) the relation between primitive and adequate emotion in transitive expression, and (4) the relation between adequate emotion and form in embodiment. The remainder of this chapter will be devoted to the first three problems, with emphasis on the third. The problem of embodiment will be dealt with in the following chapter.

Emotion and Expression

The theory of art as expression accords to emotion the primary place in art, and devotes the greater part of its energy as theory to the description and understanding of the relations, transformation, and consequences of emotion in art. Here it stands in clear contrast to the theories of art as representation and as form, which find a secondary or incidental place for emotion in art, or deny it altogether.

The emphasis on emotion requires justification, a preliminary to which was supplied by the more nearly neutral legitimization of emotion in art that was undertaken in an earlier chapter.[3] Apart

---

[2] George Santayana, *The Sense of Beauty* (New York: Scribner, 1896), p. 49.
[3] Above, Chap. 4, "The Role of Emotion in Art."

from any theory of the essence of art, it was stated in that place that emotion has important relations to value, experience, and thought, which justify and even require its entry into the aesthetic experience. It was shown that aesthetic form implies emotion, whether in sensation, the choice and methods of representation, or in the diverse types of aesthetic structure. The arguments of the adversaries of emotion were stated with some precision, and were contravened as being in error about emotion, or art, or the life of values.

These arguments were answered partly from the ground of the expressional theory of art, and the ability of the theory to supply and to give meaning to such answers is a partial justification for the central place accorded to emotion by the theory. It was stated that in expression, emotion achieves a relatively outward and public character, of interest to the behaviorist; that it becomes active and yields power, which the voluntarist values; that it consorts with and gives aesthetic status to ideas, to which the intellectualist is partial; that it achieves distance for disinterested contemplation, to allay the fears of the moralist; that it becomes significantly different from emotion in ordinary life, as desired by the formalist; and that it is purified in distanced objectivity, as a guarantee against sentimentality. If these views regarding emotion and expression are true, it follows that emotion and experience are perfected interdependently. Emotion is the immediate awareness of value, and in expression that awareness achieves its most satisfying fulfillment. Emotion supplies to art an imposing matter and problem, and expression supplies a solution equal to the task. In this solution lies the only balance between life and art that aesthetic theory can discover: through emotion art draws without limit on life, and through expression it achieves a unique status and value that sets it apart from the rest of life.

Further evidence for the centrality of emotion in the expressional account of art may be found in the barest view of the structure of expression. That structure involves an agent of expression, which is the aesthetic form, and a patient of expression, which is the matter and content of expression. It seems clear that the matter and content of expression are the center and end-value of expression, in relation to which the form is a vehicle and instrument. Something appears initially in a primitive state and clamors for fulfillment or adequacy, and the form is the instrument of the change. This distinction is not contradicted by the indiscernible fusion of the content and form in embodiment, which means that the contributions of the two constituents merge, but does not mean that the contributions are the same in function or equal in value. If, then, emotion serves as the matter and content of expression, it has paramount status in that act.

Since emotion is not the whole of experience, it may be objected that it is too narrow a term for the designation of the matter and content of expression. It may be proposed that better terms are "impression" or "passivity." It is true that the matter of transitive expression is an impression: a term as appropriate to the inward condition of transitive expression as "expression" is to the outward condition. It is also true that the inward condition is a passive condition of the mind, to the extent that the mind has not acted on it to form it. It is sometimes assumed that emotion is universally a passive condition; but its fate in expressive activity belies that assumption, as will be shown later. Emotion does not in any case exhaust the passive content of experience, and the objection has in mind those wider reaches as also appropriate to the matter of expression. Croce's treatment of impression, intuition, form, and the individual object suggests that he had in mind such a view of the matter of aesthetic expression: in which case his parallel use of *emotion* and its derivatives either indicates identification of emotion and passivity, with resultant dilution of the meaning of emotion, or indicates confusion in analysis.[4]

Passivity or impression is too wide a conception of the basic matter expressed in art. Sensory passivity begins with sensory feeling, which seldom if ever occurs to attention. The artist and appreciator inherit from ordinary experience sensory intuition and sense perception, in which sensory quality is already formed to some degree and sensation is no longer entirely passive. Perceptual objects may be said to involve expression of felt sensory qualities; but neither the form nor the expressive activity can be called aesthetic without further determinations, which include structure of a select order and emotional relevance. A block of marble and a finished statue are both perceptual individuals, but

---

[4] Benedetto Croce, *Aesthetic,* trans. Douglas Ainslie (London: Macmillan, 2nd ed., 1929), Pt. I, Chaps. i, ii; compare Chap. x.

only the statue can be called an aesthetic individual and an object of aesthetic expression. Croce apparently was willing to apply the term *aesthetic* in the more general context, subject to the proviso that the individual object be held for attention at the level of the image; but such usage, while reverting to an early meaning of the word, is too broad for the phenomena of art and beauty, just as passivity is too broad a concept for the matter of expression.

Passivity is not limited to sensation. The origin of formed and lucid ideas or concepts can be traced to a condition of passivity. The first apprehension that intellect has of the content of a specific concept is of that content in a relatively formless and passive state, which is the state in which we do not understand what we mean by an idea that has not been developed, analyzed, bounded, related, and affixed to words. This primitive object of intellect is formed and expressed by the operations just mentioned. But once more it is true that neither the operations nor the final state can be called aesthetic without emotion and a structure appropriate to it.

These negatives do not mean that the nonemotive contents of passivity have no relevance for aesthetic expression. The development of emotion is also the development of form, in which sensory and conceptual materials may be perfected as constituents of the completed form of the work of art. A poet may be said to express matter from ordinary auditory intuition in the organized word sounds of his poem, and intellectual matter in the meaningful structure of the words. But these expressive activities are parts of the activity of the creation of form and thus subordinate to form as a whole, which in turn is subordinate to the expression of the emotive content.

The expression of intellectual material in the conceptual form of a poem makes poetry somewhat similar to philosophy and science, and it has the disarming advantage that it gives poetry a content that can be removed from the poem and subjected to analysis in prose translation. The formed ideas of a poem are not an end in themselves, however, but are part of the method for the expression of an emotive content which cannot be removed from the poem without serious damage, and which therefore may be said to take the poem seriously enough to reject any alternative locus. There is no rivalry within the poem between intellectual and emotive factors. Intellectual form in poetry differs from its similars in philosophy and science in ways (exemplified by image, symbol, and narrative) which can be explained only on the supposition that it is created for the expression of emotion. The emotion that is expressed may be one that is elicited by abstract thought and is expressed in a concrete form that pays tribute to such thought. Emotion and form of this kind may be found in Shelley's "Hymn to Intellectual Beauty" and in Edna St. Vincent Millay's "Euclid alone has looked on Beauty bare."

If emotion may be accepted as the fundamental matter and content of aesthetic expression, the question that remains is whether any emotion is eligible for that status, or only emotions of a certain kind. It is sometimes believed that certain emotions are inherently aesthetic, due perhaps to delicacy or intensity, purity or loftiness. But regardless of its special characters, an emotion is not aesthetic until it is expressed; and when it is expressed, it is aesthetic regardless of its special qualities. The belief may be modified to assert that the same emotions are more competent for expression, and therefore are peculiarly aesthetic potentially. But the processes of formulation and objectification are formal in a generic sense which is receptive to an indefinite variety of emotional quality. As far as its object, pleasantness or painfulness, and inward texture are concerned, any emotion appears to be expressible and thus artistically eligible. Since embodiment is a condition of distanced contemplation of emotion, the organic sensations and the set of an emotion may have to be greatly revised to permit expression. Subject to this reservation, any emotion appears to be expressible, and thus to satisfy the specifically artistic test for eligibility.

Beyond this test is another, which may lead to preference of one emotion over another. The artist, appreciator, and critic inevitably consider an extra-artistic criterion, which is not easy to state, but may be called the meaningfulness of an emotion. This character is hinted at in the primitive state, and manifest in the adequate state, and it serves as a guide to the comparative evaluation of expressed emotions and thus of the work of art. Meaningfulness in an emotion belongs primarily to the inward texture of the emotion. It seems to be the joint product of diversity of quality in the emotion, unity of relation among the qualities, and generality of sources of the emotion in the self and the world. Meaning rises to its maximum in the intuition of depth, which appears first in the diverse qualities taken separately; second in a unity that is subtly balanced and highly organic; and finally and ultimately in a generality that is distilled without residue, leaving no boundaries or limitations but embracing whatever is bounded. The maximum, with emphasis on generality, may be illustrated in the Mozart *Quintet in G minor* mentioned earlier. Every complete work of art contains emotion in an adequate state, since the emotion is expressed; but only art of great stature has, in addition, emotion of profound significance.

Form and Expression

The primary place accorded emotion by the expressional theory, whether in the work of art or in the pages of expressional aesthetics, does not mean that this theory has less than an absorbing interest in aesthetic form. No theory can discount the complex and fundamental importance of form without being blind to the most accessible and stable datum of the aesthetic experience. Because every theory admits the existence and importance of form, whether as a matter of course or of passion, the expressional theory is not required to take any special responsibility in regard to it, but can borrow heavily from the tradition in dealing with it. This theory has an exceptionally wide position in regard to form, which spares it the controversial spirit that can readily absorb the attention of the specialist. It is clear from even an introductory view of the theory that it takes form seriously, since it regards transitive expression as mediated by form and embodiment as a fusion of emotion and form. Only through form can emotion be made adequate and brought within the compass of intelligence.

The expressional theory is able to do full justice to the sensory aspect of form, whether it appears alone or with representation. The emotional characters of sensation find a ready place in the account of emotion, whether in art or in nature. As Collingwood has said, sensa often are sterilized, or shorn of their emotional nature, by the adult or the practical man.[5] In embodiment, the pristine unity of sensation and emotion is restored, and the res-

---

[5] R. G. Collingwood, *The Principles of Art* (New York: Oxford, 1950), p. 162.

toration is taken as a model of all aesthetic experiencing. When the elements of form are limited in a given instance to sensation, as in formal art, the expressional theory can view the resulting form as sympathetically and discerningly as can formalism, without the dogmatic limitation of art to pure forms, and with the added advantage that the emotional character of the sensory design is properly located in the locus of the design and is properly accounted for in the theory.

With the representational theory, the expressional theory can accept in art the full range of representation, from the third dimension in painting to abstract concepts in poetry. Its requirement is not the use of form of a certain category, whether pure or referential, but the use of form to express emotion. Representational forms can do this as well as pure forms. In either case an emotion can be embodied for objective contemplation and a significant gain in experience and understanding, although the respective emotions will differ in their intrinsic characters and probably in their degree of generality.

The expressive use of representation affords a rationale to representation. If representation is controlled objectively, by the nature of the object chosen for representation, it must either repeat the object or convey the abstract essence and laws of the object. The sciences and philosophy undertake the second function, but it is not available to art because of the concreteness of its forms. Art then becomes in theory a repetition of nature, justified at best by the circumstance that nature often is absent. The fact that art does not in practice descend to that condition is evidence that representation is not controlled objectively. The control lies in the artist's attitude, interest, or evaluation, that is, in his emotion about the object; and this control is the ultimate guide to interpretation in representation. The expressional theory alone supplies this rationale for representation. Thus the theory can accept representational forms as sympathetically as can the representational theory, without the dogmatic limitation of art to such forms, and with the further advantage that a rationale for representation and interpretation is provided. It should be clear that the expressive control of representation does not require or favor a particular kind of representation. It does not imply the use of distorted, bizarre, fantastic, or highly private representation, as of the watches in Dali's *Persistence of Memory* (Plate 2) or of the

face in Munch's *The Cry;* and it does not require the expression
of strong or emphatic emotion, as in *The Cry* or in Van Gogh's
Crows Over the Wheat Fields (Plate 19). The expressionistic schools
in recent art are compatible with expressional aesthetic, but they
have no special privilege within this theory.

The interest of the expressional theory in structure rounds out
the position of the theory in regard to the characters of aesthetic
form. The aesthetic object is distinguished from other individuals
by superior structure, and no work of art exists without structure
of some appropriateness. But structure is of specific importance
for the expression of emotion in several ways. The elements drawn
from sensation or representation, or both, have much greater expressive power when joined in a structure than when separated.
This is particularly true of sensory elements, as has been noted
in the case of music, in which single tones have negligible emotional value in comparison with tones formed in harmonies and
melodies. Structures have a characteristic and direct emotional
value, as has been seen in the instances of harmony, balance, and
rhythm. And emotion itself is susceptible of structure and achieves
it through expression.

Through embodiment, the structuring of sensory and symbolic
elements that constitutes an aesthetic form becomes identically
the structuring of the expressed emotion. For the expressional
theory, the final locus of structure is not in the form or aesthetic
object, but in the emotion. Since, however, emotion is of itself
both tenuous and private, it can achieve and sustain structure
only by affiliation with the aesthetic object. For the same reason,
the affiliation must be of maximum closeness, which can be found
only in the condition of fusion characteristic of embodiment.
Thus emotion and structure are intimately related for the expressional theory. This intimacy supports the thesis already stated,
that types and formulas of structures evolve in the history of art
in obedience to the subtler evolution of the emotion of cultures
and periods. Emotion controls structures and rescues them from
the dogmatism of schools and the aridity of fixed rules.

The expressional theory has no special interest in the question
of the ontological status of the object whose characters have just
been described. It can accept the general thesis set forth in an
earlier chapter, that a form is an essence, or set of characters contemplated without judgment of reality. That judgment set aside,

the form may equally well be located in external physical things, apprehended through sense perception, or in internal imagery, apprehended through introspection. The distinction of the two locations and the more solid reality of the first are of no concern to the contemplator of form, who abstracts from questions of reality and of grounds that lie beyond the immediate phenomenon. This neutral attitude is confirmed within expression, for colors, tones, and words can embody emotion whether received through the senses as parts of a public world or imagined in the privacy of the individual consciousness. A poem can be read aloud from marks on paper, or be imaged intramentally, with equal competence for the embodiment of emotion, provided always that the form is present to awareness with normal clarity and stability. Undoubtedly the sensed poem is more likely to have these attributes, but that is a matter at least partly relative to the individual percipient.

If there is a strong argument for the ascription of external reality to the aesthetic object, it is to be found in artistic creation, which is transitive expression on the part of the artist. It is difficult to conceive of a painting that does not arise through close contact of the artist's body with physical canvas, brush, and pigments. This is partly a matter of convenience in the creative process of trials and changes: a process which can, however, in principle take place imaginally. It is more basically a matter of the use of the brush, which leaves evidences in the painting after creation is over. But even here it may well be that what is involved is not the demand for the external and physical, but the addition of tactile and kinaesthetic characters to the visual, which may have the same essential indifference to the criteria of reality that the visual form has.

Since the position here set forth is one of indifference to ontological status, there is no particular interest in asserting or denying either an internal or external locus for the aesthetic object. Croce regarded expression as a spiritual fact culminating in an internal image, and the sensed external work of art as a translation having practical rather than aesthetic status. The contrast arises not out of the requirements of expressive activity, but out of a special metaphysical bias.[6] And even his idealistic bias does

---

[6] Croce, Pt. I, Chap. xiii.

not properly imply the inferior status of the external object, for it automatically removes from the object as sensed the claims of material substance. The external object then becomes merely a set of determinate and unified characters, which achieve their determinateness and unity through the theoretical activity of spirit. In these respects the external object of sense perception is indistinguishable from the internal object of ordinary imaginal introspection, and Croce's preference for the latter over the former becomes groundless. An idealistic theory of knowledge has no reason to disclaim the perceptual object, for that object arises as much out of the forming activity of spirit as any other object of which spirit may be aware. But another statement by Croce does not suffer these criticisms of the contrast between the internal and external object. Croce's assertion that "intuition means, precisely, indistinction of reality and unreality, the image with its value as mere image,"[7] suggests that the special virtue of image is not to be intramental, but to indicate abstraction from the question of real and unreal. If image then means individuated essence, it may embrace both the intramental image of ordinary usage and the public perceptual object. Except for the emphasis on sensory character, the doctrine so understood appears to be identical with the notion of form as essence set forth in this book.

The Structure of Transitive Expression

The discussion of the general nature of expression has opened the way for the systematic treatment of the two main phases of expression: transitive expression and embodiment. Transitive expression was defined as the passage of emotion from a primitive to an adequate state through the mediation of form, and embodiment was defined as the perception of adequate emotion as incorporated in form. Transitive expression terminates in embodiment, which conceivably may exist without transitive expression, and which in any case proceeds as a moving equilibrium of form and emotion after development has ended. Embodiment involves rela-

---

[7] Benedetto Croce, *The Breviary of Aesthetic*, in Rice Institute *Book of the Opening*, Vol. II (Houston, Texas: circa 1912), p. 443.

tions of the finished emotion to its form, but transitive expression involves relations of the same emotion to its primitive state. These relations within transitive expression contain several contrasts: primitive and developed emotion are opposed as internal and external, potential and actual, indeterminate and determinate, obscure and luminous, and compulsive and free.

In transitive expression, an emotion which ordinarily is hidden within the artist or appreciator is externalized in the aesthetic object. The internal and external conditions of emotion in expressive activity involve a relation of emotion to space. The space in question is not the physical space of ordinary sense perception, and still less is it the physical space of natural science. It shares with the former a perceptual or fairly immediate character; but it contains psychical events which cannot be located in physical space, it is not subject to extensive quantification or exact measurement, and it cannot be investigated in any public manner. It might be called psychical space, except that physical objects appear in it, and it contains objects of memory and imagination which may depend on mind for their existence but are not as obviously psychical as are the activities by which mind apprehends them. With some ambiguity it may be called phenomenal space.

In this space, the self occupies a privileged though dark position at the center. Activity goes on at this center whenever the space may be said to occur. The activity is basically evaluative, and its most immediate content is the inward texture of emotion. Here emotion is felt as belonging to the self rather than to the objects, physical or imaginal, that partially cause it. It is in this position that emotion is relatively potential, indeterminate, obscure, and passive. This is the condition of ordinary life: that is, of life apart from aesthetic perception. But as expression occurs, emotion moves outward in phenomenal space toward the relatively objective contents of experience. Perceptual objects, such as a tree, and intuited sensa, such as the sounds of a voice, normally seem to have an external or distanced position in phenomenal space, since they are set off against the process of attending and against the emotional reaction they may induce, and engage the self usually as means rather than as ends, and are regarded as having a career somewhat independent of the self. Images have a similar position and for like reasons, except that they are not usually regarded as independent of the self: "external" in phenomenal space does not mean independence of the self or knower, as it does in physical space. But as expression occurs, the objects that enter into aesthetic form move inward, so that emotion and form join at a position which differs from that occupied by either of them in ordinary awareness. Thus sounds in music and colors in painting appear closer to the self than would otherwise be the case, and the expressed emotion appears further from the self than is customary. This reciprocal movement answers to the characteristic mode of awareness in art and beauty, in which sensory contents appear to be felt as emotive and emotion appears to be sensed.

The relatively external position of feeling in aesthetic experience need cause no questions about the ontological status of objective feelings. The emotion that is expressed is not attributed to independent physical objects, which do not feel and cannot even be certified to exist. It is attributed to apparent objects in phenomenal space. It is not, however, attributed to these objects in the sense that they are experienced as subjects or agents of feeling. Objects in general do not feel and are not experienced as feeling. Imagination could no doubt interpret them as subjects of feeling, but that would be an extra-aesthetic whimsy. No experience or supposition about subjects or agents of feeling occurs in aesthetic experience, and that is one of the objective characters of the experience.

The attribution of emotive content to objects is merely an experiencing of the emotion as though it were a quality of the object comparable, in its apparent relation to the object, to a color. The problem of the independent existence of colors does not engage the artist or the aesthetician; and it is not supposed by a subjectivistic interpretation of color that the color is sensed by the object that it appears to qualify. The apparent position of a quality affords no implications as to the actual position of the quality in the ensemble of causes and effects and cannot be contradicted by any theory as to the cause or actual basis of the quality. Reasons other than the position of an emotion in phenomenal space lead us to judge it as caused by and lodged in a self. But such knowledge is irrelevant to aesthetic experience.

The origin of an emotion in the self does not indicate how the self will space the emotion. It is probable that the most primitive experiencing contains no awareness of objects in contradistinction to subject, of boundaries and shared histories, and therefore has no distinction of position between self, emotion, and sensory qualities. In such experience, colors are as subjective in location as emotions, and the two interweave formlessly. In the organization of its world, which is largely a construction of things in the character of means to internal ends, the self objectifies the sensory qualities, stripping them of emotive value in proportion as they become parts or tokens of useful objects. A green color is objectified in a plant; as a sign of useful food, the color may lose its intrinsic emotional quality. In aesthetic experience, the self recovers the intrinsic value of sensa, which means that they move inward to become vehicles of a fresh objectification by self, the content of which is emotion. The recovery is not a reversion to primitive experiencing, for the sensa now bear the discipline of the forms contributed by sensory intuition and perceptual interpretation. Thus the position in which the self will experience its objects is variable, and it will depend on the history of the self, the purposes of the self, and the extent to which the self has itself developed.

As emotion moves from an internal to a somewhat external position in aesthetic expression, it passes from a relatively potential condition to one of full actualization. In its own character in the primitive state, the emotion already is actual; but in relation to what it may become, it is potential. This potentiality is not mere logical possibility, or absence of self-contradiction, which belongs to characters that do not become actual as well as to those that do, and thus has no principle of selection and impetus for actualization. Logical possibility belongs equally to centaur and horse and thus cannot favor the actuality of the latter. The potentiality cannot be identified simply with existential possibility, which is contained in the presence of a cause from which the existence and nature of something may be derived or anticipated.

Causality may be either statical or dynamical. Statical causality implies the concrete separateness of cause and effect; but the developed emotion is not that distinct from the primitive emotion, being rather the primitive emotion expanded in nature and shifted in position. Statical causality emphasizes the notion of uniformity of connection as the essence of the causal relation;

it is hard to verify when the terms are emotions, since emotion has a plenary individuality that resists repetition and subsumption under universals. Accompanying the individuality is a creative factor opposed to rigorous causal determination: the emergence of the actualized emotion involves no kind of necessity, for a somewhat different outcome, or none at all, is compatible with the primitive emotion.

It is possible that a concept of dynamical causality can meet these criticisms of a causal interpretation of the potentiality in question. Dynamical causality emphasizes force or power rather than uniform connection; it admits spontaneity to some extent; and it does not require a sharp separation of cause and effect. Such a concept would center about a continuing impulsion, whose career is one of growth and unfolding. At the heart of the impulsion is a telic factor, sometimes clear and sometimes vague, but consisting of a psychical pressure toward fulfillment of essence, experience, value, and self. The bearer of the impulsion is the emotion in its primitive state, and the general description of that state may vary considerably. The primitive condition may be a particular emotion derived from a particular incident, both of which may be identified in consciousness by the person involved in transitive expression, as by Goethe in writing *Werther*. It may consist of a more generalized emotion, which contains the obscure drift of many past feelings associated with a variety of situations and meditations, as for Wordsworth in writing "Intimations of Immortality." It may be a latent emotion, which in the artist is carried or represented by a pivotal sensation or thought in the approach to creation, and in both artist and appreciator becomes evident only in the process of creating or apprehending form. Whatever may be the general type of the primitive emotion, transitive expression brings into actuality characters which are continuous with the primitive emotion and founded in it, although not perceived in it and therefore not actual in that state.

The actualization of character in the emotion is accompanied by an increase of determinateness. The determinateness of the developed emotion follows from its actualization in aesthetic form, which has a higher degree of determinateness than existence usually betrays. In the condition of embodiment that is the goal of transitive expression, emotion joins with the sensory and symbolic content of aesthetic form and achieves the structure of that form. Emotion thereby shares the determinateness of the form in which it is embodied.

It has been shown that determination implies the establishment of a limit or boundary.[8] The limit distinguishes what the character or thing is from what it is not, and thus separates a character from other characters and confers identity on it. In transitive expression, the primitive emotion is relatively indeterminate. It has sufficient boundary and identity to distinguish it roughly from other primitive emotion of a considerably different character; but a more precise identification is impossible. The artist therefore can apprehend only dimly what it is that stirs him to create. As it develops, however, the emotion achieves further limitation, which separates it from every other emotion, even emotion of a kind so close as to elude the distinctions of ordinary and of scientific language. A sequence of poems dealing with roughly one emotion, or with a closely related set of emotions, such as those of love, change, and death in Rossetti's *House of Life,* can proceed at so high a level of determinateness that no poem is apt to repeat another in its embodied emotion. The more consummate the art, as in Shakespeare's sonnets dealing with time and change, the more sharp and polished is the distinction of the embodied emotion from every other emotion, whether in art or in ordinary life.

A service of determinateness may be found in the clarity with which the developed emotion is apprehended. Determination through form confers on the emotion an element of "line" that satisfies the intelligence. In its indeterminate and potential state, primitive emotion is opaque to the understanding. Within its borders, currents of emotion arise unexpectedly, move about ambiguously and interpenetrate, and subside without culmination or resolution. In this condition, emotion is dark though it may indeed be violent. But in its fully determinate state, emotion is made luminous or transparent. It arises under controls by form appropriate to the itinerary it is to follow. Its several currents or nuances have a transparent history, and an inevitable destination that is freely chosen. They grow and decline in a way that is full of meaning, which does not lie outside the emotion, but can

---

[8] Above, Chap. 3, "The Concept of Form."

be found in other sections of the emotion and in the emotion
as a whole.

The emotion thus runs its course to its final resolution, so that
it is experienced as a whole with a beginning, middle, and end.
It cannot be broken down into parts separable either for analysis
or in existence, and therefore it cannot be understood analytically
or conceptually. It has a considerably more organic kind of determinateness, which sponsors a more immediate but fully formed
understanding. Intelligibility is not limited to reason, with its
preference for identity over diversity, the universal and abstract
over the particular and concrete, and necessity over spontaneity.
Intelligibility occurs wherever there is form, the concept of which
is broader than reason, though never embracing the irrationality
of self-contradiction.

It might be supposed that emotion is the least propitious
ground for the exercise and imprinting of intelligence, since
emotion often is associated with irrational impulse, violence, and
bodily activity. But the relatively external position of emotion in
aesthetic experience means that the emotion is not identified with
the self in its practical, conative character. In its external position,
the emotion is neither a stimulus to action nor a discharge from a
critical situation. On the contrary, it has the detachment from
practical urgency typical of the more objective content of experience, such as sensation and thought. In this detached position the emotion invites objective contemplation of its nature, and
contemplation proceeds with security because of the fixation of
emotion in the objective form. Whatever violence the emotion
may have had is eliminated by the shift in position, but an
intensity appropriate to the pulsation of meaning takes its place.
The intensity is fused with clarity, and only in aesthetic experience
can the combination be counted on: ordinary living separates the
pair all too often. Thus external position joins with determinateness to make the emotion luminous and intelligible.

The intelligible character of the developed emotion is the
proximate cause of the final trait to be noted in the emotion: its
nature as active and free within the self rather than compulsive.
In the primitive condition of emotion the self is passive. The
emotion is given to it from without, rather than assimilated and
mastered, and the emotion thus is appropriately called a passion
in the self. The emotion may very well have major sources within

the self, but those sources are not connected with the self as a whole. On the contrary, they have a life of their own, scattered, furtive, and dark. Their deposit of evaluation occurs in the primitive emotion as something isolated from the self and possibly contrary to it. The emotion contains a fund of energy and meaning which should add to the power of the self, but the fund is not integrated with the self and has the effect upon the self of a burden. The potentiality in the emotion is a challenge to the self to grow in the free development of experience, but the self is unable to meet the challenge and feels contained and impotent.

In a fortunate moment, however, the self finds itself coming to terms with the alien emotion. It does so not by expunging the emotion from itself, nor by harnessing the emotion to a practical activity. Such methods would remove the burden of the emotion, but they would also remove a possible contribution to the self. The method pursued by the self in the aesthetic mode is that of the development of the emotion in form. When fully developed, the emotion is no longer isolated and scattered. It is a coherent and ordered experience. It is steeped in the forming activity of the self, which recognizes in it the fulfillment of its own activity. At the same time, it is objectified in the distanced form, where it is fixed under complete control, neither enticing nor rebelling. The emotion thus is mastered by the self: the self has power over it. The fund of energy and meaning now contributes to the self, which grows in power from both components. But the self is active and free insofar as it has power. Since the self has power over the emotion and through the emotion, the self is free in relation to the emotion, and the emotion is a free movement within the self.

The full understanding of the freedom of the self in aesthetic activity requires a distinction between ethical freedom, appropriate to the self in its interested and practical function, and aesthetic freedom, appropriate to the self in its disinterested and contemplative function. For ethical freedom, the emotion is formed conceptually, yielding an abstract grasp of the nature of the emotion and especially of its causes, effects, and value. Depending on whether the conceptual evaluation is positive or negative, the emotion is integrated as a real component of the self, or it is liquidated. In either instance the self has increase of power through the intellectual act of conception, with its extension of essence or meaning. If the emotion is integrated, its energy adds to the power of the self; if it is liquidated, the power of the self is restored that had been injured by passion. Ethical freedom was well described by Spinoza in his *Ethics,* Part V.

For aesthetic freedom, the emotion is formed intuitively, yielding a concrete grasp of the nature of the emotion in the condition of embodiment. In that condition, the emotion is neither integrated nor liquidated: it is contemplated with distanced objectivity. The self again has increase of power through the intuitive act of embodiment, with its extension of meaning or essence in a complex degree and in a highly immediate mode. Since the emotion is not integrated, its energy is not directly added to the power of the self; but the injury through passion is removed in the distanced position. This removal of passion is what is usually called the liberating character of aesthetic expression. It was experienced by Goethe in writing *Werther:* he was freed from the oppression of his emotion of disappointed love, while continuing to experience the emotion in the form of his creation. Liberation is a negative component in freedom and should not be confused with the other and positive components. Freedom is not mere liberation or release, except where nature or human nature may allow nothing more. Release may be had through animal discharge, except that discharge is temporary whereas liberation may be enduring. And further evidence for the positive nature of aesthetic freedom is found in the fact that, though the energy of the embodied emotion is not added directly to the self, it is added indirectly or in modified fashion. Though distanced, the emotion is a vital pulsation in consciousness, where it strengthens attention in a bright focus. To this may be added the power derived from beauty, which will be shown later to be an emotion distinct from the embodied emotion, and which is integrated as a real component of the self.

Transitive Expression, Creation, and Contemplation

When transitive expression has successfully completed the passage involved in the five pairs of opposites, it has issued in embodiment. Transitive expression therefore implies embodiment; but the question remains whether embodiment implies transitive expression. It is clear that for the artist, embodiment is achieved by a preceding activity of transitive expression. The work of art comes into being only by a process of fashioning and creating form, which process is inseparable from the development of emotion in the artist. But the recipient of the work of art does not in any obvious way create a form. Neither does the spectator of natural beauty. In both cases the contemplator experiences embodiment, since he perceives the form as joined with an external, fully actual, determinate, luminous, and active emotion. But the absence of a history of making raises a question as to the existence of transitive expression in the mere beholder. If such expression does occur, a further question arises as to its relation to transitive expression in the artist.

It is probable that the appreciator approaches the work of art with a primitive emotion relevant to the emotion that can be objectified in the particular work of art at hand. The experience of change, love, and deity, of struggle, injustice, guilt, and defeat, deposits in the self emotion which, whether latent or conscious in the approach to the work of art, may well be relevant to it. The immediate question here concerns the relation of the beholder's emotion to the objective form rather than to the primitive emotion of the artist. The emotion of the artist is of merely biographical interest except as it speaks through or in the form; but when that happens, the artist drops out of the picture and the form alone has authority. Furthermore, emotion has a very considerable power, not generally recognized in the theory of art, of distillation, transfer, and generalization. Primitive emotion in the beholder therefore may be relevant to the given work of art without having any great likeness to the original emotion of the artist. Granting the existence of a relevant emotion, it can be brought to a fully developed condition by the simple apprehension of a form created elsewhere, with embodiment as the special character of the developed state.

But the generalization of the theory of transitive expression to cover all instances of embodiment is a matter of some risk. The discernment of primitive emotion is necessarily not clear, and the investigation of relevance is correspondingly difficult. This dual hazard is involved in applying the theory to the creative process of the artist, but it is considerably increased in the general form by absence or frailty of evidence in the appreciator, whose introspective powers may not be equal to the task of confirmation or refutation. In addition to these difficulties concerning method, it appears that development of a primitive emotion in the beholder may be an abbreviated process, just as simple apprehension is less complex than creation. Insofar as this is true, intermediate phases may occur only in part or not at all; but a modified kind of transitive expression still occurs in the change from primitive to developed conditions of emotion. And it is conceivable that emotion may be brought into existence by and in form without any history. It is not likely that this will happen where emotion is complex. Such emotion requires maturation in the living process, which is one of cumulative experience and reflection. In this respect it has a more subtle discipline than the naked understanding. But where emotion is not complex, it seems quite possible that it should be perceived in form without any antecedent existence. Thus the discernment of gaiety in a flower, which underlies the beauty of the flower, does not obviously call for a preceding process of transitive expression; and in the actual case it does not appear to supply one.

The less certain existence of transitive expression for the beholder is an intimation that where it occurs, its nature differs from that of transitive expression for the artist. The difference comes under two headings: sensibility and imagination, whose interplay is too complex to be traced. In the artist, sensibility has more scope than in the typical appreciator. This means that his primitive emotion has more energy and meaning, and that in turn means that its potentiality is more readily recognized. The recognition calls into play powers of imagination, which are sufficiently strong in both their nature and motivation to develop the emotion through the simultaneous development of form. Neither the determinate emotion nor the determinate form exists prior to the artist's activity, and the artist alone brings them into existence. His activity therefore may be called a creation, in a more modest sense of the word than the meaning appropriate in metaphysics.

This is not, however, true of the beholder's activity. The appreciator does not make a form, whether perceptual or imaginal, but apprehends a form derived from a foreign activity. Only with this assistance from the artist is he able to experience his emotion in determinate form. For the artist, the effective start of transitive expression is the primitive emotion, and the perception of form is the end. For the beholder, the effective start is the perception of form, by virtue of which a primitive emotion is guided into a determinate state. It is true that the beholder must acquire an understanding of the form, which cannot be merely presented to him from without; and this implies a contribution from his own nature. The understanding may pass into factors of interpretation which modify or add to the form. The imagination of the appreciator must animate what is literally presented and understood, in order that the form may be fully organic and may embody emotion. The emotion can exist for the appreciator only insofar as he experiences it, and he can experience it only insofar as his own nature is capable of bringing it forth. But these factors do not destroy the fundamental difference between artist and beholder in regard to the genesis of form and emotion in transitive expression. Of these, the artist is the only creator. There is accordingly no warrant in the nature of transitive expression for the thesis that beholder and artist are identical. They probably have an identical position in embodiment; but the concept of embodiment is irrelevant to questions of genesis and therefore to questions about creation.

CHAPTER 9

Art as Expression

Embodiment and Beauty*

The Problems of Embodiment

Embodiment has been defined as the perception of adequate emotion as fused with form. Whether preceded or not by the process of transitive expression, it is the consummatory phase of aesthetic expression and the heart of aesthetic contemplation: in it, a formed and objective emotion is experienced as fused with the form through which it has these traits. This phase of expression may be viewed either synthetically or analytically. The analytic view considers the emotion and the form as conceptually separate items, and inquires into the kind of relation that unites them in support of fusion. It is concerned with the structure of embodiment. The synthetic view preserves the concrete immediacy of embodiment, with its experience of accomplished fusion, and attends to the special characters that accompany the fusion. The leading problems accessible to the synthetic view are those of beauty, which emerges out of embodiment by virtue of the structure discerned in the analytic view; of aesthetic

* The third through the sixth sections are reproduced, with revisions and additions, from a paper presented as a presidential address to the Missouri State Philosophical Association, Fulton, October, 1956; read in part at the Fifth Interamerican Congress of Philosophy, Washington, D. C., July, 1957; and published as "Beauty, Embodiment, and Art," *Philosophy and Phenomenological Research,* Vol. XXI, September, 1960, pp. 50–61.

intuition, which is the cognitive mode appropriate to embodiment; and of liberal activity, which is the principal basis of the moral status of art. This chapter will consider the structure of embodiment, beauty, and intuition; liberal activity will be deferred to Chapter 12, the first and fifth sections.

Form as the Sign of Emotion

At least three hypotheses may be advanced in explanation of the relation between form and emotion. The form may be believed to be the sign or symbol of the emotion, or the cause of the emotion, or in a relation of mutual immanence with the emotion.

The theory that the form is a sign of the emotion holds that the form refers to the emotion. The reference here intended is not one of emotional representation that is part of the form, as when a novel describes the emotional state of a man in despair. Such representation is indubitably symbolic and referential; but it occurs as a normal part of the representation of objects, which happen in this case to be emotions; and it is limited to works of art that have representational form. What is intended by the present theory is a relation of reference that occurs between the aesthetic form as a whole and the emotive position or interest of the contemplator. If the theory is true, a relation of reference would occur in every instance of aesthetic experience, whether the aesthetic object involve representation of objects or be a pure form. The essence of the theory is the assertion that when the contemplator discerns the emotive character that is appropriate as response to the form, he does not experience it as an emotion actual in his own consciousness, but apprehends it in a purely symbolic mode. The theory may or may not be couched in the language of the theory of art as expression; but when it is, it asserts that the matter and content of expression are not actually felt by the artist or contemplator, but are negotiated by signs or symbols which, for the content of expression, are the aesthetic form. The theory thus asserts that in its relation to the emotive position of the contemplator, all art is representation, though on a level distinct from and less direct than that discussed in the analysis of the aesthetic object made in an earlier chapter.

The evaluation of the sign theory may be made summarily by

considering characteristics of referential meaning set forth in Chapter 2, the fourth section:

1. Reference involves a quantitative distinction of sign and referent, so that they are numerically two. But in the experience of embodiment, the form and the emotion are fused into one object of attention.

2. Reference involves a qualitative distinction between sign and referent. The sign is always in some way abstract in relation to the referent, which has characters not conveyed by the sign. Since form and emotion are experienced in embodiment as one, there can be no qualitative distinction between them. In the aesthetic perception of a color or shape, the distinction between sensory and affective components disappears: the emotion appears to be seen in the act of being felt, and the color is felt in the act of being seen. Furthermore, the emotion is made determinate by the form and has no characters other than those conveyed by the determining form.

3. The object referred to by a sign need not exist. But the emotive content of expression does exist as a datum of the experience, and there is no respect in which expression would be improved if emotion were removed from existence.

4. Signs do not create the object that they signify: but the form is partially creative of the emotion that it expresses. By virtue of formulation in transitive expression, emotion passes from a primitive to an adequate character, and the increase of essence is due to the form. If embodiment occurs without preceding development, the embodied emotion is entirely due to the form.

5. If the referent of a sign should exist, it would still in some respect be absent from the interpreter, for whom the sign is present as a partial mediator of the absent referent. But the emotion in expression not only exists, but exists in the locus of the present form, being fused with it.

6. The passage of the distance between sign and thing signified requires some shift of attention, which takes the form of a movement of transcendence from sign to meaning. There is, however, no movement of transcendence, or of any other sort, in the relation between form and emotion.

7. Signs are subordinate in value to their referents, and have in their own character no value except as conveyors leading beyond themselves. But aesthetic form has sufficient value to lead

some aestheticians to regard it as of sole or paramount value. Without taking that position, and granting that the value of form derives finally from the emotion that it expresses, it is clear that the form is not a substitute for the emotion, and that its value rises to the value of the emotive content by virtue of identification with the emotion. Thus the form is not experienced in embodiment as subordinate to the emotion, but as one in value with it.

8. The highest virtue of a sign is to be transparent to its meaning, so that attention barely lodges on the sign and in the ideal case passes through it without notice. But form in art absorbs attention to the highest degree.

If these asserted contrasts between reference to emotion and embodiment of it are true, then the form cannot be a sign of the embodied emotion. But it may be worthwhile to examine the semiotic theory further, with emphasis on certain of the points that have just been summarized. This may be done in relation to the work of Susanne Langer, whose *Philosophy in a New Key* and *Feeling and Form* are notable statements of aesthetics in general, of a theory of art as expression of emotion, and of expression as based on a symbolic relation between form and content.[1]

In calling the aesthetic form a symbol, Mrs. Langer expresses her belief that the form neither indicates the existence of the emotion in question nor participates in a practical reaction to it. The work of art is not like tears or a cry of pain, which are symptoms of an actual emotion in the utterer, incitements to action that would remedy the state of affairs, and avenues of discharge and relief. A cry of pain is an instance of what Mrs. Langer calls "self-expression," and so are "the expressive abandon of the Indian 'Ki-yi' and 'How-how,' the wailing primitive dirge, the wild syncopated shouts of African tribesmen."[2] In this type of expression, an emotion is actually felt, and it is felt with a practical efficacy that leads to overt action. Such action has no affinity with aesthetic activity. "Sheer self-expression requires no artistic form. A lynching party howling round the gallows-tree, a woman wringing her hands over a sick child . . . is giving vent to intense feelings;

---

[1] The following four paragraphs are reproduced, with revisions, from "Semblance, Symbol, and Expression in the Aesthetics of Susanne Langer," *The Journal of Aesthetics and Art Criticism,* Vol. XIV, June, 1956, pp. 489–502.

[2] Susanne Langer, *Philosophy in a New Key* (Cambridge, Mass.: Harvard University Press, 1942), p. 216.

but such scenes are not occasions for music, least of all for composing."[3]

The kind of expression that is appropriate to art is what Mrs. Langer calls "logical expression." Emotion is said to be logically expressed when symbols are devised through which the emotion can be conceived, and the emotion is conceived when it is contemplated objectively so that its form becomes apparent. The symbol must itself have a form similar to that of the emotion, and it is through the similarity that the emotive form is made discernible, the work of art becomes a symbol of the emotive form, and the emotion is logically expressed.

> The tonal structures we call "music" bear a close logical similarity to the forms of human feeling—forms of growth and of attenuation, flowing and stowing, conflict and resolution, speed, arrest, terrific excitement, calm, or subtle activation and dreamy lapses— not joy and sorrow perhaps, but the poignancy of either and both —the greatness and brevity and eternal passing of everything vitally felt. Such is the pattern, or logical form, of sentience; and the pattern of music is that same form worked out in pure, measured sound and silence.[4]

If expression of an actual emotion necessarily were to have the attributes that Mrs. Langer ascribes to it, and were to be as opposed to logical expression as she thinks it is, there could be no question of the adequacy of her belief that emotion in art is attended to only symbolically. In her exposition, the existence of the emotion seems to become the start of a chain of undesirable characteristics. Existence always has a factor of particularity in it, and Mrs. Langer appears to enlarge on that factor in negative ways, so that the existent emotion becomes part of a private biography and is denied universal scope. We have seen, however, that an emotion can be quite actual in experience and still have general purport, and the self experiencing the emotion can detach itself from its local moorings and achieve a parallel breadth of meaning, experience, and value. Existence also is the locus of action, which is a particular sustained by particulars in the environment. Mrs. Langer interprets this to mean that an existent

---

[3] Langer, p. 216.

[4] Susanne Langer, *Feeling and Form* (New York: Scribner, 1953), p. 27.

emotion must be an incitement to practical action, including an emotional catharsis of a psychophysical sort. But we have also seen that it is possible for an actual emotion to be contemplated rather than to be acted on, and for the contemplated emotion to be preserved in the form that is the vehicle of contemplation. In general, aesthetic form is the condition by which emotion can be shorn of particularity and practicality, and be made intelligible for the satisfaction of the understanding, without also being shorn of its existence. The apprehension of emotion in form is not only an understanding of the emotion, but also a creating, living, and enjoying of the emotion. Only a nonsymbolic form is competent for both functions.

Mrs. Langer's own discussion of the aesthetic symbol, issuing out of the perceptive statement of the presentational or non-discursive nature of the art symbol, leaves some doubt as to how literally and seriously the theory of symbolic function should be taken. In *Philosophy in a New Key,* meaning was said to be not a quality of the sign vehicle but a function, or pattern of relationship, based upon the vehicle; and meaning was attributed to all symbols. In *Feeling and Form,* it is stated that the symbolic function of music

> is only loosely called meaning, because the factor of conventional reference is missing from it. . . . Music has import, and this import is the pattern of sentience—the pattern of life itself, as it is felt and directly known. Let us therefore call the significance of music its "vital import" instead of "meaning."[5]

Mrs. Langer continues to speak of the work of art as a symbol, though in the immediate sequel she makes further qualifications in regard to sign-function. The "nondiscursive form having import without conventional reference" is presented "not as a symbol in the ordinary sense, but as a 'significant form,' in which the factor of significance is not logically discriminated, but is felt as a quality rather than recognized as a function."[6]

These modifications of theory are an attenuation of the doctrine of the symbolic relation between form and feeling. But the statement that significance in art is "felt as a quality rather than

---

[5] Langer, *Feeling and Form,* pp. 31–32.
[6] Langer, *Feeling and Form,* p. 32.

recognized as a function" points to an intimacy of relation between form and feeling that is obscured, if not denied, by the
idea of symbolic relation. So close a relation appears to be anti-
thetical to the distinction in number and quality of sign and
referent, and to transcendence and transparency in the sign. The
last pair of attributes of reference is recognized by Mrs. Langer
when she speaks of words as being ideal signs because "in themselves they are completely trivial"[7] and therefore do not detain
attention in its passage to the referent. Such an account of the
sensed content of words does not apply to poetry; and in general
it does not apply to the alleged vehicle of symbolism in art, which
is the created form. But the value of the form is not something
contradistinguished from that of the expressed content, as though
the form were an ornament of intrinsic and separate charm. The
form has high value because there is no movement of transcendence from it to the emotive content; the emotion is not only actual
in the experience, but immanent in the form.

The difficulties of the sign theory are increased by passing from
the general question of reference to the specific question of how
reference is to be accomplished in the relation of form and emotion. Reference may be through either conceptual or imaginal
signs. For Mrs. Langer it is the first. Presumably this means that
a work of art is somewhat indeterminate in its meaning, conveying only as much character in the emotion as can be found in
all instances of the class. Insofar as a musical composition, for
instance, should take joy as its object, and signify only what is
generally to be found in joy, reference would be conceptual. But
in Mrs. Langer's view the object of musical conception is not the
content of emotion, whether specified for a particular instance or
generalized for a class; it is the form of emotion, involving elements of "growth and of attenuation, flowing and stowing, conflict and resolution." If these forms are conceived, they too should
be signified in somewhat indeterminate fashion, embracing only
what may be found in all instances of growth, or of flowing, or
of conflict. But the flow of emotion relevant to a particular composition is a highly specific flow, like the tonal pattern that is
said to represent it, and it is differentiated from all other instances
of flow. It is therefore not appropriate to say that it is conceived.

[7] Langer, *Philosophy in a New Key*, p. 75.

To be so determinate, a form of feeling must be inseparable from the emotional content of which it is the form. This corresponds to the inseparability of the tonal structure from the tones of which it is the structure. If the qualitative wealth of emotion and of sensation is incorporated in the symbolic scheme, as seems necessary to do justice to the forms of emotion and of sensation, signification of the former by the latter would be imaginal rather than conceptual. Such a mode of signification would explain not only why a highly determinate form of emotion is dealt with, but why the form should be of emotion in the first place rather than of some physical or biological process. Growth and flowing and conflict are not limited to emotion, and it is because of the qualities of tonal sensation that tonal conflict, for instance, specifies emotional conflict. The musical composition may therefore be proposed as an image of the emotion.

Here other difficulties arise. Although there is resemblance between the structure of the music and of the emotion, it is not possible to find resemblance between tonal quality and emotive quality. Undoubtedly there may be a causal relation between the two, but it does not depend on likeness. A sound and an emotion are both qualitatively unique, and for that matter belong to distinct families of quality. Beyond the problem of resemblance lies the problem of distinguishing between emotion as actual and emotion as symbolized imaginally. Since emotion is an intramental content, the distinction is not as clear as it may be for image and sensation. Common sense can readily distinguish between the image of water and actual water. But the only distinction that suggests itself for the distinction of imaged emotion and actual emotion is that of faintness—intensity. This is a distinction of degree, not serviceable for the distinction between the unreal and the real. Furthermore, it contradicts the clarity of emotion in the aesthetic experience, as shown in the analysis of transitive expression. It gives a certain mediocrity to the referential account of art, since it makes the superiority of symbolized over actual emotion to consist in diminished strength of the object. In sharp contrast, the theory of the embodiment of actual emotion asserts an emotion of subtle intensity, which is clarified for objective contemplation in the form that expresses it. Perhaps the theory of emotive reference is a halting description of emotion in this objective condition, which mistakes distanced emotion for unreal emotion.

PLATE 13. *El Greco*, Cardinal Don Fernando Niño de Guevara *(1596–1600)*. *The Metropolitan Museum of Art, Bequest of Mrs. H. O. Havemeyer, 1929. The H. O. Havemeyer Collection.*

PLATE 14.   Youth Sleeping under a Willow Tree *(Persia, Safavid period, late 16th century).* *The Cleveland Museum of Art, Purchase from the J. H. Wade Fund.*

PLATE 15.   Chartres Cathedral, *nave (12th–13th centuries). Photograph No. 168978, Marburg-Art Reference Bureau.*

PLATE 16. Pablo Picasso, Guernica (1937). On extended loan to The Museum of Modern Art, New York, from the artist, P. Picasso, Permission SPADEM 1968 by French Reproduction Rights, Inc.

This error is avoided by a nonreferential theory of the form as sign of the emotion, which places the symbolic relation in the pragmatic function of the sign. The emotion is then said to be the pragmatic rather than the referential meaning of the form. The pragmatic meaning of a sign may readily include emotion as one of the effects upon the interpreter, and the emotion as thus described is necessarily actual in the experience of the interpreter. But pragmatic meaning is a kind of meaning, and therefore shares the distinction and duality of sign and what is meant that inheres in meaning. It also embraces transcendence of attention from the sign to the pragmatic meaning. It makes no provision for objectification of the emotion in the sign: it is as compatible with discharge as with embodiment. Like referential meaning, it fails to do justice to the special traits of embodiment.

Apart from the special context of aesthetic expression, it does not seem appropriate to speak of pragmatic meaning in instances where there is no reference to support the sign-function. Pragmatic meaning is collateral to referential meaning, being made of effects upon the interpreter that are brought about by interpretation of referential meaning. If something does not refer, but has emotional effects, there is no reason to speak of the latter as a pragmatic meaning. If sign-function should occur, as it can between any two terms that interpretation should choose to connect, it would be referential rather than pragmatic. Since formal art does not refer to objects, the emotion that it expresses may well be called a pragmatic content by persons partial to the term, but hardly a pragmatic meaning.

The Mutual Immanence of Form and Emotion

The concept of pragmatic meaning affords a transition to the second theory of the relation between form and emotion in embodiment. The causal theory asserts that the relation between form and emotion in embodiment is sufficiently accounted for by the supposition that the form is the cause of the emotion. This supposition undoubtedly is true: the intuition of a color, or of a sequence of tones, or of a stanza of verse is the proximate cause of some appropriate related emotion. But the theory is not therefore adequate. The emotion is also a cause of form. Primitive

emotion is an impetus and partial guide to the imagination in
the creation of form; and adequate emotion is the cause of the
animation of form and of the intuition of form as a truly organic
whole. The theory of unilateral causality must therefore yield to
one of causal reciprocity. But the revised theory is also insufficient
for the description of the phenomena of embodiment. Causes and
effects are at least partly separate; but within the experience of
embodiment there is no gap between form and emotion such that
either might be experienced as the cause of the other: on the
contrary, there is an intimacy of union that defies a merely causal
analysis. The causal theory, original or revised, is appropriate for
the genetic account of embodiment; but it does not describe the
finished fact of embodiment.

The intimacy of union in embodiment that neither the semiotic
nor the causal theories approach is the special concern of the
theory of the mutual immanence of form and emotion. This theory
accepts the theory of causal reciprocity, but states beyond that
theory that form and emotion move from opposite positions to a
common position in phenomenal space, and there interpenetrate,
yielding a very close fusion with preservation of their individual
natures. The theory accounts for various features of aesthetic expression which the alternative theories seem to ignore. We have
seen that in the aesthetic perception of tones, colors, and words,
the separation of the formal and affective components disappears:
the emotion is heard, seen, or verbalized in the act of being felt,
and the tones, colors, and words are felt emotionally in the act
of being sensed or understood. Emotion is actualized in the form
that brings it into being. It is made determinate in form: separation of the emotion from the form causes vagueness and attenuation in the emotion. Emotion animates the form and helps to
make it an organic whole. In transposition of emotion and form,
each penetrates the other. In actualization and determination,
form penetrates emotion. In animation and unification, emotion
penetrates form. Thus form and emotion are immanent in each
other.

The theory of mutual immanence does not assert the identity
of form and emotion in embodiment. The form and emotion are
determinate beings, which do not melt into each other. The form
itself is not an identity: a sound has pitch, volume, color, and
duration, which are fused in auditory perception but nevertheless

are discriminable even in embodiment; and emotion has a similar relation to form as a whole in the experience of embodiment. This organic union of emotion and form is the special concern of the theory of mutual immanence, and the basis for the emergence of the quality that constitutes beauty.

Beauty: Embodiment and Emergence

Although the two principal terms in popular aesthetic discourse are art and beauty, there is little agreement about the relation between these terms. The common view, held by the layman and many aestheticians, asserts that art aims at beauty and that beauty has one of its most illustrious exemplars in works of art. Opposed to this view is a characteristic doctrine of the Platonic aesthetics, which has been shown to separate art from beauty, praising beauty and disparaging art: beauty is formal, universal, and absolute, but art is imitative, particular, and relative. In recent times there has come into prominence a third view, which is likewise opposed to the common one, but reverses the Platonic order of the value of the two terms. According to this view, the essence of aesthetic value consists in a property other than beauty, such as expression or pure form; and beauty either is a contingent attribute of some works of art, as in the statement by Ducasse that expression is beautiful only when the emotional content is pleasant, or it belongs outside of art and is probably inferior to it, as in Bell and Collingwood.[8] Available to this theory, and sometimes hotly advanced by its proponents, is the opinion that ugliness has positive aesthetic value: ugliness may be an alternative attribute derived from the basic aesthetic character, as when the expressed emotive content is unpleasant; and it may in the extreme case be regarded with veneration as having a depth or complexity that beauty cannot have. In this last instance there occurs a kind of aesthetic diabolism, provocative, paradoxical, surely mistaken in its conclusion, but sometimes highly perceptive in its data.

Amid such disagreement about basic terms, the only recourse is to look for a third term which should mediate between art and beauty and shed light upon their relation, whether positive or

[8] Above, Chap. 1.

negative. The concept of expression has sometimes been proposed by parties to the controversy: but there is reason to believe that the term has not been analyzed with sufficient care to establish an organic relation with beauty in the affirmative case, or compelling reasons for disavowal in the negative case. Thus Croce, Ducasse, and Collingwood share a philosophy of art as expression; but the simple statement of Croce that expression is beauty has been met by the only slightly more complex rebuttals of Ducasse and of Collingwood, that expression need not be beautiful or that beauty has no adequate relevance to expression. This book will also propose the concept of expression, but sharpened to indicate as clearly as possible how beauty is related to expression. We have seen that aesthetic value lies primarily in the phase of expression that has been called embodiment, which has a structure of a certain kind. We may now develop at length the view that aesthetic value consists in a quality that emerges from embodiment. This emergent quality of embodiment is beauty.

The emergent nature of beauty begins to be apparent when the question is raised: Of what may beauty properly be predicated? The common answer undoubtedly is that beauty belongs to the form. This reply is adequate for common purposes, but it does not hold up under analysis. The form by itself, without emotion, is not beautiful; it is a purely natural event, and it may be a potential for aesthetic value in an appropriate context; but it cannot achieve aesthetic value without the presence of emotion in that context. Nor is the emotion the immediate vehicle of beauty. Beauty does not belong to emotivity as such, or to any privileged type of emotion, but only to emotion as formed; and when the emotion is formed, attention in the enjoyment of beauty focuses indivisibly on the emotion and the form. It appears, then, that the vehicle of beauty, of which beauty may properly be predicated, is neither the form nor the emotion, but the fusion of them: beauty belongs to the condition of embodiment rather than to either of the constituents of embodiment. Since beauty is something new in relation to those antecedents and founded upon their collective action, it may be said to emerge from them in embodiment.

The concept of emergence is often applied in vitalistic philosophy, which asserts the emergence of life as a new kind of reality from suitable antecedents. A general theory of emergence can be stated, and illustrated in the instance of life for heuristic reasons, without commitment to vitalism. For such a theory, emergence is a relation that occurs within process under certain conditions.

1. Emergence requires two or more antecedent factors. Without such multiplicity, emergence could occur only by a leap of sheer creation. But emergence is not entirely mysterious, for it has more ground than does pure creation. In the case of life, the antecedents are a collection of molecules with physicochemical properties.

2. To support the creative function in emergence, the relation between the antecedent factors must be relatively intense: that is, the factors must have a maximum number of points of interaction. The molecules supporting life are very complex, and their mutual relations in a cell are in keeping with that complexity.

3. The character that emerges must have basic novelty in relation to the antecedents, distinct from mere combination, and it must be continuous with them. The novelty testifies to the emergent, and the continuity to the nature of emergence as having a ground to which the emergent is closely related. Life is thought by the vitalist to have a new and distinctive nature, which is not merely a complex combination of physicochemical properties. But it exists only in close relation to its antecedents.

4. The emergent quality must be holistic. The antecedents are plural, but the emergent is single and qualifies them indivisibly. The quality of life is simple in contrast with the multiple antecedents and qualifies them as a whole.

These requirements seem to be met by beauty in its relation to embodiment. As has been shown, beauty cannot arise out of form or emotion singly: it arises out of the interplay of form and emotion in embodiment. And this interplay not only involves the fairly tight relation of causal reciprocity; it also involves the mutual immanence of the two factors, yielding fusion for the production of a common heir.

It may be shown that the quality of beauty in any individual occasion is different from the form and emotion and continuous with them. The essence of beauty is an emotion of joy, which is new in relation to the antecedent form and emotion. This joy has two aspects. The formal aspect has its basis in the generic fact of embodiment. It is the same in kind in all occasions of beauty, regardless of the nature of the form or emotion. It results from the mere fact of embodiment and testifies to the imperative need for the kind of awareness in which emotion is formed for objective contemplation. It varies only in degree, which depends mainly on the adequacy with which the emotion is embodied.

Under the formal aspect is a material aspect, which consists in the immediate awareness by the self of the value of the specific content of the embodiment. The material joy of beauty varies in nature with the embodiment. Whereas the formal beauty of the Grieg *Lyric Pieces* is comparable with that of the Beethoven *Hammerklavier Sonata,* the material beauty of the first is inferior to that of the second in texture and meaning. The two aspects of beauty are not isolated from each other: they color each other in the single emergent quality of beauty. And the new quality is continuous with the form and emotion. The formal joy testifies to the unique fact of embodiment, and the material joy to the nature of the embodiment. Inseparable from its source, the joy of beauty shines upon embodiment, giving it a radiant transparency, objective, fixed, and inviolable.

The singleness of beauty, despite the complexity of its basis, is appropriate for the holistic nature of beauty. Not only is beauty equally dependent upon both the form and the emotion, but it qualifies the two indivisibly. Beauty is the unitary sense and appreciation, direct and unalloyed, of the oneness of form and emotion in embodiment. It is at the instant of fusion that beauty appears as a radical creation; beauty is the primary synthetic character in embodiment.

Further Traits of Beauty

In this conception of beauty as the emergent quality of embodiment, certain further characteristics of beauty may be emphasized. Beauty is an emotion, which should not be confused with the emotion that is embodied. The original emotion is logically prior to embodiment; the emotion of beauty is posterior. The original emotion may have important similarities to emotion as found outside of the aesthetic experience, though now made adequate through embodiment; beauty has no similar outside of the aesthetic experience and is wholly autonomous. The embodied emotion may have a history of development, as is indicated by the possibility of transitive expression; beauty has no history and no development. The original emotion may be painful; but in beauty, the formal joy contains no pain.

Since beauty is an emotion, it is clear that beauty is an axiological entity: for emotion is an immediate awareness of value. More precisely, beauty is an object of value, a process of evaluation, and a seizing in immediate enjoyment of what is valued in that process.

It is not necessary to show that beauty is valued along a spectrum that ranges from simple personal adornment to some of the major achievements of civilization. As a process of evaluation, beauty is directed toward embodiment, in relation to which it is an implicit judgment of approval. The formal joy in beauty contains a direct assent to the mere fact of embodiment, which precedes any discursive judgment about the value of embodiment and serves as a guide to such a judgment. The material joy of beauty contains an implicit judgment of approval of the emotion as embodied. This judgment does not concern the emotion as a stimulus or goal in the sphere of practical action. In that sphere, the emotion may be futile or destructive, and only a discursive judgment is competent to determine the value that the emotion may have. In embodiment, on the other hand, the condition of adequacy, involving distance, clarity, and freedom, enables the emotion to be abstracted from practical relevance and to be contemplated for its individual coloring in experience. In this immediate and terminal sphere an intuitive judgment is alone competent: a discursive judgment would destroy both the fusion necessary to the emotion being judged and the material joy that contains an immediate awareness of the value of the emotion.

In this intuition, the value of embodiment is not merely asserted: it is grasped and lived through. The judgment in beauty is indexical: it occurs only in the presence of the embodiment whose value is asserted. The judgment is a factor within the experience of beauty, and beauty occurs only when embodiment occurs. Beauty implies not only the existence and proximity of the object that it values: it also implies the seizure or consummate enjoyment of the valued object, for beauty emerges out of the embodiment that it praises. Beauty thus illustrates an ideal of human experience: the act of evaluation is competent to its task;

the object valued is apprehended immediately rather than through surrogates; and the object valued is owned and enjoyed in the act of valuing it.

From its status as an emotion it follows that beauty is subjective, that is, existent only in or for a mind. The same conclusion follows from the dependence of beauty on embodiment, which contains the emotion antecedent to that of beauty. Since the aesthetic form of itself is not beautiful, whatever objectivity the form may have does not lessen the subjectivity of beauty. In the absence of emotion a form that has in the past embodied emotion may be said to be a potential for embodiment; and in respect of the form, beauty may be said to be objective potentially. This does not lessen the subjectivity of actual beauty. Beauty therefore does not belong to nature conceived as a physical or neutral process. But this does not mean that beauty is unreal, or foreign to nature.

Every finite thing has its appropriate conditions for being real, defined by its essence and supplied by its environment. The conditions for the reality of beauty include the presence of a mind; in that context beauty is made actual and enjoys, as concerns the compass of experience, a sufficient degree of reality. Since finite minds arise as organically out of the process of nature as do atoms and cells, beauty may appropriately be ascribed to nature in an enlarged sense of the term. The subjectivity of beauty does not interfere with an ontological status for beauty in a panpsychistic view of nature, or with a similar status for beauty in a theistic view of the purposive creation and ordering of the world. In both of these philosophies mind is basic, pervasive, and controlling: and there is nothing in the subjectivity of beauty to prevent beauty from playing as large a role in the world order as these philosophies may be disposed to grant.

Formal Beauty, Perfection, Pain, and the Ugly

Various objections to the identification of beauty with expression may be anticipated, as they must by any attempt to understand a phenomenon as elusive as beauty. We may consider three criticisms that arise from sources friendly to an expressional aesthetic.

The first objection agrees that embodiment, or some other version of expression, is sufficient for beauty, but denies that it is necessary. A common form of this view is that there are two kinds of beauty: one expressive, the other formal. For expressive beauty there are a form, an emotion, an expression or embodiment of the emotion in the form, and an attitude of contemplation of the form as expressive of the emotion. Except for the absence of the theory of emergence, this half of the account is schematically similar to the theory advanced in this book. But formal beauty is thought of in quite different terms. For formal beauty there are a pure form; pleasure, which is not expressed; and a similar attitude of contemplation. Formal beauty is identified with pleasurable contemplation of form, apart from expression and emotion.

Surely these omissions are in error. The line between pleasure and emotion is a thin one and not essential to an expressional aesthetic. Pleasure is a part of positive emotion, and it is doubtful that it occurs in abstract purity. Pleasures are differentiated by further qualities, which tend in the direction of emotion. The pleasure of a formal design, to which exponents of this theory appeal, is conditioned by the experience of the design; and that experience provides an individuating inward texture in the pleasure, as in the case of emotion. But even if the pleasure in formal beauty were distinct from emotion, there is no reason why it should not be embodied, and there is good reason why it should be. If the pleasure is purely and entirely the result of the stimulus value of the form in the moment of contemplation, with no antecedent anchorage or rooting in the mind or experience of the percipient, there is reason to deny transitive expression, but none to deny embodiment.

Embodiment is the condition in which emotion, or pleasure alone for that matter, is perceived as fused with form: it implies nothing in regard to prior development and personal history. And embodiment supplies factors which go beyond the simple fact of pleasurable contemplation of form and which are required for the maximum value in contemplation and in form. If the pleasure is not embodied, it has neither the distance nor the fixity that perfect contemplation: short of embodiment of the pleasure, contemplation wavers and is more easily tempted to pass over into practical function. A dualism of form and pleasure is set up, which contradicts the intuited unity of aesthetic experience. The pleasure must lack the formal quality of "line," that goes with adequate determination, which in turn requires fusion with the form. As long as the pleasure is experienced as the effect but not as the fused partner of the form, the form must lack the quality of radiance appropriate to beauty, which is conferred by the joy that emerges at the moment of fusion. In general, there is a clear distinction between a pleasant and a beautiful design. The difference is that in beauty, the pleasure is embodied, and a joy results which illuminates and deepens the experience from which it arises.

The second and third criticisms hold that expression is necessary but not sufficient for beauty: some further character than expression is required for beauty; and in the absence of that character the expression is neutral or even ugly. The second criticism identifies the added trait with "perfection of form": when expression is through a form that is perfect, it is beautiful; when the form is lacking in perfection, it is neutral or ugly, though still entirely expressive. The third criticism identifies the further trait with pleasure in the embodied emotion: when the adequate emotion is pleasurable, the expression is beautiful; but when that emotion is painful or unpleasant, the expression is ugly.

The objection based on the notion of perfection of form appears to identify beauty with a classic style, in which harmony and poise are dominant. Beauty of this kind may be found generally in Raphael, Spenser, and Mozart, and exceptionally in Mahler's *Fourth Symphony* and James Joyce's *Chamber Music*. But such a style defines a tendency within the field of beauty: it does not define the field, and the tendency itself has some obscurity. Harmony and poise are somewhat variable terms, and what appears classic to a later generation may not seem so to the generation of the artist or to the artist himself. If a romantic beauty does not participate in these qualities, it is not therefore an impostor or usurper. Romantic beauty contains factors of conflict and tension, as in the last movement of Beethoven's *Ninth Symphony,* Part V of Eliot's *Waste Land,* and Rouault's *Crucifixion* (Plate 17). Conflict and tension give complexity and sometimes strength to a form. In the extreme case the result may loosely or mistakenly be called ugly: but it is more appropriate to identify it with what has been called "difficult beauty." Picasso's *Guernica* may be an example (Plate 16).

Beauty is not incompatible with strength, but may absorb it to the advantage of both. To set up a bifurcation of beauty and strength is to give beauty clear sailing into the inane and to reserve strength for philistines. In the experience of difficult beauty, elements that have a high degree of tension and incipient disruption are nevertheless united into a form, but united among many fronts rather than just a few. Such a form can embody its appropriate emotion, and from the embodiment emerges an emotion that rejoices directly in the fact of embodiment and massively in the complexity of the embodiment. This generality of beauty answers to the realization that perfection of form is either a highly general term or a misnomer. Not even for a classic beauty are there rules or standards defining perfect form. In default of discernible standards, form must be conceived of as perfect insofar as it is sufficient for the adequate embodiment of emotion. There is no embodiment completely adequate to the potential of the emotion but imperfect in form.

If all embodiment is beautiful as far as variations in form are concerned, it will not be surprising if beauty cannot be excluded from some instances of embodiment on the score of the embodied emotion. Painful or unpleasant emotion, which the third criticism assigns to embodiment that is ugly, is usually the burden of difficult forms; and the beauty available to such forms indicates that the negative character of the emotion is not sufficient to set up a rival aesthetic value. To this indication may be added evidences from the side of the emotion. Tragic art and sublimity in nature involve some aspect of pain in the emotion, which is present not only in the early phase of transitive expression but also in the most mature form of the adequate emotion of embodiment. Nevertheless, such embodiment is indubitably beautiful: far from being ugly or neutral, it appears to have a special claim on beauty, as will appear in a later chapter.[9] A subtle interplay of pain and pleasure is characteristic of tragic art. But it is not limited to the aesthetic domain. Human experience seldom is merely pleasant or painful. In proportion as experience is profound, the distinction tends to blur. Art especially taps experience of such depth; and beauty profits from it with equal comprehensiveness. It is therefore impossible to show that beauty is limited to the embodiment of pleasurable emotion.

[9] Below, Chap. 11.

An explanation of the ugly is to be had not by using the general concept of painful or unpleasant emotion, but by appealing to a highly specialized species of such emotion. What distinguishes the ugly is not a difficult form, or a negative emotion as such, but a negative emotion in the form of loathing. What makes an object ugly is the disposition of the object to cause a feeling of loathing. But such a feeling does not look toward or achieve embodiment. It is a practical emotion in its essence, which leads to destruction of the object or removal of the percipient. An artist guided by a feeling of this kind seeks to expunge it from his consciousness rather than to develop it and to fix it in a form. The feeling of loathing is the diametrical opposite of the joy of beauty: one emerges from embodiment as its signal achievement; the other is wholly incompatible with embodiment.

Aesthetic Intuition

The emergence of beauty completes the object of awareness in embodiment, which may be summarized as consisting of form, embodied emotion, and emergent beauty. The awareness in turn may be described as an intuition, which may be called aesthetic intuition in distinction from the sensory intuition of an earlier chapter. Like sensory intuition, aesthetic intuition stands between feeling and conception. Intuition generally is immediate and particular, like feeling and unlike conception, which is mediate and universal. But it is also formed and clear, like conception and unlike feeling, which is formless and obscure. Intuition is formed immediacy, and this dual character applies to both sensory intuition and to aesthetic intuition.

The distinction between sensory and aesthetic intuition is a matter partly of the character that is formed immediately, and partly of the complexity and perfection with which the immediate forming takes place. Sensory intuition is of sensory qualities that are formed in relations of space and time, which bound a character from other characters in space and time and give it unity in the same media. Aesthetic intuition is of emotional qualities that are formed by embodiment in the aesthetic object or form. The primitive emotion of transitive expression is merely felt; the adequate emotion of embodiment is intuited. And to this distinction of quality is added one of degree. The shape of any pebble on a beach and of a statue both involve sensory intuition: the one taken in isolation, the other in support of aesthetic intuition. But the statue has more parts, which are more tightly unified. It seems clear that the structural advantage of the statue derives from its relation to emotion, which brings to the occasion an aspect of value that requires a maximum of forming for its expression, and justifies the labor of creation and contemplative attention needed for the form.

Granting that aesthetic intuition is formed immediacy of a more perfect sort that is directed toward emotion, the special traits of aesthetic intuition follow. Aesthetic intuition is a highly organic awareness. By virtue of organic unity, a given part of a form is interdependent with other parts and flows beyond its normal boundaries into the other parts. Awareness thus moves readily from one part to another, and the awareness of any part yields an immediate sense of the presence and contribution of other parts. The result is an immediate awareness of the form as a whole. But the form is fused with emotion, and the emotion brings to awareness the trait of immanent or intrinsic interest. The embodying form is not a means to something else, in relation to which it would be a transition and mediation; it is an end, in which attention rests in immediate fulfilment. Immanent interest therefore is a part of aesthetic intuition. In turn it contributes to the individuality of awareness characteristic of the intuition. An individual is unique in some relevant way. The uniqueness of the aesthetic object is due to the determinateness of its parts, which are not reducible to types; to organic unity, which makes the whole more determinate than its parts and even less reducible to a type; and to immanent interest, which means that the value of the object is not reducible to that of any other object. The aesthetic individual is an organic unity of intrinsic value, and aesthetic intuition proceeds as an awareness of such individuality. But so perfected an awareness is clear to an exceptional degree, and the clarity penetrates the entire individual. Aesthetic intuition therefore has the final attribute of insight or luminosity. It is a grasp of the entire nature of the object, in the mode of effortless fruition. Aesthetic intuition thus is immediate formed awareness that is qualified by organicity, immanent interest, individuality, and luminosity, all of which perfect immediate awareness on a complex level.

The attributes of aesthetic intuition have been stated with emphasis on the aesthetic object or form, which is more negotiable than emotion by the discursive language of aesthetics. But in the experience of embodiment, intuition is realized as having its proper object in the adequate emotion, which furnishes a content of intuition in relation to which the form is a method. Aesthetic intuition is of an emotion made adequate through fusion with form: it is only in embodiment that an emotion can be apprehended with formed immediacy rather than be merely felt. This intuition of emotion is the universal and primary knowledge in art.

It seems clear that aesthetic intuition is limited to embodiment. Awareness of emotion in the mode of formed immediacy takes place only in the condition of embodiment. Intuition therefore does not embrace transitive expression; and if it does not include the latter, it cannot be equated with expression as a whole, as Croce asserted.[10] To do so is to pass from intuition as a certain kind of awareness, to intuition defined as the history and process by which the awareness comes into being. Intuition may be so defined by stipulation; but that would be pointless, since the term *expression* takes care of the need. Intuition thus has an important part in the experience and the theory of expression: but it is a part only.

[10] Benedetto Croce, *Aesthetic,* trans. Douglas Ainslie (London: Macmillan, 2nd ed., 1929), pp. 8–11.

PART III

Art and Values

CHAPTER 10

Criticism

Questions and Positions

The analysis of art and the interpretation of art prepare the way for the last and most synoptic task of aesthetics, which is to understand the relation of aesthetic experience to values. On no theory of the nature of aesthetic experience can this relation be absent from the interpretation of the fundamental nature of art; but for the expressional theory it is present with exceptional pervasiveness and vigor. That is due to the role accorded to emotion by this theory and to the centrality of value in the experience of emotion. If art is expression of emotion, and emotion is value or disvalue immediately apprehended, then art is expression of value, and the concept of value dominates aesthetic experience from the first impulse toward creation to the last moment of contemplation. This dominance is internal to the experience and helps to define the essential and general nature of art.

Given this schooling from the interpretation of art, the expressional theory is well prepared for the study of the diverse relations to value that come to view after the general nature of art has been defined. With the analysis and interpretation of art now accomplished, we may consider the problem of criticism, or the comparative evaluation of works of art, and the further problems of the relation of art to pain or evil, to morality and the conduct of life, and to religion. These problems will be pursued with emphasis on the expressional theory: the theory will shed light on them, and they will in turn round out the theory.

Criticism is concerned with the interpretation and especially with the evaluation of particular works of art. It is not a part of aesthetics, which is a general theory of art, and which mentions particular works only as illustrations of some aspect of theory. Criticism is like creation and contemplation in its direction toward the particular work of art, and in an implicit form it is inseparable from them. But when it is explicit, and discernible in its own right, it has a discursive and mediate nature that contrasts with creation and contemplation and resembles aesthetics. Criticism has its basis in aesthetics. As a logical foundation for the interpretation and evaluation of a given work of art, the critic must consider two general questions which arise within aesthetics and are answered, if at all, within this discipline.

The first question is whether there is in art universal value, by virtue of which men generally may be expected to agree that one work of art is good and another is inferior. If there is such value, a discerning critic may claim the assent of other appreciators, expect to find it insofar as they are competent, and anticipate error of judgment whenever there is disagreement. If there is no universal value, judgment of value has no special competence and is not liable to error, but is merely a report on a private liking. Of such a liking it is interesting to know that it exists, but irrelevant to inquire whether it is right or wrong.

If the first question is answered in the affirmative, the second question may then be asked: whether rules or principles can be stated, by virtue of which the value of a given work of art can not only be affirmed rightly, but can be demonstrated, so as to require the assent of other persons. If rules can be stated, they will give support to the thesis of universal value. But if they cannot, that thesis may still rest on a conception of good taste. By this conception is meant an intuition of value, which is regarded as right in its discernment, but as not susceptible of formulation in rules or precepts: for every rule is a concept.

In regard to this pair of questions, three positions may be distinguished, perhaps loosely but surely usefully. What may be called absolutism in critical theory is the view that works of art have universal value, which may be demonstrated by rules of unimpeachable authority. One instance of this view, fresh and vigorous despite its rigid and closed nature, may be found in Lessing, whose *Laokoon* legislated sharply the proper spheres of poetry and of visual art, and whose *Hamburgische Dramaturgie* claimed guidance for contemporary German drama in principles exemplified in Sophocles and systematized by Aristotle. In the latter work Lessing wrote:

> However, I do not hesitate to acknowledge (even if I should be derided for it in these enlightened times!) that I regard it [the Poetics] as being as infallible as the Elements of Euclid still are. Its principles are just as true and certain, only to be sure not as comprehensible, and therefore more exposed to sophistical mis-interpretation. Particularly of tragedy, of which time has favored us with a pretty complete account, I am confident that I can prove irrefutably that it cannot depart one step from the model of Aristotle without declining in like measure from its own perfec-tion.[1]

At the opposite pole is relativism in critical theory, which denies universal value to the work of art and therefore rejects the apparatus of rules. A strong statement of this view was made by Ducasse:

> If the critic possesses an extensive and intimate acquaintance with works of art, and his faculties through much observation and comparison have become sensitive to facts and differences which would pass unnoticed by others, he may then similarly be able to take the plain "consumer" of art upon a personally con-ducted tour of a given canvas or symphony, and call his attention to features which he might otherwise overlook, or which it might take him much time to discover for himself. But of course, once such features are pointed out and perceived, the "consumer" must do the rest. That is, the question of their aesthetic worth is one that he must decide for himself. The critic's judgment of it rep-resents neither more nor less than the judgment of anyone else; namely, it represents his own preferences only, and is in no sense to be regarded as "authoritative" or binding on anyone. For in matters of aesthetic taste it is as with taste in matters of cookery.[2]

---

[1] Gotthold E. Lessing, *Hamburgische Dramaturgie,* Vol. II, *Sämtliche Schriften,* Vol. X, ed. K. Lachmann (Stuttgart: Göschen, 1894), Secs. 101–104, p. 214.
[2] Curt J. Ducasse, *The Philosophy of Art* (New York: Dial, 1929), p. 8.

Between the extremes of absolutism and relativism lies a third position, which may perhaps be described as a modified absolutism. This theory of criticism holds that there is universal value in works of art, but that it cannot be set forth in rules. It speaks for the common attitude of artist and contemplator, which desires and anticipates general agreement in the enjoyment of a work of art, and bases the anticipation on the intuition of a significant distinction between the pleasure of the beautiful and the pleasure of the merely agreeable. But it does not sanction the use of rules, which attempt to ground a pleasure that is spontaneous when real, and which confine both artist and contemplator. Like the other positions, modified absolutism has a range. A strong version may be found in Kant, whose *Critique of Judgment* asserts an a priori and necessary basis for the universality of aesthetic judgment.[3] For reasons which will appear presently, a more modest version will be proposed in this chapter, which will assert an empirical and contingent universality. Such a universal is equally responsive to the serious claim for agreement among appreciators of art, and more in accord with the complexity both of art and of human nature. In support of this position, we may examine the arguments that may be made by the relativist against the position of the absolutist. Four arguments will be considered: that aesthetic experience is subjective; that aesthetic evaluation is subjective; that contemporary creation is polemical and contemporary criticism is weak; and that the work of art is a unique individual.

The Intersubjectivity of Aesthetic Experience

The first argument of relativism in critical theory is one which has its basis in general epistemology, where it asserts that all contents or objects of experience, including those of aesthetic experience, are subjective, or dependent upon an apprehending mind. Accepting in spirit the relativistic arguments of dualism and of idealism in epistemology, the relativist in critical theory may assert that the aesthetic object or form, and *a fortiori* the embodied emotion and emergent beauty, are subjective and consequently, he supposes, variable among persons and private. These arguments are

---

[3] Below, "The Intersubjectivity of Aesthetic Evaluation."

persuasive, for they assert in essence two notions, one of which is verified in routine experience, and the other of which has a high degree of probability in metaphysics. The one assertion is that contents of experience, such as the apparent size and shape of a table, vary with the character of the experient, such as his distance and angle to the table. The other is that experience presupposes effects upon the experient, which are received in accordance with the character of the experient and may therefore be modified, distorted, or added to. If these arguments are true, it may well be that the aesthetic object is partially or entirely subjective. And it may be more extensively subjective than most objects of experience, for a painting consists of colors, and a musical composition of tones, which are usually labeled secondary qualities in recognition of the maximum probability of their subjectivity. Physics has no place for these qualities, while asserting the objectivity, or independence of the apprehending mind, of their causes in appropriate forms of wave energy.

Whatever extent of subjectivity may be required of aesthetic experience by epistemology and physics, it does not automatically justify the relativistic thesis in critical theory that different appreciators cannot have substantially identical experiences of a given work of art. Subjectivity is compatible with intersubjectivity, or the likeness of experience of an indefinite number of subjects or persons. Literal objectivity, or status in an object that is independent of the knowing mind, is not required for science, philosophy, or criticism; what is required is intersubjectivity, whether this be taken as something self-sufficient and terminal, or as evidence of something literally objective. But intersubjectivity follows from subjectivity whenever the subjective causes of the content of experience are the same in kind. Given that sameness among different persons, a subjective content of experience may be as universal and dependable as the most limpid property of an independent thing. Thus variations in the appearance of a thing to a given person do not imply further variations among several persons; the original set of variations may be repeated among all subjects, due to similarity of their condition. It is therefore necessary to inquire into the extent of such similarity among aesthetic experients, or appreciators of a given work of art, as a ground of the intersubjectivity of aesthetic experience, which would refute the first argument of the relativistic critic.

The intersubjectivity of the sensory content of aesthetic form is

difficult to verify with rigor. It is not possible to insert oneself
into the sensory apprehension of another person or, for that
matter, into any conscious process of another mind, to compare
the qualities there manifest with those of one's own experience.
Comparative description of the sense data of two persons is not
adequate, for the idiosyncrasy of sensory quality forbids reduction
of a quality to simpler characters that might conceivably be shared
by the persons. Mere community of labels is not sufficient, for two
persons using the word *green* to label the hue of a given region of
space may mean by that word different sensory qualities, having
been taught the use of the word by acts of pointing which established a place but merely assumed a hue. There is no logical connection, that is, no intrinsically necessary connection, between a
light wave of certain dimensions and a visual sensum of a certain
hue. If similar waves of light, reflected from an assumed external
and independent object, lead to similar hues, it must be due to
similarity in the processes of sensation among various percipients.
Such similarity cannot be verified in practice, and probably not
in theory. Thus it is indeed difficult to be certain of the intersubjectivity of the sensory content of the work of art. And yet, there
are only ghostly reasons for questioning it. The character of sensory
feeling is not conditioned by experience, as through learning, and
thus is removed from the most potent cause of variation in human
response. It is a fact of constant experience that people communicate with one another in the realm of sensory experience.
The communication has gaps and blind spots, but it is massive
and dependable: it furnishes as high a degree of universality as
the critic needs.

The represented content of aesthetic form has a less favorable
claim on intersubjectivity, since it depends heavily on experience
which is conditioned by time, place, culture, or social pattern
and individual circumstance. If representation is arbitrary, as is true
for the most part in literature, the language has to be learned
and its subtleties thoroughly domesticated. If representation is
iconic, as in painting and sculpture, the objects referred to may
be unfamiliar or their implications obscure. Every man may recognize a cross; but only persons familiar with Christian culture will
understand its general significance in painting with a Christian
subject, and only persons well versed in that culture will follow
the detailed symbolism that may be used. But these disadvantages

may be considerably compensated in art. Despite differences in time, place, culture, and individual circumstance, there are basic similarities in human nature and the situations in which it finds itself. Birth, sexual love, death, and deity; struggle, achievement or defeat, and disillusionment: these provide a universal condition of man, which the artist taps in proportion to his ability, with confidence that he will be widely understood. What is specialized in this condition either may be grasped by an act of sympathetic historical imagination, aided by appropriate learning, or it may be dissolved by a more abstract penetration, which passes from a special vehicle to a general essence. Thus a person removed from the ideas and sentiments of Christian culture may with a little trouble identify them in a painting of the Crucifixion, or he may ignore them and discern a more essential representation of human nobility and suffering.

The highest degree of intersubjective grasp in aesthetic experience may be anticipated for structure, on the ground that it consists of relations and that relations may be constant while terms differ. But the truth of this anticipation may be limited by two matters. One is that the awareness of structures requires sustained and directed attention, which may be missing in many acts of aesthetic appreciation, with consequent lapses of understanding. This limitation is reparable in principle. Another, and more essential limitation, is that a given structure in art is a structure of specific terms, which may be colors of certain hues and intensities, or tones of certain pitches and volumes, or ideas interpreted in a certain way. The specific nature of harmony, balance, and evolution depends on the specific nature of the terms, and shifts with variations of perception and interpretation. In general, structure in art is concrete rather than general and becomes general only as a formula which is separable from the aesthetic experience. But the concreteness of structure aids intersubjective understanding of the experience, for the syntax of a work of art may shed light on the nature and meaning of a term through its relation to other terms.

Without consulting either the artist or the historian, the intelligent appreciator can expand his grasp of the work of art by comparing part with part, using each part as a lever for the negotiation of other parts. This internal grasp of the nature of the work of art makes the work more self-contained and consequently more public. It frees the work of art from the more casual, arbitrary, and private elements which may easily enter aesthetic awareness. The test of what belongs to a given work of art is to discover what may be assigned clearly to a given element and to discern what may be integrated with other elements. The second part of the test extends and checks the first. Thus structure makes public recondite modes of interpretation. In poetry, symbol, metaphor, myth, and partial allusion are saved from the death of private fantasy by the discerning pursuit of structures of meanings. This pursuit may be taken to be a large part of what Greene called the re-creative function of criticism, which establishes in each appreciator the individual and complete work of art.[4] Such criticism is a major support of the intersubjectivity of aesthetic experience.

For an expressional aesthetic one component of aesthetic experience remains to be considered: that is emotion. This may be thought to be highly variable among persons, and the variability may be alleged, with reason, to disqualify emotion for serious attention in the definition of aesthetic experience. But the adequate emotion of aesthetic expression, or embodiment, has a claim on intersubjectivity comparable to, and interdependent with, that of the other parts of the experience. It has been seen that the emotional character of a sensum is so closely and directly related to the sensory quality as to make it reasonable to suppose that the two are in some respect identical. Whether this supposition is true or false, the intersubjectivity of sensation in the work of art is virtually equivalent to the same status for emotion induced by sensation in the aesthetic experience.

Emotion based on representation is admittedly in a different situation, for the same object or event in nature or society may evoke different emotions in different persons, and artistic representation has no means of overcoming such difference of response. But the intersubjectivity of artistic representation was found to have a basis in the likeness of human nature and of its situations, and emotion based on subject matter can have a comparable intersubjectivity based on the community of human nature in its profounder aspects. Faced with the same basic objects and situations of experience, men at different times and places have a consider-

---

[4] Theodore M. Greene, *The Arts and the Art of Criticism* (Princeton: Princeton University Press, 1940), Chap. xx, pp. 369–373.

able community of emotional response. Thus death is not only a universal human occurrence, but it is awaited with regret by those who have lived well, with partial relief by those who have no hope, with indignation by those who find in it injustice or cruelty, and with some degree of anxiety by men of every condition.

In tapping these common sources of common emotional response, the artist justifies his implicit conviction that what he expresses is not for himself alone, but for men generally. But the community of emotion among men is greater in art than outside of art. The effectiveness of structure in securing a common grasp of the work of art, and in dismissing private and irrelevant elements from the form, extends to the emotion also. A major cause of private variation in emotion among appreciators is a similar privacy and variation in apprehension of the form. The service of structure in promoting intersubjective awareness of the form extends to emotion. For it has been seen that the adequate emotion of embodiment is made determinate and clear by the form in which it is embodied. The close relation of emotion and form in expression is assurance that emotion in art has an intersubjectivity comparable to that of the form.

The Intersubjectivity of Aesthetic Evaluation

The second argument of relativism in critical theory stems from general theory of value, where it asserts that all values, including aesthetic values, are subjective. It holds that values are created rather than discovered by the act of valuation, whether that act be implicit or explicit, impulsive or deliberate. Thus it asserts that values are doubly subjective, being subjective responses to objects that are themselves subjective. From this status of values it infers variability of values from person to person, and it feels secure in the inference because of the nature of the subjective process involved in valuation. This process is not of a cognitive order, such as reason, which might be universal among men; on the contrary, it is conative, being described by such terms as will, desire, or interest, and satisfaction or pleasure, which are thought of as eminently distinct from reason and thus highly variable.

This argument also is highly persuasive in its initial assertion.

Apart from mental function of some sort, whether subhuman, human, or divine, the concept of value lapses from meaning. It is impossible to conceive of anything as valuable or disvaluable in a world entirely divested of mind. The characters of an object that is valued may conceivably exist in the absence of mind, and they may be said to be valuable potentially; but the potentiality is definable only in relation to mind, rather than to other objects, and mind thus remains a necessary condition of value.

The aspect of mental function involved in valuation clearly is conative. Given an interest of any sort, value springs into existence; given a plurality of interests, whether in one person or several, harmonies and conflicts of values arise. Reason is necessary to adjudicate conflicts and to secure harmonies of values; but it can act only on behalf of interest even when it criticizes interests, for its criticism is based on an interest in the maximum compossibility of interests. The thesis of the conative subjectivity of values thus is not only credible, but apparently necessary for the conception of value. It does not, however, entail the variability of values from person to person. If interests are common to many or all men, values will be similarly common. But interests are grounded in, and perhaps ultimately constitute the essence of, human nature. The community of human nature, which is empirically evident on some level and to some extent, is a basis for a significant degree of inter-subjectivity of values. The fact that valuation is not fundamentally an act of reason does not interfere with this. For in its essence valuation is nonrational rather than irrational; and the community of human nature is not limited to reason: if indeed it may even be found there. The way therefore is open for a consideration of the problem of intersubjective evaluation in the aesthetic sphere.

It is necessary to establish first what it is that is valued in the aesthetic experience. The character that comes most directly to the attention of the value consciousness is beauty, in which aesthetic experience and aesthetic value are consummated. Speaking loosely or hurriedly, it is sufficient to say that it is beauty that is valued: and the pleasure of beauty, described earlier as a formal joy, is an intrinsic value and needs no further justification. But beauty is the emergent quality of embodiment, and its pleasure is an assent to embodiment. In the experience of beauty, embodiment is valued, and axiological attention thus shifts to embodiment as the source of value. Embodiment is a fusion of form and emotion. From its more patent character, and its literally visible or audible basis, form commends itself as the proper carrier and seat of aesthetic value. If, however, form serves for the embodiment of emotion, it is the servant of the emotion. It follows that the ultimate object of approval or disapproval in the aesthetic experience is an emotion. It is in our judgment of the worth of the expressed emotion that we have the basis, if any, for our claim on the similar judgment of others on the work of art in question, and for our further judgment that the given work is better or worse than some other work of art. In practice, however, it makes no difference whether criticism is directed toward the emotion or the form, since the two are fused in the salient fact of embodiment. In practice also, it is necessary to be guided immediately by form in the critical process: for the form is the basis of the intelligibility of the emotion, is therefore the method by and in which the emotion is approached, and is consequently the vehicle and direct target of critical inspection and evaluation.

The problem of the intersubjectivity of aesthetic evaluation thus becomes the problem of the intersubjectivity of the evaluation of emotion or, more directly, of form. And here a number of difficulties arise in the way of the affirmation of intersubjectivity.

The value of the emotion in aesthetic experience cannot be settled by the rational technique of showing that the emotion is a means to a further end, the value of which happens already to have been agreed upon. The emotion is not a means, the value of which can be determined by objective causal analysis. It is an end, which has value in itself or not at all. Since the most cogent method for securing agreement in interpersonal evaluation is to show the usefulness of the object in question for achieving an end which is not in dispute, aesthetic evaluation suffers accordingly.

The value of the emotion cannot be justified empirically by a census leading to the empirical generalization that all persons do, as a matter of fact, similarly value the emotion. Apart from other difficulties, a census is not necessary, for routine experience shows that appreciators of a given work of art do not agree about the value they set upon it. That disagreement is the source of the problem of the intersubjectivity of aesthetic judgment. Undoubtedly it is based at least in part on variation in experience of the form and the emotion, which means that difference is not in the evaluation of a single emotion, but in the experience of two distinct emotions. It cannot, however, be assumed that disagreement is based wholly on such variation, without begging the question of intersubjectivity of evaluation in general.

In default of the descriptive mode of reason and experience, which purports to show that something is, recourse may be had to a prescriptive mode, which alleges that something ought to be. The critic may therefore say, as he often does, that others ought to find value in the emotion, or form. But this obligation is difficult to define and to justify. It cannot be a hypothetical ought, which is the assertion that one ought to value the means to an acknowledged end, since the emotion is not a means. It must therefore be an unconditioned ought, to value the emotion as an end. But an ought derives from a value, and the statement that one ought to value something is no more than the tautology that it would be valuable to find value in something. Insofar as the statement goes further than this, it is to assert a requirement or command on behalf of the value. Such a requirement is meaningless in the aesthetic sphere, for no one needs to be commanded to pursue and enjoy a pleasure, and the experience of pleasure is a spontaneity beyond the control of choice.

A final attempt to secure intersubjective evaluation of the emotion, or more readily of the form, may be made by the citation of rules observed by the form. Apart from the problem as to whether there are rules available and useful for criticism, which will be discussed in a later section, it is evident that the use of rules would merely postpone the issue: for a rule would be an analysis of some specific aspect of the form, the value of which is generalized beyond the scope of the particular form. But the intersubjective value of the stated aspect is not secured by the repetition of the aspect in many works of art. It can only be approached by methods such as those already discussed, which here are directed to an analyzed factor of a work of art rather than to the work as a whole.

Despite these difficulties, some progress may be made toward the general affirmation of the intersubjectivity of aesthetic evaluation. Although the emotion is an end which cannot, like a means, be an object of demonstration, it has the advantage that the compass of its value is limited to its own nature. No indefinite ramification of consequences is involved, concerning which there may never be complete knowledge and thus no security for a

certain judgment of value. Whatever is relevant to the value of the
emotion is present in the experience of the emotion, where it is
self-contained and, by virtue of embodiment, fully clear and intelligible. Furthermore, and also in support of the preceding advantage, the emotion as embodied has a distance from the self of
the contemplator, which removes it from the practical and moral
function of personality. The aesthetic evaluation of an emotion is
not of something which is to be included or excluded from the
self: for the emotion as embodied rides at a distance, where it
raises no issues as to ideals and patterns and harmonies of personality. The aesthetic evaluation of suffering, fear, or jealousy
does not entail an evaluation of these emotions for the normal
conduct of life. The distance of aesthetic emotion thus helps to
simplify the problem of intersubjective evaluation.

To go further toward solution of the problem, it is necessary to
appeal again to the community of human nature and interest,
which was the basis of the intersubjectivity of aesthetic experience,
and apart from which no intersubjectivity of aesthetic evaluation
can be found. That community provides the ground for agreement among different persons about the value of an emotion as
embodied in a particular form. The empirical fact of disagreement among appreciators, insofar as it actually touches on evaluation rather than on experience, indicates diversity of interest in
regard to the instance of embodiment. Assuming equal and competent penetration of the instance in the parties to the disagreement, there is no way to eliminate the disagreement short of
censorship or propaganda, neither of which is suitable to criticism.
But when the embodied emotion answers to an interest that is
common, it will be evaluated in common also. And this happens
in proportion as the emotion has the character of meaning described
in an earlier chapter.[5]

Meaningfulness of emotion was said to consist not in some
particular quality of an emotion, which might or might not
engage some interest, but in diversity of quality, unity of relation
among the qualities, and generality of sources of the emotion in
the self and the world. Meaning thus is the basis of the spread of
relevance of an emotion, and that spread is the assurance that a
common interest will be served by the emotion. The spontaneous

---

[5] Above, Chap. 8, "Emotion and Expression."

claim on general agreement that appears to be an integral part of the aesthetic consciousness is not an assertion that others ought to value likewise, but a conviction that the emotion has an order of meaningfulness that would secure the interest of anyone by whom the emotion was experienced and understood. The perception of such meaningfulness distinguishes aesthetic value from the value of the merely agreeable, such as may be found in foods, wines, or physical exercise.

The intersubjectivity here provided is empirical and contingent. It is based on experience of human nature and human interest as having a substantial degree of community. It depends on that community and is subject in principle to change, since there is no absolute need for human nature to be what it is rather than otherwise. Thus it stands in contrast with the Kantian view, which asserts an a priori and necessary basis for the universality of aesthetic evaluation. For Kant, aesthetic pleasure is based on the intuition of the form or abstract structure of the object, without consideration of the sensory matter or quality of the object or of a purpose advanced by the object. Since the form alone is judged, the faculty of judgment is invoked only in respect of the conditions of the general use of that faculty. These conditions have to do with the interplay, in every instance of empirical knowledge, of the cognitive powers of the imagination, which unifies the manifold of sense in intuition, and of the understanding, which unifies the product of the imagination in conception.

When the form of an object stimulates the optimal interplay of these powers, the form is apprehended as subjectively purposive for the faculty of judgment, and pleasure arises in that faculty as the determining mark of the interplay. Since the pleasure arises from cognitive powers, which must be as universal as the knowledge they produce, the pleasure is itself universal. For Kant, then, the universality of aesthetic evaluation is based on the implicit knowability of the valued form: a relevance which is not cognitively explicit, since the form does not actually engage the understanding and conception, but which is nonetheless cognitive in its subordination to the requirement of the understanding.[6]

This theory of the universality of aesthetic evaluation, which is

---

[6] Immanuel Kant, *Critique of Judgment,* trans. J. H. Bernard (New York: Hafner, 1951), Pt. I, Secs. 6, 11–12, 18, 21–22, 31–38, 56–57.

integrated carefully with the theory of knowledge and, it seems, with the transcendent metaphysics of the most influential system of modern philosophy, is open to several objections from the field of aesthetics. It disregards the sensory content of the aesthetic object in favor of the bare structure, though sensory content is a primary part of the object, and the structure that pleases in a given object is a structure of sensory contents. In regard to structure, it favors unity over diversity and harmony over balance, thus simplifying the structural opportunities of art: and that is inevitable if the understanding is to be satisfied, since the understanding favors unity to the point of reducing given unities to simpler unities and has no interest in a balance that strains toward disruption. It provides no evidence that the optimal interplay of imagination and understanding will be at the same point or ratio for all men; so it is possible that two persons guided by the same principle of interplay will differ in their evaluation of a given object, the one finding and the other missing the optimal interplay in that object.

Though the cognitive process may be intersubjective, it is not clear that the process or its result will be valued intersubjectively, as in a pleasure experienced by all men in the satisfaction of the cognitive requirement. And if all men should, by some transformation from their present condition, value and be pleased by the cognitive suitability of a form, the value and pleasure would appear to be slight in comparison with the wealth of value and pleasure to be found in art, which draws on every quality and motive of human experience. To know is not the only purpose of men: and that is particularly so when the a priori functions of knowledge are separated from the empirical content that is known.

Contemporary Conflict and Historical Agreement

The third argument of relativism is concerned with the conflicts and acknowledged weakness of contemporary aesthetic evaluation. It points to the hesitancies, disagreements, and errors of contemporary criticism, learned and distinguished though it may be, and to the polemics of artists against each other, though artists are of all men presumably the closest to the forms and emotions in dispute. The critic who has to judge a new work of art, and especially a work that is novel in its form, may readily prefer a lesser to a better work, or value the better work for lesser reasons. So accomplished a student of music as Hanslick, who was adept both at aesthetic theory and at practical criticism, mentions without distinction musicians who have survived the intervening decades and musicians who are now museum pieces. It is well known that inferior poets have been acclaimed in their day, whereas superior poets have had routine praise, or have languished in the shade, or have received bitter abuse.

To this incompetence of contemporary criticism must be added the frequent intolerance of each other, or of alien schools, that is found among artists. The "invectives of one school against another," which Santayana rightly thought are "artistically often signs of health,"[7] are common in each succeeding generation of artists. One may consider the extent to which painters, who of all artists are the most vocal and disputatious in the current century, abandon the masters of their early instruction in pursuit of a new form, only to divide vigorously among themselves as to the direction that the new generation should take. With a new surge of creative energy old idols fall, particularly those dominant in the preceding generation. Thus critics err, and the privilege of genius is to be insulted by genius.

The facts are as stated, but they do not warrant the conclusion that relativism draws in favor of the inherent privacy and variability of aesthetic evaluation. They require a sober and modest view of the intersubjectivity of aesthetic evaluation, but they do not demand sheer relativism. The weakness of contemporary criticism indicates at least two facts about such criticism. One is that the disinterested attitude required for good criticism often is subverted by personal bias arising out of friendship or animosity toward individuals, or out of sheer closeness in time and space to a school or theory. The other is that a novel form and emotion are not easily understood and adequately experienced, and the critic evaluates something that he only partly grasps. These causes of inadequate criticism are automatically removed by time.

The polemics of artists against each other have a simple basis, which lies outside the philosophy of criticism. Partly from egocentric involvement with his own fortune and fame, but more

_____
[7] George Santayana, *The Sense of Beauty* (New York: Scribner, 1896), p. 44.

PLATE 17. *Georges Rouault,* Crucifixion *(c. 1918). Henry P. McIlhenny Collection, Philadelphia, Pennsylvania.*

PLATE 18. *Fra Angelico*, The Madonna of Humility *(15th century)*. *National Gallery of Art, Washington, D.C., Andrew Mellon Collection.*

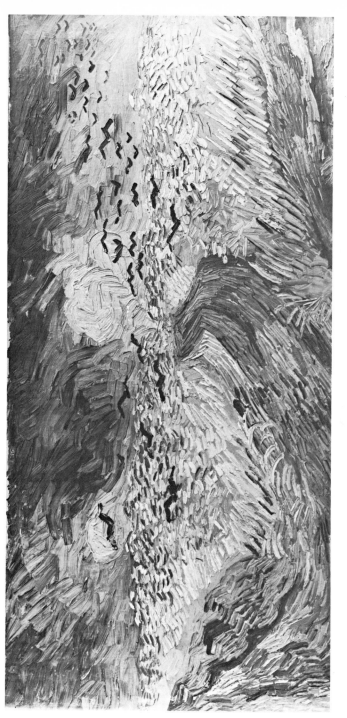

PLATE 19. *Vincent van Gogh, Crows over the Wheat Fields (1890). Collection Vincent van Gogh Foundation, Amsterdam.*

PLATE 20. *Andrei Rublëv,* Old Testament Trinity *(c. 1411). Tretjakoff Gallery, Moscow.*

substantially from the sheer vigor and consequent concentration of the creative process, the artist is liable to exclusiveness in his interest and thence to blindness in his judgment on others. But no artist works without a tradition; and the work of many artists shows either strong influence of the preceding generation in an early piece, or a new and more discerning evaluation of an artist of a distant time. Whatever his manifestoes or depreciations, no artist creates for himself alone; and in proportion to his serious- ness, he creates in hunger for an audience limited by no time or place. For the artist, art is never comparable to cookery.

This attitude of the artist is vindicated by the extension of time beyond the immediate present. As the decades and genera- tions pass, a sifting occurs in aesthetic evaluation, by virtue of which the majority of works of art drift into obscurity or perish, and only a minority survive. Time becomes the sternest of critics, and the greatest. This happens through the domestication of new forms and emotions, so that they are more widely understood and experienced than at birth. It happens also, and more profoundly, through the recognition in certain works of art by succeeding gen- erations of breadth and depth of meaningfulness, whose extent is attested by the verdict of each additional generation. What is meant here is not routine acceptance or praise of classics, but the fresh appreciation, and often the novel interpretation, of the classics by persons active in the creation and criticism of their time. In this appreciation and interpretation, the quality of mean- ingfulness that was the theoretical basis of intersubjective evaluation becomes the actual recipient of such evaluation. Time thus cor- rects its initial errors and becomes the most solid adversary of relativism.

The Particularity of Aesthetic Forms

The fourth and final argument of relativism in critical theory asserts that aesthetic form always is particular and that in conse- quence no rules or principles can be stated for the evaluation of a given work of art. It asserts that every work of art is unique, thus incomparable with other works of art, and thus incapable of subsumption under rules for the determination of comparative value. The argument may be made by persons who deny the intersubjectivity of evaluation of aesthetic form, and may be alleged as a basis for the denial. But it may also be made by those who accept the intersubjectivity of aesthetic evaluation, and who believe that the community of aesthetic evaluation is not based on or supported by rules, or fettered by dogmas. As so proposed, the argument in effect asserts that although one person's judgment of a given work of art may entail or make a claim on another person's judgment on that same work, judgment of a given work entails no judgment by the same person as to the value of another work of art. There are no general rules or effective similarities among works of art, by virtue of which the agreement or disagreement of one work of art with another justifies the conclusion that the one is of similar or differing value from the other.

This final argument of relativism appears to be sound in its basic contention. It is not hard to find in aesthetic experience strong evidence that rules are neither sufficient nor necessary for the value of a work of art. The evidence may be found either deductively, from the basic nature of art, or inductively, from a consideration of rules that seem to have some credit in the history and criticism of art.

The intuited individuality of aesthetic experience indicates that rules are not sufficient for the establishment of aesthetic value. We have seen that an aesthetic form is an individual, which is apprehended by an act of intuition. The conception of individuality in the object, and of intuition in the mode of apprehension of the object, are identical ways of asserting that no universal, or set of universals, can define a work of art. This does not mean that universals are irrelevant or unreal in aesthetic experience. It means that a given universal is exemplified with a nuance of character that is not expressed in that universal or any other, and that a number of universals are combined in a set or totality which has novel character in relation to the components. In general, aesthetic form slips beyond the grasp of the universal because of the plenary determinateness of its parts, and because of the organic unity of the whole into which the parts enter. It therefore follows that the same rule, or collection of rules, can be exemplified in two works of art, while the latter are of quite different orders of value. Though obeying the same rules, the two works are of dissimilar value because the rules are abstract in comparison with their applications; and it is the latter that must be judged.

That rules are not necessary for the value of a work of art may be seen in the phenomenon of artistic genius, which presides over the creation of works of art. Genius implies the capacity to bring forth something new, which therefore is not produced by the application of rules. Talent proceeds by the application of rules and thus makes nothing essentially new. Since the command of rules yields skill and can be acquired, talent embraces art in the generic sense of acquired skill. Genius therefore transcends art, though making use of it en route, and artistic creation combines art with a factor of novelty. Artistic creation has a subtle tension between art and genius, which baffles the historian and the critic, but delights the appreciator. The tension may be mitigated somewhat by the fact that the skill in art is partly a skill in modifying a rule to suit the particular material or need at hand, so that art is distinguished from pure theory or abstract rule and is to be thought of as these modified subtly in practice. Art thus moves slightly in the direction of genius.

It may be proposed that genius also involves rules, which are innate or natural rather than acquired. This was the view of Kant, for whom genius is "the innate mental disposition (*ingenium*), through which nature gives the rule to art."[8] But this view is open to objection. Believing correctly that every art implies rules, and that aesthetic evaluation cannot be based on rules derived from concepts, Kant sought the rules for artistic genius in nature. But if genius starts where art ceases, the dependence of art on rules does not entail a similar dependence of genius. If nature is appealed to as the source of a rule which is nonconceptual, what is meant is a rule in the sense of a direction rather than of a universal principle, and the rule supplied by nature would not be of the kind pertinent to criticism. Whatever the basis of genius in nature (and the mystery and power of genius are enlarged rather than explained by the appeal to nature), genius remains as that factor in artistic production for which rules are not necessary. We may go a step further and say that they are regarded by genius as alien to its nature and as obstacles. Thus genius in artistic creation devises forms for which no rule can be found, and does so often over the dead bodies of rules handed down by tradition.

[8] Kant, Pt. I, Sec. 46, p. 150.

To such evidence from the fundamental nature of art may be added the evidence provided by a sampling of rules, which again indicates that rules are neither sufficient nor necessary for the value of art. A rule of importance in Greek drama was the principle of the unity of time, which limited the extent of represented action to one day. In comparing tragic and epic poetry, Aristotle with some reserve stated the rule: epic poetry differs from tragedy

> in its length—which is due to its action having no fixed limit of time, whereas Tragedy endeavours to keep as far as possible within a single circuit of the sun, or something near that. This, I say, is another point of difference between them, though at first the practice in this respect was just the same in tragedies as in epic poems.[9]

The rule of diurnal unity was illustrated in Sophocles' *Oedipus Rex* and in Lessing's *Emilia Galotti,* and it is impossible to trace the brilliance of the one, and the mediocrity of the other, to the observance of the rule. It was violated in serious drama from Shakespeare to Ibsen to Arthur Miller, and the excellence of these writers does not suffer on that account. The reason for this variety in regard to the rule is not hard to find. The rule has justice only as a principle for the unity of action, to which it may supply the virtue of concentration. But unity of action does not depend upon this rule, having more general sources in unity of character, in selection of events, and in the conjoint evolution of character and events. When character changes in some unified way, and events interact organically with character as its causes and effects, action has as much unity as is necessary for imposing drama, and the unity is entirely integral to the action. If action is concentrated within a short and arbitrary interval, it may lose integrity. In such concentration there may be virtuosity, but at the expense of truth and depth. That these losses are avoided in *Oedipus* is due to a distinction which undercuts the application of the rule. Represented action may be either explicit or implicit, manifest or latent, enacted on the stage or reported retrospectively. All of Oedipus' life is involved in the play; but it is represented implicitly through a series of retrospective discoveries, and only that series is concentrated in the assigned time. The

---

[9] Aristotle, *Poetics,* trans. Ingram Bywater, *Works,* Vol. XI (Oxford: Clarendon Press, 1924), 1449b.

ascending crisis of discovery would be melodrama without the cumulative weight of the promethean past of Oedipus, and the final acts of renunciation would be extravagant without the same foundation. Thus the aspect of the play that observes the rule depends on another aspect that does not, and the scope of the rule is significantly limited. This distinction has all the more force in many of the plays of Ibsen, in which unexcelled dramaturgy melts the past and present into each other. Here the past is not thrust into the present through isolated discoveries, but grows with quiet strength through the entire tissue of the enacted present, so that the present becomes a process of realization of the past and therefore of the self. In so organic a process it would be meaningless to try to confine the present action to any given interval, for the present cannot be defined.

A rule setting the bounds of poetry in relation to visual art was proposed by Lessing. Observing that the medium of poetry is "articulated tones" ordered successively in time, and that the medium of painting and sculpture is "figures and colors" ordered coexistently in space, Lessing held that successive objects, or actions, are appropriate subjects for poetry, and that coexistent objects, or bodies, are appropriate subjects for painting.[10] He therefore disagreed with the judgment of certain of his contemporaries, who believed that a good poet must also be a good painter; on the contrary, he held that the poet must avoid sustained description of things. A poem describing a floral scene generally fails to give a unified picture of such a scene; for by the time the description is finished, the earlier images usually are forgotten, or are remembered without vivid synthesis. The coexistence of bodies collides with the consecutiveness of speech, and a unified picture is displaced by piecework.[11] In support of this thesis Lessing cited Homer, whom he found to describe only continuing actions, to describe bodies only as sharing in actions, and then to describe bodies only with one or at most with two traits. Homer describes a ship merely as black, or as well-ruddered and black; but he dwells on such actions as launching or landing a ship.[12]

[10] Gotthold E. Lessing, *Laokoon, Sämtliche Schriften,* Vol. IX, ed. K. Lachmann (Stuttgart: Göschen, 1893), Pt. I, Sec. 16, pp. 94–95.
[11] Lessing, Sec. 17, pp. 102–104.
[12] Lessing, Sec. 16, pp. 95–96.

This restriction on the subject matter of poetry is persuasive when the intent of the poem is to narrate an action, as in epic or dramatic poetry. In such poetry, the form in which emotion is objectified consists basically of a continuing series of events, and the strength of the form requires that the forward movement of events be interrupted as little as possible. Thus description of bodies in a condition of stasis must be held to a minimum, and that condition must be converted to one of kinesis by using the body to support the action. But the restriction is irrelevant in lyric poetry, in which events, whether continuous or not, are incidental parts of the form, and emotion is objectified in images, metaphors, concepts, and the entire sensuous content of the presented form. Here many coexistent parts, or details, are held together in the temporal succession of words and lines, and earlier parts are not lost with the appearance of later parts.

Explicit memory of earlier images may or may not fade, but the images survive effectively through two means. One is the syntax of the poem, to which each image delivers itself to achieve immortality within the confines of the poem. The other is the objectified emotion. The emotion of a unified line, stanza, or poem is indivisible, despite the great complexity it may have. In the reading of the poem it suffers no discrete distinction of past, present, and future. It survives subtly, effectively in memory when the landmarks of form have disappeared. Since the image fuses with the emotion that it objectifies, it survives vicariously in the emotion. For these reasons the successive nature of the poetic medium is no bar to the vivid description of coexistent elements. Apart from theory, the proposed rule is sufficiently refuted by the common practice of poets. In the opening lines of the second stanza of Keats's "Ode to Psyche," images from several senses are joined in complex and vivid description of a single scene:

> 'Mid hush'd, cool-rooted flowers fragrant-eyed,
> Blue, silver-white, and budded Tyrian. . . .

In a quite different poet, the rule again is denied by the opening score of lines of Part II of *The Waste Land*, "A Game of Chess."

Complete use of the medium was proposed by DeWitt Parker as one of several principles for the evaluation of all of the arts.[13]

---

[13] DeWitt Parker, *Principles of Aesthetics* (New York: Appleton-Century-Crofts, 1946), p. 110.

In keeping with this rule, Parker judged normal verse to be superior to free verse, since it makes fuller use of the rhythmic possibilities of language. The advantage of the rule is its liberality, which gives the artist maximum opportunity in contrast to the restrictive nature of many rules. But the weakness of the rule stems from the same trait, for the rule expresses no more than a generous hope for art and gives no specific guidance to the critic. The definition of the medium is a matter in some instances of controversy or of local practice, as in the use of song in ancient drama or of painted surfaces in ancient sculpture. The rule does not provide for evaluation of different partial uses of the medium, or of the respective claims of breadth of use of the medium at a nominal level and selective use at an intense level. It appears to rate program music above absolute music, opera above symphony, and symphonic music above chamber music: contrary as such preferences are to many discerning tastes.

In place of a rule about the maximum use of elements available to a given art there may be proposed a commonly received principle, that the first concern of every work of art is to be unified, and that greater unity is the major source of greater value. There can be no doubt about the importance of unity in defining both art and a measure of its comparative value: works of art are distinguished from works of nature more obviously by their greater unity than by their human source; the skill in art is as much a skill in fashioning order as of handling the elements appropriate to the given art; and the value of the elements in the finished work of art depends heavily on the order given to them. But there can be no unity without diverse parts; and the principle of unity either tends to favor itself at the expense of variety, or it leaves unanswered the question of the relative claims of unity and diversity when, as readily happens, the opportunity to increase one becomes the requirement to decrease the other.

Within the field of unity, problems arise as to the value of types of unity. Harmony and balance urge their respective claims, but neither can be pushed very far without loss to the other. The rule of unity tends to favor harmony, for harmony admits less diversity than does balance, and subordinate rules of unity can be stated more readily for harmony than for balance. But balance contains greater diversity not only in the elements that are related, but also in the points of relatedness among the elements, and the rule therefore tends to discourage the more subtle and organic modes of unity: that is, the more unified though less formulable unities.

The preference for formulas of forms, which are generalized versions or models of forms, is a further weakness of the rule. Formulas never reach the intimate individuality of the actual forms of works of art; a dozen or a hundred instances of a generalized form vary in their individual character and value, and the formula that applies to all cannot distinguish and order their individual values. Formulas are known by an act of analysis, which breaks a whole into distinct parts; but this operation misses the organic flow of the actual forms of art. And formulas usurp authority, become the cant of criticism, and arrest experimentation with new forms. For all of these weaknesses of formulas the remedy is the intuition of the artist, appreciator, and critic: an intuition schooled in formulas and developed by repeated encounters with living works of art, but going beyond these to make a fresh approach suitable to the uniqueness of every work of art. The finality of intuitive discernment for the artist and the appreciator leaves the critic with no stronger option. It is compatible with the foregoing acceptance of intersubjectivity in aesthetic experience, aesthetic evaluation, and the history of art; but it disclaims doctrinaire methods in art, and it therefore modifies absolutism without converting it into relativism in critical theory.

CHAPTER 11

Art and Pain: Tragedy

The Problem of Painful Art

The problem of pain, suffering, evil, or disvalue in art arises from two considerations. One is that much art is concerned with pain or evil. Painting represents not only fertile lands, and women at the height of their natural beauty, but also the ravages of war, faded courtesans, and a crucified god. Music expresses not only fulfillment and joy, but denial and sorrow at the passing of love, at the approach of death, and at the heart of reflective consciousness. The novel and the drama represent not only conflicts that are resolved happily, but conflicts that end in desolation and death. In all of these instances there is pain in the primitive emotion of transitive expression and in the adequate emotion of embodiment. The contemplation of the finished work of art registers as a sustained object an embodied emotion that is charged with pain. But this use of painful subjects and forms, and ultimately of embodied emotion that is painful, is attended by positive value. The art of pain pleases; it impresses us with its depth of meaning; it has exceptional beauty, which may be at once tender and ravaging. Thus it happens that pain and evil, which are avoided by the wise man outside of art, are embraced by him within art. This being so, it appears that art must have some peculiar efficacy, by virtue of which our attitude toward pain is changed from fear and aversion to exalted interest.

Since the interest is exalted, and occurs in the highest instances of art, and is pursued by wise men as well as by other men, we may rule out at the outset the hypotheses that the interest in pain and suffering is sadistic or masochistic. Cruelty, or delight in the pain of others, is incompatible with aesthetic contemplation, in which the appreciator steeps himself in the form, the action, the human characters, and therefore has yielded the vantage point of his private self, from which alone he can exult in the pain of another. Pleasure in one's own suffering is morbid and stagnant. Sadism and masochism contradict the clear nature of art as experience that is open, expansive, and creative: a condition of vigor and health for the creator, the appreciator, and the society in which they live. All the more, then, they contradict the nobility of the art of pain, which has no room for the mean callousness of sadism or the base groveling of masochism.

Four hypotheses suitable to the stature of painful art may be proposed for the explanation of the value to be found in the aesthetic presentation of pain. Schopenhauer held that the value of painful art lies in the resignation that it vividly illustrates. Diverse moralists locate the good of such art in the enhancement of morality that they find in it. Aristotle taught that the value of painful art consists in the catharsis of pity and fear. And Nietzsche held that pain may be a condition of the ultimate good of power. These four views have been listed in the order of the scope and freedom they accord to painful art in the development of vital experience, whether within the frame of works of art or in the conduct of life as a whole. Schopenhauer denies life; Nietzsche affirms it generally and ecstatically; and between these poles the moralist appears to hold art and life in tighter reins than the Aristotelian critic.

The four theories also are directed toward painful art in its most emphatic and systematic form: the art of tragedy, in which pain is consciously regarded as the dominant condition of human life and as the major challenge to the artist's thought and formative power. The art called tragedy usually is identified with tragic drama, which from Aeschylus and Aristotle to the present has had a distinguished tradition of art and of theory about the art.

The tragic spirit, however, has had a second major exposition in music. The tradition here is short and recent, as is the art itself in its developed form. But the sensibility of tragedy was avowed in Beethoven, Brahms, and Mahler, and the philosophy of tragedy of Nietzsche was steeped in the experience of music. A philosophy of painful art may therefore concentrate on the art of tragedy and include in that term both tragic drama and tragic music.

In keeping with this program, and in order to afford data for the evaluation of theories, the discussion that follows will make use of certain works of drama and music whose diversity within the common field of tragedy will serve as a corrective against narrowness in the understanding of the field. In *Oedipus the King* of Sophocles, a king at the height of his power suffers self-blinding and exile following the discovery of his past, in which he had ventured more than even a king may hope safely to achieve. In Shakespeare's *King Lear,* an aged king who had resigned his powers to ungrateful and treacherous daughters passes through madness and dies, having discovered too late the fidelity of the daughter he had disowned. Ibsen's Hedda Gabler, in the play of the same name, terminates an existence of proud boredom and strong contempts in a suicide of the same temper. In *Riders to the Sea* an impoverished mother bows her head to the sea, which had taken her husband and sons, whose livings had depended on the sea. And in Arthur Miller's *Death of A Salesman,* a man of small capacity and many slogans and illusions breaks over rejection by a greatly loved son, and finally acts on the belief that his death would benefit his family more than would his life.

Beyond these works for the theatre, in a medium that represents no persons, situations, or actions, Beethoven's *Symphony No. 3* (*Eroica*) and *Piano Sonata No. 29* (*Hammerklavier*) express with unsurpassed brilliance and depth a tragic attitude toward life. In the second movement of the *Eroica,* a colorful pain is absorbed in a young energy and the will exults in conquest. In the third movement of the *Hammerklavier* sonata, pitiless calamity is met by an unyielding will which looks steadily into the heart of immovable fate. Beyond these outposts the tragic spirit cannot go. It is indeed true that Beethoven went a step further. In the later quartets, pain and the will are transformed by an act of inward grace, and the categories of struggle, conquest, and defeat melt away. Into this strange land, of the most remote beauty, no concept enters: but those that approach have left behind the philosophy of tragedy.

Tragedy as Resignation

The theory of tragedy as resignation holds that tragedy teaches the wisdom and advances the practice of resignation to the suffering and evil of existence. The tragedy is said to do this by showing persons of fortune and passion renouncing their goals after a siege of struggle, suffering, and disaster. The hero comes to the point where he sees desire and action as vain; he therefore disavows these, reduces or eliminates pleasures as well as pains, and slows down the pulse of life. The spectator who truly follows the play sympathizes with the hero's resignation and discerns the wisdom of it. This gain in wisdom by the spectator is the good in tragedy and the source of tragic pleasure. The good here achieved is not merely theoretical, such as might be had from aphorisms or chapters in the ethics and metaphysics of resignation. It is also practical. The vividness of the drama impresses the will of the spectator with a momentary stir of resignation, and the image of this experience may persist after the aesthetic experience is over as a motive to further practice.

The philosophy of resignation was stated at length by Schopenhauer, who brought to it eloquence if not conviction. The foundation of the philosophy, as set forth in *The World as Will and Idea*, is the thesis that reality is will, which is an endless blind striving incapable of satisfaction. The pain of the will is compounded by the conflicts of individual wills, whose distinction and egoism are appearance rather than reality. In a moment of insight, the wise man sees through appearance, individuation, and egoism and realizes the universality and unity of all suffering. The insight, fortified by experience of unusual suffering, quiets the will as such, and removes further suffering.

> In this individual it [the will] stands out forcefully, in that one more weakly; in varying degrees it is brought to reflection and moderated through the light of knowledge, until finally, in a particular instance, this knowledge, refined and heightened by suffering

itself, reaches the point where appearance, the veil of Maya, no longer deceives it, the form of appearance, the principle of individuation, is seen through by it, the egoism based on the principle perishes; so that the previously forceful motives henceforth lose their power, and instead of them the complete knowledge of the essence of the world, operating as a tranquilizer of the will, brings about resignation, the surrender not merely of life, but of the whole will to live. Thus we see in tragic drama the noblest persons, after long struggle and suffering, finally renounce forever the aims they have hitherto so violently pursued, and all the enjoyments of life, or surrender life itself willingly and gladly.[1]

Thus the true meaning of tragedy is "the deeper insight, that what the hero atones for are not his particular sins, but original sin, *i.e.*, the guilt of existence itself."[2] In support of this conclusion Schopenhauer quoted the Spanish poet Calderón:

> *Pues el delito mayor*
> *Del hombre es haber nacido.*[3]

Schopenhauer's view of tragedy is not unpersuasive. It has a certain magnificence about it, which suits the tragic spirit; for it contemplates the whole of reality and appearance, assumes a tremendous transformation in the will, and teaches men neither to rant nor to whimper when confronted with the evils of existence. It is ethically mature in its advice to accommodate the self to matters that cannot be changed. It is ethically precarious when the accommodation becomes so habitual that it extends to matters that can be changed. But the ethical advantage or disadvantage of resignation is mainly extra-aesthetic, whereas the worth of the theory as an explanation of tragic art must be assessed in direct relation to the art. Here the theory runs into difficulties, some general and some located in individual works.

The general difficulties were well stated by Nietzsche. The experience of tragedy is a tonic, according to this writer[4]; and anyone

---

[1] Arthur Schopenhauer, *Die Welt als Wille und Vorstellung*, Vol. I, *Sämmtliche Werke*, Vol. II (Leipzig: F. A. Brockhaus, 1891), Bk. III, Sec. 51, p. 299. *The World as Will and Idea*, trans. R. B. Haldane and J. Kemp, Vol. I (London: Routledge, 1957), p. 327.

[2] Schopenhauer, *Die Welt*, Bk. III, Sec. 51, p. 300. *The World*, p. 328.

[3] "For the greatest crime / Of man is to have been born."

[4] Friedrich Nietzsche, *Der Wille zur Macht*, Vol. II, *Werke*, Vol. XVI (Leipzig: Kröner, 1911), Bk. III, Sec. 851.

who has felt the profound, serene elation of a tragedy well performed must agree with this description. The experience is hardly
one of resignation of will and of life, for it is filled with energy
and assurance, and it defines the perfection rather than the with-
drawal of activity. If it be proposed, in a paradoxical spirit, that
tragic art brings about the joyful surrender of all joys, the answer
must be in two negatives. The elation as experienced does not
have surrender as its target: it has an opposite target, which will
be defined under the fourth hypothesis. And where the will moves
joyfully to some great sacrifice, it does so with a positive good in
mind, in which affirmation of the will is represented. A martyr
embraces the flame in pursuit of eternal bliss; a nun who turns
from the man she loves does so for the greater bridegroom, Christ;
the hero who rushes into mortal danger does so for the sake of
those who will remain in life and in volition, or on behalf of an
honor that is the first affirmation of his will while he lives.

A further difficulty of a general sort is that tragedy flourishes
at a time of expansion and fulfillment of the society in which it
arises. Such were the times of Aeschylus and Sophocles, in the
fifth century before Christ, and of Shakespeare, about the year
1600. Neither Greece nor England was at its respective time in a
period of decline in temporal power or of negation in attitude
toward life. But if tragedy were an art of resignation, then it
should be contemporary with nihilism and decadence, as Nietzsche
pointed out in further criticism of the theory.[5]

Beyond the general weaknesses are conflicts of the theory with
actual works of tragic art. Oedipus destroys his sight and goes
into exile, and these are great renunciations; but he does so with
an energy hardly smaller, and certainly more fierce, than that
with which he solved the riddle of the Sphinx, killed his father,
married his mother, and brought on the discovery of his crimes.
The energy is one of expiation, not of resignation. King Lear
prefers madness to a conscious collapse of will in tears; and over
the dying figure of Cordelia he utters exquisite praise of her
womanly grace, and expresses a fragment of bitter satisfaction in
having cut down her hangman. His friend Gloucester attempts
suicide, feeling that his life is as dark as his blinded condition;
but failing, he abandons what he would consider to be total re-

[5] Nietzsche, Bk. III, Sec. 851.

nunciation, and resolves to endure to the end. Endurance is not resignation: it lies within the positive compass of the will. Hedda Gabler chose death to an existence that offered neither the freedom nor the beauty that she desired; in dying, she did not renounce these, but affirmed them with her usual curt decisiveness. Willy Loman died without any mitigation of the will to live; he expected his death to confer a benefit of the kind that he had regularly looked for in life. And it is impossible to find in the *Eroica* or in the *Hammerklavier* sonata an attitude of resignation. The conquering will of the one and the unyielding will of the other are far from the categories of defeat or acceptance, of passivity and encompassing mildness.

Only in *Riders to the Sea* do these attributes occur. The bereaved Maurya says:

> They're all gone now, and there isn't anything more the sea can do to me. . . . It's a great rest I'll have now, and great sleeping in the long nights after Samhain, if its only a bit of wet flour we do have to eat, and maybe a fish that would be stinking. . . . Michael has a clean burial in the far north, by the grace of the Almighty God. Bartley will have a fine coffin out of the white boards, and a deep grave surely. What more can we want than that? No man at all can be living for ever, and we must be satisfied.[6]

This is one of the saddest of tragedies, and sadness is an infirmity in the tragic spirit. The play may show that resignation is available to tragedy as a source of value, though it cannot show that it is the general and essential source. And even in *Riders to the Sea* there may be more than resignation, as a later view may perhaps show.[7]

Tragedy as Moral Instruction

The moralistic account of tragedy asserts that though the hero meets with disaster, the moral law does not, and the disaster of the hero enhances our appreciation of the moral law. The en-

[6] John M. Synge, *Riders to the Sea*, in *Five Great Modern Irish Plays* (New York: Modern Library, 1941), pp. 188–189.
[7] Below, "Tragedy as Power."

hancement may occur in either of two ways. In the lesser case, the hero is in harmony with moral principles, and the pain of his undoing is mitigated or dissolved by the survival of the moral principle. The principle may be advanced by the individual's sacrifice, or it may appear to have an eternal being which is better appreciated in contrast with the passage of individuals. In the major case, the hero collides with moral principles, and his disaster is punishment for wrongdoing and is vindication of the moral law.

The lesser case is seldom appealed to in the philosophy of tragedy. It invites division of our interest, even of our moral interest, since the hero deserves well in the light of the moral law but receives poorly. Satisfaction in the survival of the law is sharply curtailed by the pain of those who are identified with it. It is more likely that the tragedy of the actively good or the passively innocent will suggest a world in which principle is not represented in power. In such a world, whether metaphysically in the "nature of things" or psychologically in the laws of human motivation and behavior, there will be either a neutral place for the moral law or a sense of demonic opposition to it. Then the disaster of a good individual will not evoke a compensatory satisfaction in respect of moral law; rather, his loss will be generalized as a complaint against the cosmos and as uncertainty about the principle. This is the procedure of naturalism in literature when it goes so far on behalf of morality as to assess the moral standing of its characters.

The major case is often argued by those who have a didactic interest in art. Regardless of the kind of interest taken in art, art cannot be shorn of moral responsibility, as the following chapter will further show; and the most ready way of handling this responsibility is to create or discover in art situations in which the good are rewarded and the evil are punished. Tragedy is then asserted to be concerned with the second half of this realm of judgment. The thesis has some merit in the actual works of tragic art, for the hero usually has one or more flaws of character, and a connection can reasonably be alleged between his infirmities and his suffering. Despite this, the moralistic account of tragedy in its major phase also is unsatisfactory. It suffers from a number of general difficulties, and it is not sustained by examination of works of tragedy. In addition, it presupposes a philosophy of the function of the moral in art which is open to criticism in general aesthetics, as will again be shown in the next chapter.[8]

1. The paramount aesthetic function of sympathetic penetration of the form is weakened by the moralistic interest, which shifts attention from persons and actions and the emotion integrated with them to a law that stands apart from them. The formal penetration and identification are necessary not merely for technical understanding, but also for that larger understanding that drama offers of the springs of human action and of the compulsions and harassments under which men labor. Given such understanding, the impulse to judge and to condemn declines and benevolence grows in its place. But there is no higher moral perspective than that of benevolence, and thus the moralistic approach to tragedy tends to defeat its highest purpose.

2. In all genuine suffering there is dignity, regardless of the moral fault of the sufferer. To think of the suffering primarily as deserved destroys this dignity and lowers visibly the level of dramatic appreciation. In the face of great pain, a moral judgment seems carping and somewhat small.

3. Individuals become means and the moral law the end in the moralistic account. Our grief in the disaster of a person is swallowed up in our pleasure in the vindication of the moral law; this means that the individual is of subordinate interest to the moral principle and is a means to the dramatic exposition of the latter. But a sensitive morality finds no higher end than the individual; and this must be particularly true in the drama, in which the individual is in effect all individuals. Thus the moralistic account again subverts its higher perception.

4. The moral law is an abstract entity. Whether objective or subjective, eternal or mutable, intuited or reasoned, the moral law is a principle or body of principles, and therefore is relatively indeterminate and remote. It has neither flesh nor blood. But aesthetic interest in general, and emotion in particular, are directed mainly to the concrete and particular: in the drama, to persons, actions, and emotions that are specific and vital. It is not aesthetically possible to generate as much interest in abstractions as in concretions. The moralistic approach thus must be content with a certain mediocrity of aesthetic attention. But the

[8] Below, Chap. 12, "Art and Moral Instruction."

fact of aesthetic experience is otherwise; and the conclusion is inescapable that the source of aesthetic pleasure in tragedy is not in the fate of the moral law.

5. The acceptance of moral principles varies in place and time. Whatever the intrinsic content and reality of such laws may be, the impact on men is neither universal nor constant. The conception and evaluation of wisdom, courage, temperance, justice, benevolence, pride, and humility vary among nations and periods of history. Great art, however, reaches a depth of indubitable experience that is amazing in its universality. Thus there is tension between the moral parish and the aesthetic cosmos, and the second may suffer from narrow ties with the first. To the extent that this is true, the enjoyment of tragedy must have some other basis than moral assertion.

6. The moral life has more complexity and intrinsic conflict than are allowed for in the moralistic theory. As Nicolai Hartmann has shown with great insight and system, conflict in the ethical domain is not only between good and bad impulses, but also between impulses of which both have the sanction of the moral ought: higher and stronger values, goodness and nobility, fullness and purity stand in antinomial tension with each other.[9] The moralistic approach would be more discerning if it should look for such conflicts in the tragic situation; for whether experienced or not by the protagonist, they have a bearing on the judgment to be made of his actions. The *hybris* of Oedipus in solving the riddle of the Sphinx, which contradicted the values of measure and human modesty, contained the value of power in the form of knowledge and was needed to relieve the land of its disaster. This excess of self-assertion was the ultimate cause of his downfall, which therefore has a source that is morally mixed. Hedda Gabler may readily be looked upon as a selfish and ruthless woman, who loved no one. Her disdain for her husband and Mrs. Elvsted, and her destruction of Lövborg's manuscript and ultimately of Lövborg, violate basic precepts of tolerance, justice, and benevolence. But they have roots in her worship of a bold freedom and beauty, which led her to be impatient of mediocrity and to consider life itself expendable. Her mistake was in not

[9] Nicolai Hartmann, *Ethik* (Berlin: de Gruyter, 1926), pp. 193, 498, 513, 554–55.

making certain that Lövborg shared her motives in the situation at hand. Like many of Ibsen's protagonists, she manipulated another in the interest of a rigorous ideal. In seeking freedom without reservation she defeated freedom. But what she could not accomplish through Lövborg she accomplished in herself, when, with symbolic rightness, she put a bullet into her head. At this conclusion she showed that her ruthlessness might well be resoluteness, and that in her demands she made no distinction in favor of herself.

7. In many instances where suffering can be correlated with moral flaws, it is far out of proportion to the flaw. The punishment is greater than the crime, so that our moral sense is rather outraged than satisfied. If King Lear is rash, there is no reason why he should pay so bitterly for it: far greater vices have no worse return. The price paid by Willy Loman for his son's discovery of his infidelity would have been no greater had Willy's flaw been accompanied by wholesale indifference to his family; indeed, the greater evil would probably have led to no suffering at all.

8. Finally, there are the many instances in which suffering has sources apart from moral defects, and in such instances the pleasure of tragedy cannot be found in the enhancement of the moral law through exposure of a wrongdoer. If a moral issue is raised, it is not by the vice of the actor, but by the severity of a world in which innocence is so dealt with. Oedipus killed his father and married his mother in ignorance. Lear and Gloucester made mistakes of judgment about their children, and Cordelia suffered alienation and then death through no fault of hers, moral or intellectual: indeed, her virtue led to the initial mishap. Tesman and Mrs. Elvsted sustain losses that arise not out of their natures and decisions, but out of those of their associates, to whom they had committed their loyalties and welfare. Such collateral wreckage occurs generally in tragedy, and it offends the moral sense. In *Riders to the Sea* there is no visible vice or error in mother or sons, but an inescapable natural force, morally neutral, brings destruction. And in the Beethoven compositions, as in music essentially, no moral situation can be stated: there are only a will, its pain, and what the will does about the pain. Here the tragic spirit at its most intense point is also perfectly general. Its concern is not with certain wills, that is, those that have contingent

defects of virtue or of knowledge, but with all wills. The problem of suffering is inherent: its gravity and challenge are increased accordingly, and the moral issue and judgment disappear entirely.

Tragedy as Catharsis

The theory of catharsis asserts that the value of tragedy consists in the removal or purification of certain emotions in the spectator. The dramatic representation of suffering brings forth negative emotion in the beholder, and thus far tragedy is solely bad. But the same representation then produces a change in the emotion, which is accompanied by pleasure; and this change or catharsis is the source of good in tragedy. The theory was stated by Aristotle in what is no doubt the most celebrated sentence in the literature of aesthetics or criticism:

> A tragedy, then, is the imitation of an action that is serious and also, as having magnitude, complete in itself; in language with pleasurable accessories, each kind brought in separately in the parts of the work; in a dramatic, not in a narrative form; with incidents arousing pity and fear, wherewith to accomplish its catharsis of such emotions.[10]

The general structure of incidents, or plot, of tragedy is determined by the requirement of pity and fear. "A good man must not be seen passing from happiness to misery"; such a situation "is not fear-inspiring or piteous, but simply odious to us."[11] An "extremely bad man" should not be represented as making the same passage. Such a plot "may arouse the human feeling in us, but it will not move us to either pity or fear; pity is occasioned by undeserved misfortune, and fear by that of one like ourselves."[12] The plot that remains to tragedy concerns "the intermediate kind of personage, a man not preeminently virtuous and just, whose misfortune, however, is brought upon him not by vice and depravity but by some error of judgment."[13]

[10] Aristotle, *Poetics,* trans. Ingram Bywater, *Works,* Vol. XI (Oxford: Clarendon Press, 1924), 1449b.
[11] Aristotle, 1452b.
[12] Aristotle, 1453a.
[13] Aristotle, 1453a.

The rules of plot indicate the relation of this theory to the moralistic theory. The rule concerning the good man provides that tragedy should not offend the moral sense of men, and that concerning the bad man indicates that pity is based on a moral judgment. But the scope of the moral judgment is restricted by the third rule. If the misfortune of the hero is due not to vice but to error of judgment, there is no moral issue in it, and consequently there is no satisfaction of the moral law to furnish the basis of tragic value.

Further independence of moral consideration is apparent in the theory of catharsis. This term is interpreted in opposed ways by students of Aristotle. The view of catharsis as purification supposes that emotion is cleansed of its inferior elements. The theory of catharsis as purgation holds that emotion is drained off with consequent relief. The one is ethical, involving insight into the nature and grounds of pity and fear and achieving a lasting alteration of emotive disposition. The other is quasi-medical; it is subintellectual and physiological; the result is temporary, though subject to repetition. Light on this conflict is not available in the *Poetics,* the extant text of which makes no reference to catharsis after the definition quoted above. But Book VIII of the *Politics,* which treats of education and the place of music in education, discusses a kindred subject in terms that favor the theory of purgation.

Aristotle there divides melodies into "ethical melodies, melodies of action, and passionate or inspiring melodies."[14] He proposes three benefits from the study of music: education, purgation, and relaxation and intellectual enjoyment. In education the ethical melodies and modes are to be used. The educative and ethical function of music is considerable:

> Rhythm and melody supply imitations of anger and gentleness, and also of courage and temperance, and of all the qualities contrary to these, and of the other qualities of character, which hardly fall short of the actual affections, as we know from our own experience, for in listening to such strains our souls undergo a change.[15]

[14] Aristotle, *Politics,* trans. B. Jowett, *Works,* Vol. X (Oxford: Clarendon Press, 1921), 1341b.

[15] Aristotle, *Politics,* 1340a.

But the end of purgation is distinct from that of education and uses distinct melodies:

> For feelings such as pity and fear, or, again, enthusiasm, exist very strongly in some souls, and have more or less influence over all. Some persons fall into a religious frenzy, whom we see as a result of the sacred melodies—when they have used the melodies that excite the soul to mystic frenzy—restored as though they had found healing and purgation. Those who are influenced by pity or fear, and every emotional nature, must have a like experience, and others in so far as each is susceptible to such emotions, and all are in a manner purged and their souls lightened and delighted.[16]

The musical treatment of pity and fear thus involves their steep arousal, leading to discharge of tension and relief from the emotions, in a pattern similar to that of sexual excitement and release. It appears, then, that the related treatment of pity and fear in tragic drama is an act of purgation rather than of purification.

This does not mean that dramatic catharsis is merely physical or physiological. The purgative melodies are said to afford an "innocent pleasure," by which evidently is meant a pure pleasure: that is, a pleasure unmixed with the pain of prior toil, and appropriate to the intellectual enjoyment of leisure. They are performed for the "free and educated" spectators at the theater. For the uneducated masses another kind of music is to be played. This popular music has for its end relaxation or amusement, which are appropriate for those who need relief after toil. It is said to be suited to the minds of the uneducated: "for as their minds are perverted from the natural state, so there are perverted modes and highly strung and unnaturally coloured melodies."[17] The music of frenzy and purgation thus appears to be neither perverted nor highly strung. It has a significant place in the life of reflective man, and in its healing function it may be regarded as moral in the widest sense of the term. The same is true of tragic catharsis, which is the end of an art that Aristotle regarded very highly. Thus the contrast of purgation and purification is measurably softened.

The spiritually favorable account of catharsis makes it eligible

---

[16] Aristotle, *Politics*, 1342a.
[17] Aristotle, *Politics*, 1342a.

for serious consideration as the explanation of the positive value of tragedy. The intensity of the experience, from arousal of commanding emotions through discharge to welcome peace, is relevant to the tragic experience, which has as much intensity as art can offer. And the theory allows more freedom to art in the portrayal of human existence than does the moralistic theory, and more vitality in that portrayal than does the hypothesis of resignation. Despite these merits, the theory of catharsis is inadequate in at least four ways. It misrepresents the emotional content of tragedy; it provides for a comparatively negative outcome of the experience; it presupposes an erroneous view of the nature of the aesthetic attitude; and it contradicts certain features of transitive expression.

The emotion of tragedy is not one of pity. Pity is an emotion of sorrow felt by a person in fortune for another who is thought to be unfortunate and, in that misfortune, lacking in strength. It implies an undesirable kind of distance between the persons, and it occurs most readily in those who have to take advantage of the exposure of another in order to be assured of their own strength. Thus it fails to see the dignity of genuine suffering, and in place of that power it substitutes a specious strength in the pitier. Nor is tragic emotion the nobler pity (putting aside labels) of compassion. In this emotion there is sorrow without distance; and there is no false ascendancy, for compassion recognizes the community of all persons in pain and in weakness. In that recognition of frailty, compassion, though admitting the dignity of suffering, does not rise to the perception of the further reaches of power in the painful experience of the tragic personality. Pity and compassion thus fall short of the kinetic stature of the tragic emotion.

And fear has a like deficiency. Unlike courageous affirmation in the face of contrary power, fear is prepared to yield. If the spectator properly has no separate self, he would feel fear only as the hero experiences fear. But though the tragic hero is beset with troubles and has little or no hope for improvement in the future, he spends little time in fearfulness. He suffers the present and laments the past, but he does not brood upon or cower before the pain of the future. Neither Oedipus, nor Lear, nor Hedda Gabler, nor even Willy Loman feels marked fear. Only in Maurya is this emotion significant; and in her case fear seems to be transformed into a lament on a future so surely divined as to be accomplished fact. For this reason the actuality of the son's death makes no fresh impression on her, and resignation comes quickly.

As a consequence of the description it makes of the emotional content of the tragic experience, the theory of catharsis provides a negative rather than positive view of the achievement of tragedy. The emotions of pity and fear are purged; and the self is left in an emotionally neutral state, as though the tragedy were itself, after all, a cipher. It is true that the purged condition is pleasant; but the only pleasure inherent in it is that of relief from the prior stresses of pity and fear: the pleasure has no significance of its own. And if the tragic emotion is one of pity and fear, it is better that it be purged than that it be allowed to persist; but the removal of an evil is not a positive good.

The best that can be said for this negative outcome is that it does not presuppose deliberate arousal of the emotion to be purged. Pity and fear are not created by the tragic spectacle. Catharsis does not have the absurdity, imputed to one version of it by Ducasse, of putting on "a shoe that pinches in order to have the delightful pleasure of taking it off."[18] It appears rather that pity and fear are abiding dispositions which burden the routine life of men. Here they are similar to hidden anxieties and tensions, and they may well be the equivalent in Greek thought of the generalized anxiety stressed in recent psychiatry and existentialist philosophy. If this be so, tragedy for the theory of catharsis has the merit of making a contribution to the treatment of a problem that it does not instigate, since the dispositions to pity and fear antedate the performance and are temporarily softened by energetic release. But if this role be assigned to tragic art, it is still negative and not equal to the high positive value set upon the art.

Such a role, however, is incompatible with the aesthetic attitude. In contemplation, an emotion is actual but not in the condition of arousal; it is experienced objectively as embodied in the form. Arousal is subjective, transitively interested, and involved with body; contemplation is objective, disinterested, and detached from body. The theory of catharsis calls for emotion in the condition of arousal rather than contemplation, and this is not true of the aesthetic experience. Furthermore, it calls for dis-

---

[18] Curt J. Ducasse, *The Philosophy of Art* (New York: Dial, 1929), p. 251.

charge of the emotion, so that the emotion leaves consciousness and the appreciator has no further relation to it. But emotion in aesthetic experience is preserved in the form that gives it expression; embodiment is not discharge. These theses about emotion, contemplation, and expression were developed in earlier chapters of this book; they center about a view of aesthetic experience as nonpractical, and this view is by no means a monopoly of the expressional theory of art. In regard to both arousal and discharge, then, catharsis differs from the general attitude of the aesthetic experience.

The theory of catharsis has a disarming affinity with the expressional theory, since it emphasizes emotion, asserts a change in emotion as a result of aesthetic operations, and concludes on a note of freedom in relation to the emotion. These similarities should not be permitted to obscure significant differences between catharsis and transitive expression. In catharsis, the determination or growth and definition of essence in emotion is relatively slight, and so is the clarity with which the emotion is apprehended. The spectator consumed with pity and fear does not have an adequate experience of them, and his concern is not to have such an experience but to be purged. Here the only alternatives are emotion as aroused and as nonexistent; given such choices, and the undesirable emotions of pity and fear, the option is for nonexistence through release. And the purged condition is free in a sense different from, and simpler than, that of aesthetic freedom. It is solely a negative freedom, consisting in the removal of the passivity induced in the spectator by the emotion; it does not achieve, or even attempt, the positive freedom of aesthetic experience, in which the energy and meaning of the embodied emotion are made available to the self. Its negative freedom is achieved in a different way from that in which the aspect of negative freedom is had in art. In transitive expression, the passion upon the self is removed by distanced fixation of the emotion, in which position the emotion is still actual to enrich the self and thereby its power. But in catharsis the passion is removed by destruction of the emotion. The character of the negative freedom in catharsis prevents the development of positive freedom.

The theory of catharsis is contrary to a number of basic aspects of aesthetic experience, and it does not measure up to the opportunities either of art or of tragic art. But it must not be forgotten that it has the authority of the second of Western philosophers, who in the field of the theory of art excelled even his teacher. We may not, like Collingwood, dismiss the theory of catharsis as a theory of the pseudo-art of amusement;[19] on the contrary, it approaches art with serious purpose and full relevance.

Tragedy as Power

The last of the hypotheses about the positive value of painful art is the most complex in its psychology and aesthetics. It asserts that pain has an intimate, constructive relation to pleasure and good and is by no means to be shunned as the opposite that precludes good. This favorable relation of pain to value lies ethically in the emphasis on the good of power and psychologically in the affiliation of pain with power. The relation is not limited to aesthetic experience. But it rises to its most significant point in art, by virtue of the contemplation of painful power by means of aesthetic form. In such contemplation tragedy consists.

For the initial exposition of the theory of tragedy as power we may turn to Nietzsche, whose perception in this area is unexcelled. The major sources are the early *Birth of Tragedy* and the late, posthumously edited *Will to Power,* Book Three. In both of these books the psychology and aesthetics are underlaid with a metaphysics of voluntaristic idealism, which is not necessary to the theory of tragic power, but amplifies it by giving the accounts of human experience and of art deep roots and thus making tragic art universal and drastically necessary. The two books differ somewhat in both metaphysics and aesthetics, due to the span of years between them; but they have in common an impassioned occupation with will, power, pain, and art, and the relatively sober contribution of the later book to the first three topics is a helpful balance to the poetic splendor of *The Birth of Tragedy.*

The basic thesis in the philosophy of Nietzsche is that reality is will. Will is power in act; it is endowed with the axiological character of striving; and it is essentially and generally nonconscious, which means that pleasure and pain, symbolized goals,

---

[19] R. G. Collingwood, *The Principles of Art* (Oxford: Clarendon Press, 1950), pp. 51–52.

deliberation, and choice are secondary to it and even epiphenomenal. In *The Birth of Tragedy,* will is one, but internally contra-
dictory; in *The Will to Power* it is many, and these wills are
spoken of as "dynamical quanta, in a relation of tension to all
other dynamical quanta":[20] here each will is a power in search of
increased power, which is to be had by the incorporation of other
wills in a scheme of organization dominated by the will in question.
Unlike Platonic ideas, will changes; unlike material atoms, it
changes essentially and internally. Reality, then, is a vast sea of
willing and change. But will brings forth reason as an instrument
of partial mastery of the environment of wills, and reason is useful
because it imposes upon the flux simplifying forms of the static
and homogeneous. Space, time, substance, and causality therefore
are appearances, as is everything conceptual, general, and abstract. But when reason takes the guise of reasoning upon the
will's own impulses and values, it fumbles in comparison with
instinct, in which will moves more directly and darkly. In this
theory of the dominance of the nonrational lies the metaphysical
foundation of tragedy, since it undercuts the optimism of intelligence. Neither nature nor man can be understood, controlled,
saved.

The good for Nietzsche is power and whatever advances power.
Pleasure and pain do not constitute the good and its opposite.
Pleasure and pain are not motivating or causal; pleasure is a
feeling of the increase of power, and displeasure or pain is a feeling of inhibition or decrease of power; and as feelings they are
items of consciousness and epiphenomenal. A feeling of power does
not have power; the power and thus the good lie outside the
feeling. "Pleasure and displeasure are bare consequences, mere
concomitant appearances,—what man wills, what each smallest
part of a living organism wills, is a plus of power."[21] As a concomitant of power, pleasure undoubtedly is a sign of good; but
this does not mean that pain indicates disvalue.

Pain is a prior condition of value, power, and pleasure. "The
will to power can externalize itself only against resistances; it
therefore seeks for that which resists it."[22] But resistance means
an at least momentary inhibition of power, and the feeling of this

[20] Friedrich Nietzsche, *Der Wille zur Macht,* Bk. III, Sec. 635.
[21] Nietzsche, Sec. 702.
[22] Nietzsche, Sec. 656.

condition is pain. "Pain, as inhibition of its will to power, is thus a normal fact, the normal ingredient of each organic happening."[23] When the will surmounts the resistance by incorporating the resisting power, it has an increase of power and the experience thereof is pleasure. Readiness to tackle pain is thus an antecedent condition of value and pleasure, and here the idolatry of pleasure leads to loss of good. The same is true of the more complex levels of human activity. Nietzsche observed that in the creative man, "the embryo of the man of the future," all shaping forces directed toward the future may be found, and consequently conflict of forces and pain. "This is the deepest interpretation of suffering: the forming forces collide with each other."[24] Here the great good of creation presupposes pain from sources within the creator.

Pain enters, sharpens, and strengthens pleasure in the Dionysian experience of ecstasy, which is the major topic of *The Birth of Tragedy*. The Dionysian festivals of ancient Greece celebrated the suffering of the impassioned god, in whom all suffering was fused.[25] Viewed concretely and contingently, this pain is that of human sensibility in a world which has no concern for human happiness and offers no security against bitter disappointment and death. Silenus, companion of Dionysus, described the condition of man when he said that it is best not to be born, and next best to die soon. But seen more abstractly and essentially, the pain is that of change or becoming generally. Throughout reality, nothing is fixed and secure; everything ceases and gives way to novelty, which also ends. Here there is a double pain. The present moment and the essences or meanings that it contains are lost in the passage toward the future; this is the pain of destruction. In dying, they resist the mobile impetus that creates the next moment; this is the pain of creation. The solution to this dual suffering is to be found in the ecstatic conversion of pain into pleasure, in a process of affirmation through transcendence.

Ecstasy was not analyzed by Nietzsche. We may propose that it is an intense pleasure founded on passage beyond established limits. The ecstasy of erotic love threatens to break beyond the ceiling of consciousness, and the ecstasy of mystical love may

[23] Nietzsche, Sec. 702.
[24] Nietzsche, Sec. 686.
[25] Friedrich Nietzsche, *Die Geburt der Tragödie, Werke,* Vol. I (Leipzig: Naumann, 1899), pp. 72–74.

do so. The Dionysian ecstasy embraces these, but extends to all change, which takes the present moment and its meaning as a limit to be transcended. The Dionysian affirmation of change regards the present moment and its essence as an obstacle to be surmounted; goaded by the pain of resistance, it rises upon the energy of that pain and marshals its resources to overflow the present in the creation of new essence. It regards destruction as a phase of transcendence toward the new being; by this good it uses the pain of loss to intensify creation rather than to subtract from it. Thus the pain of transcendence invests it with high energy, which appears in ecstasy as intense pleasure.

Since the energy involves the conversion of pain to a positive end rather than its elimination, the pain appears in the pleasure as a coloring that gives it massiveness and sharpness not to be found in pure pleasure. But the pain is in a relation of tension to the pleasure, and threatens to break apart from the pleasure, which seeks to overcome the threat to its maximum state by embracing its opposite. No pain is as great as that of passage to nonbeing, and pleasure seeks its own destruction in its imperious desire for pain. Thus ecstasy involves transcendence of pleasure toward both pain and nonbeing. This is a second transcendence in ecstasy, which occurs not in the changing situation on which the pleasure is founded, but in the pleasure itself. And while the first transcendence is achieved in all change, the second is not achieved but is taken as an ideal; it is approached with increasingly concentrated pleasure, but with haunting awareness that consummation would eclipse consciousness and thus pleasure and pain alike.

A further source of pleasure in pain occurred in the unity or community of the Dionysian festivals. Ecstasy was not experienced in solitude; it was the joint property of many people dancing and singing together. Man was united with man in an act that dissolved individual boundaries and differences and merged all into one indivisible humanity. Pain is less grim and hostile, more fluent and amenable, when shared. And this community of pain went a step further to its ultimate limit in the unity of man with nature. The suffering of individual man, and his endurance and triumph in individual change and insecurity, were identified with the suffering and change of the one primordial will through the image of the satyr, which was part man and part nature. Pain could not be abolished; but it could be made significant by sympathy with life in the ground of things. Through this identification came the "metaphysical comfort" that life "despite all change of appearances is indestructibly powerful and pleasurable."[26]

The experience of unity might be expected to support ecstasy, causing it to appear more readily and to have greater scope. Like ecstasy, unity involves the transcendence of limits, which in this instance are the boundaries between man and man and between man and nature; unity therefore involves its own ecstasy. In the passion to overpass limits the Dionysian philosophy reveals itself as the advocate of the indeterminate and formless: first in change, which is indeterminate at the point between the present moment and its successor; and second and more deeply in unity, in which the individual will embraces the indeterminate totality of the one will and loses its own determinateness thereby.

The Dionysian principle of power specified through pain, ecstasy, and unity supplies the inspiration and basic content of tragedy. But it cannot of itself produce tragedy, for this is an art and thus formed and determinate. The formal principle for Nietzsche came from an opposed source, the Apollonian. Apollo was the god of dream and of prophecy, the visionary discernment of the future. More deeply, he is the deification of the principle of individuation.[27] The practical corollaries of emphasis on this principle are self-knowledge, measure, and control. The theoretical significance of individuation is its identity with the principles of determinateness and of a unity based on determinate, separate parts. Individuation is formation; but Nietzsche arbitrarily identified form and individuation with visual form, and thought of Apollo as the god of the visual arts. Since reality is indeterminate volition, individuality and form are appearances, images, illusions: for which the dramatic term is dream. In this dream world, action, power, and commitment of self do not occur; the Apollonian spirit rests in the detached contemplation of images, in which it is contained, measured, and saved from pain.

Tragic drama arises out of the union of Dionysian will and Apollonian form. The Dionysian role is enacted by the chorus, which sings, chants, dances, and weaves about in ecstatic identifi-

---

[26] Nietzsche, *Die Geburt der Tragödie*, p. 55.
[27] Nietzsche, *Die Geburt der Tragödie*, pp. 35–36.

cation with Dionysus and the universal will, becoming, and pain that he represents. The chorus as a musical community is suited to the Dionysian role. In contrast to the protagonists, it is an unindividuated whole comparable to the indeterminate totality of the one will. Its musical function gives it direct access to the will, in contrast to the limitation of language or speech to appearance. On this basis the Apollonian spirit builds the form or structure of protagonists or characters, actions, dialogue, and scene: all determinate and illusory. Thus tragedy "may be interpreted solely as a manifestation and picturing of Dionysian states, as visible symbolization of music, as the dream world of a Dionysian ecstasy."[28] The Dionysian spirit contemplates itself in the fixed forms of Apollo, beholding its commitment detachedly. The artist in Greek tragedy is

> simultaneously an artist of ecstasy and dream: so we must think of him as, in Dionysian intoxication and mystical self-transcendence, alone and apart from the revelling choruses, he sinks down and, through Apollonian dream influence, his own state, i.e., his unity with the innermost ground of the world, is revealed to him in a symbolic dream picture.[29]

In the essential theses of this complex theory, Nietzsche has surely provided the basis for the solution to the problem of painful art. But full assent to the theory of pain as good through power requires certain stipulations, which will partly subtract from and partly add to the theory as stated by Nietzsche.

As noted before, the metaphysic of the will as the basic reality is dispensable. It is significant in metaphysics, since it is rich with suggestions about the nature of both the real and the apparently real; but in aesthetics it is not necessary. All that is required here is the will of man. But the generalization of the concept of will has value metaphorically, since it states in its symbol the universality and necessity of suffering. From these attributes follow greater significance for suffering and deeper involvement with the problem: both of which increase the power of the tragic experience in the spectator or appreciator.

[28] Nietzsche, *Die Geburt der Tragödie,* p. 101.
[29] Nietzsche, *Die Geburt der Tragödie,* p. 25.

Parallel to the shift from the will in the cosmos to the will in man is a shift from the will as essentially nonconscious to the will as conscious. It is the conscious will that suffers in the full sense of the word. This will alone concerns the artist and appreciator directly; if an unconscious will is of interest, it is because of its effects on the conscious will. This is to say that the good lies within the field of consciousness or experience: only an item of which we are conscious can be intrinsically good or bad.

If power is to be good in itself, it must appear in consciousness rather than at a darker level. But the experience of power does not generally define the good; that role belongs to pleasurable experience and its emotional constellations. The difference practically between the two conceptions may not be great, since for Nietzsche pleasure is a symptom of the feeling of increased power,[30] for Spinoza it is the emotion by which the mind passes to greater perfection,[31] and for Aristotle it enhances the activity that it accompanies.[32] But power is subordinate to pleasure and of no value apart from pleasure. It may be an antecedent means, bringing about an experience which is pleasant. It may be a concomitant means, entering the pleasant experience. And it is a component means, entering the pleasure itself. It there defines, at the minimum, magnitude of pleasure through the primary attribute of intensity and secondary attributes of massiveness, sharpness, and urgency of set. Here power is near to being an end; but it is such not as an alternative to pleasure, or as the referent of pleasure, but as pleasure made most pleasurable. This view of power agrees with the interpretation of ecstasy made above. In ecstasy, pain becomes a source of power in pleasure and thereby an ingredient of the greatest pleasure. The theory of tragic value as power is a theory of tragedy as pleasure of a certain high degree and, as is true of intensive magnitudes, of a certain quality.

The aesthetic of tragic pleasure is complex, and the aesthetic of ecstasy is as complex as its psychology. A profound elation, charged with power and the sense of motion, is felt by the spectator; its sources must be traced in the hero and the spectator.

[30] Nietzsche, *Der Wille zur Macht,* Bk. III, Sec. 688.

[31] Benedictus de Spinoza, *Ethics,* trans. A. Boyle (London: Dent, 1934), Part III, Prop. xi, note.

[32] Aristotle, *Nicomachean Ethics,* trans. W. D. Ross, *Works,* Vol. IX (Oxford: Clarendon Press, 1925), 1175a.

For the hero, the generalized transcendence of change, emphasized in the cosmology of the Dionysian spirit, does not significantly occur; this transcendence is not concrete enough to define the tragic problem, which concerns not change in general but the passage of high values in a specific human situation. The more specialized passage is not embraced on the wheel of change, or welcomed as a prelude to other values; it is struggled with in an affirmation of the will as it already exists. Thus the hero does not pass limits in regard to objects about him. His task is to maintain what he values against the evils that surround him. He fails in circumstance, which is a weakness, but succeeds in a deeper essence, which is a point of power. In his decision or desire or emotion, in his personality or bare stream of consciousness, he manifests a noble strength which rises above shortcomings, errors, and defeats.

Such power is readily recognized in Oedipus, Lear, and Hedda Gabler, who are persons of stature acting vigorously in a crucial situation. It is less evident in Maurya, who may seem to be merely resigned, and in Willy Loman, who is sometimes dismissed as a cipher. But Maurya's resignation is one in which acceptance leavens defeat, and the acceptance of great loss with love continuing has in it personal strength as well as the negative action and wisdom of resignation. And Willy commits himself without reservation first to the dynastic love of a son, and then to despair and subsequent death mainly because of rejection by the son.

It goes without saying that the *Eroica* and the *Hammerklavier* sonata reveal in abstract terms a strong will. In all these instances, then, there is magnitude of spirit, which rises to various degrees of transcendence as the will seems to pass normal human bounds in its desire and commitment, its lament, defiance, endurance, or acceptance, its contrition. But the pleasure appropriate to power, and particularly to transcending power, is submerged in the pain with which the hero is engaged. The sheer intensity of his pain, abstracted from its set against the hero and its token of equally intense resistance in the situation, is a good of power. The hero is too involved in his pain to make the abstraction. The pain can be a good to him only if he can rise upon its energy to overcome the evil situation. But the intensity of the pain and resistance forbid this. The hero thus feels no joy in his affirmation and no ecstasy. These must arise in the spectator as an original fact of the aesthetic experience.

The experience of the spectator is painful, since he is steeped in the dramatic form and therefore in the pain of the hero. But the pain of the spectator is adequate in the condition of embodiment in form. From this adequacy a number of benefits follow. In the distanced contemplation of embodiment, the pain is shorn of the violence and sting that it has for the practical, committed self. It is a free movement of the contemplative self, and so does not oppress the self as an alien element. The meaningful intensity of the pain can now be experienced in its own right, and its distanced power felt as a pleasure. In the full determinateness and clarity of embodiment, the pain acquires further significance from the realization of the profundity of the issues involved and of the universality and necessity of suffering: this significance is a source of power and pleasure. The spectator also shares the affirmation of will in the hero. Since the pain surrounding the hero's affirmation has been transformed for the spectator in the ways noted, the power of the sympathetic affirmation is clearly defined and pleasant.

In this experience of pain and affirmation, the spectator becomes sharply aware of the immensity of the human situation and its pain and desire; his emotion of pain, power, and pleasure moves toward transcendence. In this movement he is greatly supported by the perfection of the dramatic form. The bright incantation of verse, and the mobile swiftness of events well articulated and strongly evolved, seize upon the spectator's emotion, which is carried in a burst of power that passes all limits and attains a serene ecstasy. Here is the tragic emotion, as it is embodied in the dramatic or musical form. But from the embodiment arises beauty. The formal joy of beauty is gratitude for embodiment. No embodiment achieves as much as the embodiment of pain, in which evil is transformed into good. Tragic beauty therefore contains formal joy to an unusual degree. Gratefully it embraces the pain that is the condition of its highest state: it embraces its opposite in an effort to surpass its own limit. This is why tragic beauty is the highest and most severe form of beauty; it is beauty seeking to transcend itself by union with the pain on which it is founded. But if beauty should achieve that goal, its formal joy would be shattered and beauty would cease. With unerring perception tragic beauty probes the limits of beauty but does not violate them.

CHAPTER 12

Art and Morality

The Scope of Moral Experience

The concept of morality may be understood either narrowly or broadly. In its narrow sense, moral value is an attribute of certain kinds of actions, such as the actions of justice, courage, and temperance, and of the choices from which they issue. Like all values, moral values have the dynamic character of a special sort that may be labeled oughtness. This trait is a persuasion on all axiologically sensitive beings toward the realization of the value; but for the narrow conception of morality, the persuasion rises to a command which must not be ignored: oughtness takes on the nature of binding obligation. The command would not be necessary if the person making the choice were inevitably determined to enact the value, and it would not be sufficient if he were similarly caused to flout the value. Moral obligation thus implies freedom in the sense of equal ability to make the choice or not. Temperance as a moral value presupposes that the individual has equal capacity to choose the temperate or the intemperate act. But if he freely violates the obligation, a penalty is incurred. This penalty does not consist simply in the loss of the rejected value and in the nature of the accepted disvalue, and it need not include the external and artificial penalties of public opinion and the state; its essential component is the emotion of guilt. What distinguishes this remarkable emotion is that the pain it contains is accompanied by a set toward endurance of the pain until some appropriate adjustment is made, and that the set contains an at least implicit judgment of oughtness. Morality in the restricted sense thus emphasizes actions, obligation, freedom of alternatives or indifference, and susceptibility to guilt.

Division arises within this concept as to the validation of the moral judgment. One school, following the method of intuition, asserts that the value of the commanded action, or duty, is self-evident, intrinsic, and categorical; it belongs to the action or choice and is not founded on consequences of the action in general, or on the promotion of human happiness in particular. The opposed school, following the method of reason, holds that the value of the action is evidenced by the consequences, among which happiness usually is emphasized; the value is extrinsic and hypothetical, though completely obligatory because the value of the consequences is not in doubt.

The strength of the second view is that it bases duty on the related concepts of desire, interest, pleasure, and happiness, which are necessary and sufficient to give content to the concept of value. The weaknesses of the view are that reason can err in estimating consequences, and that the target of rational calculation may be egoistic rather than social happiness and interest. These defects, however, are less by far than those of the first school. If the intuition is as pure as it is claimed to be, and is not the rational experience of generations of men disguised in a condensed rule of which the premises are suppressed, it offers no shelter against fanaticism and against rigidity in the face of changing conditions of life, and no method for resolving the conflicts of intuitions. Stripped of relation to interest and happiness, the asserted value loses all meaning. And the theory disregards the coherence of moral choice and action with the stream of experience of the self, which needs support from moral conduct and must be subject to the same standards of evaluation as the decisions and acts participating in it and supporting it. The result is a bifurcation of means and ends, of moral command and intrinsic enjoyment, of oughtness and appreciation. The bifurcation in turn vitiates that comprehensive harmony in self and experience which even a narrow conception of morality must wish to respect. To avoid these evils, the ethics of moral action must be one of reason, consequences, and happiness rather than intuition and inherent rightness.

With this interpretation, the concept of moral value widens, since the ends directly served by moral choice and action are integrated with the latter. The self is seen to be moral not only when it acts temperately, but also when it enjoys the fruits of temperance. There is no reason to halt the process of enlargement and integration short of the whole of experience in the self. Here the wider concept of morality can be defined. It applies to thought, emotion, and impulsion as well as to choice and action. It preserves the general character of oughtness, but discards the notion of obligation and command. The freedom it contemplates is not that of alternatives in choice by the self, but that of activity and power in the self; the first freedom puts a gap between the self and its contents, while the second assimilates contents to the self. Emotion and thought cannot be commanded and chosen, at least not directly: but they are subject to an ought nevertheless, and they can enter into the freedom of the self through the enlargement of its power. Here morality is not the consequence but the cause of freedom. And the penalty for immorality is neither external punishment nor the dark unreason of guilt; it lies in the pain of value lost and of disvalue consummated. For the essence of morality in the wide sense is the maximum possible synthesis of unity and variety in the self and among selves in society. The immoral self suffers a loss of unity or variety or both in its experience; and this loss is felt, whether clearly or dimly, as pain in the self.

The formula of the maximum synthesis of unity and complexity may be implemented by the proposal that morality in the wider sense participates in the mode of experiencing that may be called liberal activity. This perfect mode of experience may embrace equally emotion, thought, and action, and preferably the synthesis of all three in complete experience. Experience is liberal to the extent that it has form, organicity, generality, emotion, immanent interest, transcendence, and freedom. Many of these terms have already been defined in the theory of art of this book. What remains is to apply them in the present context and to clarify terms that may not have been made explicit earlier.[1]

Liberal activity draws upon the forming not only of the

---

[1] A further statement may be found in "Liberal Activity and the Liberal Arts," *The Journal of General Education,* Vol. VIII, April, 1955, pp. 177–188, from which part of the following paragraphs is taken.

sensuous and representational elements appropriate to the arts, but also of the abstract thought of the sciences and philosophy, the practical thought that is subordinate to action, and action itself. Action does not become form in the full sense of the term, since it is rooted in a time, place, and causal context. But it may be made determinate and unified. When a courageous act is distinguishable from a rash act and is informed with the sense of the benefit hoped for in the facing of peril, it is more liberal than it would otherwise be. The unity of action is increased by organicity, as when actions are reciprocally modified and strengthened in a program of action, and the ends served by the program clarify and motivate the acts. Like even the process of thinking, action is a particular; and like thought, it is most commanding when it rises to the universal or general. As theory takes an interest in general concepts and general relations between concepts, which make thought reasonable and necessary, so action looks toward ideals and rules which are distant from the time, place, and person of the action, and which make action reasonable and necessary. It is clear that at all steps action becomes liberal through its affiliation with thought, and that practical thought becomes liberal through its union with abstract thought.

Emotion in liberal activity belongs both to the end served by action and to the action itself when organically united with its end. Emotion also accompanies liberal thought, as in admiration or sympathy for truth, or reality, or the unfolding or elegant or necessary structures of thought. However adequately formed action or thought may be, they are merely muscular or technical without emotion. Given form and emotion, action and thought are of immanent or intrinsic interest. This is readily seen in abstract thought, which is embraced by the scientist and the philosopher for its own sake. It is not as clear in action, which frequently has its justification in a state of affairs that lies beyond it. In relation to that state, the action has transitive interest. But in liberal activity, the action is organically united with its end in a whole which has intrinsic interest, and the interest spreads to all of the parts in proportion as the union is close. The action is not gone through with impatience or patience: attention dwells on it gratefully, discovering at least traces of the emotion that originates in the end. And the action may very well have interest and emotion of its own, for there is nothing in usefulness to prohibit the intrinsic charm of what is useful. In liberal activity every means is an end, and every end is a means in a larger occasion of liberal activity.

Transcendence in liberal activity is found in the relation of the self to the world of its formed experience. The self looks beyond itself to the objects that it has formed and finds its fulfillment in them. Through the principle of generality, the self passes beyond the myopia of the particular, by which it was originally limited, and dwells in a world other than itself and greater. The self achieves objectivity in the sense of impersonality, in which vanity and special privilege are replaced by comparative measure of self. But transcendence is not self-negation. Through organicity, the self is identified with the world it discovers and is fulfilled in it. Liberal activity celebrates the passage of the self from the sheer immediacy of the present moment and appetite to whatever lies beyond it. Transcendence has degrees which are aesthetic, ethical, and religious, as the sequel will attempt to show.[2]

Having obtained transcendence and its prior conditions, the occasion of experience is fully liberal and the self involved in it is free: the self has power; it thus is active of itself; and so it is self-determining in the only sense that joins the self to its acts rather than separates it from them. In deference to form, it appears that whatever happens is limited, has points of contact with other happenings, and is passive because of these two facts. Liberal activity does not escape this description, but avoids submission to it by further forming. Granting that the self can be self-determining only if it embraces the whole of what is, liberal activity secures a rapport between the self and the world, as a result of which the action of the world upon the self becomes the action of the self instead of its passion. The agent of this rapport is form, through which feeling, and the self in it, pass from passivity and impotence to activity and power.

Through generality and organicity, form present to the occasion of experience expands throughout being to the maximum universal and returns with it to the occasion. Form thereby becomes a native and intrinsic principle in the occasion. But feeling develops through form, and moves through form out of its first darkness

<hr>

[2] Below, "Art and Liberal Activity"; Chap. 13, "Religion and Art."

and toward a universal sympathy, which identifies the feeling with
the power of the world and internalizes that power in the act of
the liberal experience. Through the internalization, feeling becomes
a native and intrinsic principle in the occasion. But the occasion
of liberal activity is nothing but its feeling formed. Since these
elements have become autonomous principles, the occasion has
become self-governing and therefore free. Freedom likewise has
degrees that are aesthetic, ethical, and religious, and it has been
described here in its maximum degree in order to emphasize its
essential principles and to state its target.

Alleged Contrasts of Moral and Aesthetic Experience

Having sketched, though briefly, the nature of moral experience,
we may consider the question whether art engages and is subject
to the moral concept, or stands apart from it in a world of its
own on which moral principles may not trespass.

It is sometimes asserted that moral experience is mainly negative, being concerned with evil and suffering and their elimination
and with restriction on human appetite, choice, and action. The ten
commandments of the Mosaic code are largely explicitly negative,
beginning in most instances with the prohibition "thou shalt not."[3]
The moralist appears to be occupied with slapping the wrist, if
not whipping the back, of his human subjects. In contrast, art
is positive. It yields the joyful good of beauty, contemplates
with avid interest the entire range of human desire, invites
the expansion of the self and even its luxury and voluptuous-
ness. If the Ten Commandments define the attitude of morality,
Hofmannsthal's *Death of Titian* speaks for the aesthetic life. But
this contrast is not sound. It presupposes the narrowest emphasis
within morality and is refuted by the wider concept and liberal
activity. Morality negates only to achieve a positive end, and its
method becomes more moral, and productive, as negatives pass
over into affirmative understanding and freedom. And art has
its negations. Creation may struggle as with a demon, and contemplation requires a discipline of attention and learning in many
instances. Art deals with the pain as well as the pleasure of exist-

[3] Exodus 20.

ence, and more than any other activity it finds the line between the two indefinable. The artistic representation of desire does not necessarily mean the exposure of the self to every desire: disinterest is distinct from practical interest, sympathetic insight from temptation.

It may also be asserted that moral experience is mainly instrumental while aesthetic experience is terminal and consummatory. When concerned with positive good, moral experience embraces actions and disciplines which are means to ends that lie beyond the typical view of the moralist. But art, expression, and beauty are ends and never means. This distinction also is inadequate. It is somewhat true of the narrower view of morality in its instrumental phase; but even there the means is judged by its end, and the end is one scrutinized by the moral code. It is entirely false in regard to the moral scheme of liberal activity, in which ends and means are organically united and immanent interest is dominant. Though art is a self-sufficient end, it has effects beyond its borders which are good, and these may be anticipated by the creator and contemplator without impairment of the intrinsic value of the experience.

A distinction which has more promise is one that begins with the assertion that moral experience is real whereas aesthetic experience is imaginary. The moral situation is substantial, but the work of art is a mere appearance. What moral experience does with its real situation is to commit the self in choice and action. A decision for or against a course of action is made; the self assumes responsibility for the decision; and the decision may affect the self throughout its nature and into the distant future. In contrast, aesthetic experience is detached. An impersonal self contemplates disinterestedly a vivid but impersonal emotion in the distanced condition of embodiment. Here it achieves the savor and sheer impression of an experience, which may give way to a contrary impression without rule and even without contradiction, since the impressions are autonomous and are not governed by some unitary thing. A poet may express today the total joy of love and tomorrow the total sorrow of love, for his aim is the sharp statement of a fleeting impression rather than the profound statement of an abiding truth. Morality, however, is concerned with what endures and its fixed, dependable relations. Without disenchantment or problem, a poet may find a woman exquisite on one view and dull on a second, since he is concerned with two independent images rather than one person; but the moral agent will find here a severe problem, as he deals with a continuous person with implications for the future: and the woman will indeed be satisfied with no other approach. Thus moral experience is integrated with experience, the self, and the world, while aesthetic experience stands aloof in a world of its own.

Not a little can be said for this argument. Moral experience is indubitably real, committed, and continuous, and it is plausible to say that aesthetic experience is the diametrical opposite. But the description of the aesthetic experience has been overstated. The work of art is not an appearance, but an essence for which the judgment of reality has been neutralized. It does not stand in contradistinction to the real. Whether appearance or essence, however, the work of art engages reality through its expressed emotion and the universal truth of what it may represent. Depending on the meaningfulness of the emotion and the extent of the represented truth, some works of art have slight contact with reality, and others have so solid an anchor as to be taken for reality at its most real. Art therefore is not limited to the sheer impression of things. But when it takes such a subject, it presents it with such formed perception as to make it a part of the real, without suggesting that it is more than a modest part. The moralist may profit from this aesthetic of the impression, for it may occasionally save him from unnecessary disillusionment and teach him the complexity of reality.

The detachment of art does not prevent attachment in two ways. Though uncommitted to the form and emotion that he contemplates, the contemplator is committed to the experience of contemplation, as is clear enough from his resentment of interruption of the act. During the act the stream of his consciousness is filled with a form and an embodied emotion on which he makes critical demands, in order that the stream be as valuable as possible. And after the act the aesthetic experience has consequences, which are received with as practical an import as those of any moment or hour of experience. Though an embodied emotion of despair, excitement, or love does not persist afterward as an aroused emotion, however faint, with a set toward certain actions, the experience of vital harmony during the act has beneficial effects later. Thus the isolation of the form and emotion in the experience of embodiment does not mean the isolation of the experience from the remainder of experience. Aesthetic experience does not stand alone, uncommitted, wraith-like.

If the arguments for the separation of art from moral relevance fail, the major question of the moral topic may then be raised: How does art fulfill a moral function? Here three answers may be considered: that art is moral as innocent entertainment, as moral instruction, or as liberal activity.

Art and Entertainment

So casual and floating an experience as entertainment needs no analysis and is seldom mistaken by those who have it. Entertainment is pleasure of a relatively passive kind and of little scope. It may be vivid and engrossing, as for an audience at a musical comedy, or mild and peripheral, as for a housewife who likes to have near her a color or a shape, a flower or a bowl. It is entirely sincere, making no claim to be more than what it is. In the arts, at least, it is pure in the sense of having no painful or bad consequences; it may instead be relaxing, freeing the mind of toil and anxiety.

Entertainment is a parcel of happiness and therefore has value. In a world of much pain, tension, and uncertainty, a modest pleasure is not to be despised, as though men were gods with all being at their command. A pure happiness is in itself moral, for the formula of unity in complexity serves happiness as the end in which this structure ideally is immanent, and happiness is a cause of unity. A moment or hour of entertainment is therefore moral, and art as entertainment serves morality in its own process. And after the aesthetic experience is over, this aspect of art may have a further moral function. Those who have been happy may look upon each other with less severity, and relaxation may be followed by renewed vigor.

Despite these advantages, the theory of entertainment is not adequate either morally or aesthetically, and the two deficiencies are interwoven. The pleasure of entertainment is received rather than achieved, and this is the passive element in it. Entertainment relies heavily on the direct stimulus value of art, and very little on the imaginative understanding of the appreciator. The form is barely touched in its sensory, representational, and structural richness. Meaning vanishes; instead, there is emphasis on novelty and exaggeration and on forms that do not tax attention. When form suffers, however, emotion loses also in meaningfulness and objectivity. The pleasure of entertainment therefore is modest in scope, since its sources are similarly impoverished. But if the pleasure is passive and lacking in complexity and tightness, it is moral only in a modest degree. And for those who can rise to a higher pleasure, that is, one more active, complex, and unified, arrest at the level of entertainment may possibly be described as immoral: though surely not as a cause for guilt!

Art and Moral Instruction

The theory of art as moral instruction asserts that art is moral by teaching the appreciator truths about moral value and the moral life, which remain with him after the aesthetic experience as a guide to the conduct of life. The essence of many of these truths may be found in sermons and books of ethics as well as in works of art; but works of art have the advantage of concrete application and vividness, and they may sweeten the moral truth with the incidental pleasures of art. The story of a novel may drive home a point about the evil of pride or envy, jealousy or adultery, more effectively than a sermon, and do so with more human interest. Thus moral instruction may coincide with entertainment. But if the work of art deals with evil without in some way indicating that it must be shunned, it is immoral, for it may encourage in the appreciator the same evils. It is then subject to suppression, and art in general to the scrutiny of the censor. If the censor is sufficiently stern, he may believe that the artistic representation of evil is so tempting that neither disastrous results nor homilies will counteract it. Art then can be moral only if it shows good men receiving the reward of their virtue. Of this sort was the moralism of Plato when he proposed, as discussed earlier, that poetry should be limited to hymns to the gods and praises of famous men.

The subject and temper of moral instruction may vary between two extremes, which coincide roughly with the narrower and wider views of morality. Moral instruction may emphasize basic rules of behavior, or it may spread over the subtle range of the problems of human desire and satisfaction. It may make sharp distinctions between good and evil, or it may find them to be intermixed due to circumstances or even to the essential nature of the values concerned. It may represent punishment as externally invoked for an evil which in itself may charm, or it may find that punishment comes inevitably as the internal consequence of evil. It may speak for tradition and official authority, or for the experimental probing of an individual who has found a new map or a new wilderness. It may state its precepts explicitly, or allow them to be inferred from the course of a plot or from symbolism. And it may welcome the censor, or it may hold that the issues and especially the nature of art make censorship unnecessary if not an affront. To the extent that the positions first stated in each pair collect together, the result is moral instruction as preachment; the opposite is moral instruction as wisdom.

The criticisms of the moralistic interpretation of tragedy made in the preceding chapter hold generally for preachment. To the extent that this position becomes paramount, sympathy is weakened and dignity lowered; individuals become means and abstractions dominant; the variability of moral judgment and the complexity of moral experience are overlooked; and art neglects the great extent to which either there is disproportion between virtue or vice and happiness or suffering, or there is no moral rule involved in the complex grounds of happiness and grief. In its more resolute forms, preachment is not deterred by these criticisms. Unlike the moralistic theory of tragedy, which claimed to be an explanation of actual works of art and was bound by them as data, moralism in this context is free to amend or to condemn art in part or as a whole. When it proceeds to do so, aesthetic destruction results. Poverty in the theory of morals leads to poverty in the practice of art. But the good of art is so apparent to those who understand it that they cannot consent to any sacrifice of art. And there is no moral need to correct art, for art can be assured of moral function as it stands.

This requirement can at least partly be met by the position of wisdom. To the extent that wisdom surveys all objects that form or deform the self, and looks for the concrete causes of good and evil in the complex tissue of human nature and circumstance, it will not sacrifice sympathetic penetration of aesthetic form, lose sight of human dignity, or submerge individuals in abstractions. Aware of the complexity of the moral cosmos and of the self, wisdom will not be dogmatic, and it will not see merely good or evil when the opposite is also present. Thus wisdom will be sensitive to the many situations in life and in art in which no formulable and practical precept is violated, but desire nevertheless is shipwrecked by unavoidable ignorance, or by the inevitable differences of free personalities, or by fatalities inherent in desire itself. Where it cannot formulate specific counsel, wisdom may still serve morality through growth in benevolence, understanding, humility, and respect for freedom. These may be exercised in many instances of aesthetic experience, and they may survive to influence the conduct of life.

Wisdom therefore may exist in art without injury to art, though the artist and the contemplator must be aware of the tension between wisdom and art that is due to the tendency even of wisdom to issue in precepts that become separate from the aesthetic form and an end unto themselves. With the tension understood, wisdom may not only enter art as an incidental part, but become a major accomplishment of art. Moral insight integrated with the form does not lose its identity, but defines the only kind of discursive truth proper to art. Beyond the immediate knowledge of embodied emotion, art can seek knowledge only mediately. It does not attempt to be history, and it is interested in general truths about man and nature and whatever may lie beyond nature only as they bear upon values in the formation of selves. Thus the discursive knowledge of art is exclusively moral. Every insight that a novelist gives us into character, motive, and action is moral and a part of wisdom. Literary art abounds in knowledge of this kind, and to cite examples is to pick out pebbles in the sand. But in no artist is moral understanding as reflective, articulate, and complex as in Goethe. Here art and life were joined in a continuous examination and practice of ends and means for the enrichment of experience. A single truth may be illustrated from his *Torquato Tasso:* it concerns the perils of solitary introversion and fantasy:

> *Auf diesem Wege werden wir wohl nie*
> *Gesellschaft finden, Tasso! Dieser Pfad*

Verleitet uns durch einsames Gebüsch,
Durch stille Thäler fortzuwandern; mehr
Und mehr verwöhnt sich das Gemüth, und strebt,
Die goldne Zeit, die ihm von auszen mangelt,
In seinem Innern wieder herzustellen,
So wenig der Versuch gelingen will.[4]

And the interplays of desire and knowledge, of the individual and society, of suffering and redemption are pursued at length in *Faust,* through successive stages of intellectual love, erotic love, and universal benevolence. Here wisdom is communicated in its largest compass, though not without a reminder of the tension between art and instruction.

Despite the merits of moral instruction in the form of wisdom, certain limitations may be asserted. Though wisdom may be assimilated formally, it may still be alleged to be a supra-aesthetic element imported into art from other domains. A poet is properly expert in words, a musician in tones, and a painter in colors; and all three are accomplished in the embodiment of emotion in the structures made from these respective media. The arts are defined by this kind of capacity. But no man is an expert in wisdom; and among men, the scientific psychologist is least ignorant of human nature and the philosophical student of ethics least ignorant of values and morals. The artist therefore must borrow from such sources, and his wisdom must be both secondhand and incidental to the essence of art. Thus the tension between art and moral instruction has a deeper cause than the tendency of the moral idea to become an end in itself and to be abstracted from the work of art; the cause lies in the nature of wisdom as independent of art.

In reply to this argument it should be noted that a novelist, for example, is expert in constructing forms which involve not only words and plots but characters. A character is a section of human nature in pursuit of a constellation of values. The making of this aspect of form is thus the making of a psychologico-moral entity. There are not two sides to the novelist's activity, of which one is

[4] Johann Wolfgang von Goethe, *Torquato Tasso,* Act II, Scene 1, lines 970–977. "On this way we shall never find company, Tasso! This path leads us astray through lonely thickets and silent valleys. The spirit becomes more and more spoiled, and strives to reconstruct in itself the golden time that is lacking outside: little as the attempt will succeed."

intrinsic and concerned with words and plot, the other extrinsic and concerned with psychology and ethics. For the making of characters the novelist is not limited to what he can learn from others. His characters are too concrete to be borrowed from the relatively abstract investigations of psychology and philosophy, and too living to be assembled logically from the supply of those abstractions. They are derived from his own observations of men, including himself, and the observations are made concrete and fluently meaningful by the same emotional perceptiveness that is required for embodiment of emotion. In the arts, then, both the forming and embodying functions contribute to the growth of wisdom.

A more significant criticism of wisdom as the essential moral function of art arises from the fact that wisdom is not generally available to the arts, since it usually requires representation of persons, situations, actions, and general ideas. Wisdom then is excluded from formal art, whether it be a building, a rug, or music without words or program, and it may be excluded from abstract art if the representation is too indeterminate to embrace morally relevant content. It is difficult to see how a building can directly teach love of the spirit rather than of the body, or love of the eternal rather than of the temporal. It then is necessary to conclude either that some art is inherently amoral, or that wisdom does not exhaust the moral potential of art. The second alternative is preferable to the first, which would make some arts inferior because of failure to perform an important function open to art. But wisdom perhaps can be rescued for formal art through the assistance of the embodied emotion. Without any representation, literal or symbolic, a building may teach through the emotion it expresses the wisdom of measured poise or of man's need to transcend himself in pursuit of an invisible and infinite good. In this way music may also participate in wisdom. In the expressed emotion of Beethoven's *Quartet in A Minor*, Op. 132, can be discerned the wisdom of an immeasurable peace that lies beyond defiance and defeat. No doubt wisdom in these arts labors under special difficulty, since it presupposes the most difficult and hazardous kind of interpretation, which has for its object an emotion. And the mere act of interpretation may here be unwarranted, since it presumably takes as its starting point an emotion already made determinate in the immediately experienced condition of embodiment, and subjects it to mediate apprehension through the form of a special concept. But it cannot be denied that men of combined musical and moral discernment find the act of interpretation, and the resulting wisdom, natural and fairly intersubjective.

A final objection that may be made to wisdom as the basic moral character of art is that it places the moral status of art mainly outside of art. Wisdom may be learned in art, but it is practiced and realized outside of art in the conduct of extra-aesthetic life. A man who achieves a moral insight through art does not set about practicing the insight in appropriate changes of his character in art. And the truth that was so clear and persuasive in art may languish in the routines of daily existence. Wisdom may become inoperative and therefore not truly wisdom, which means the power to realize the value that has been understood. Then the moral value of art is stillborn.

In deference to this criticism and to the one preceding, and without impugning the importance of wisdom as a part of art and of the moral value of art, we may look within the aesthetic process for a moral value that is completely general in art, fully realized within the borders of art, and not subject to the gap that often separates moral theory from moral practice. This value may be found in liberal activity. The aesthetic experience is an instance of liberal activity, and therefore it is inherently moral.

Art and Liberal Activity

The liberal character of form is more complete and pure in art than in any other human experience, and it offers a strong indication that art is inherently moral. Neither in the structures of general theory, nor in those of practical thought, choice, and action, are parts so diverse in nature, unifying relations so close, and both parts and relations so sharply and fully determined. Moral conduct of the most developed sort, motivated and unified by general principles, is schematic and at the same time rambling in comparison with aesthetic form. The model of the special sciences, mathematics, lacks the resources of sensation and emotion on the one hand, and emotion and aesthetic imagination on the other, to furnish parts that are diverse in quality and unified with full respect to their qualitative richness.

The unity of art is supported by an exceptional degree of organicity. Moral conduct naturally seeks to be organic through the mutual enhancement of actions and of ends and means. But it is limited in its accomplishment by ignorance of values, self, and circumstances, by infirm resolution of will, and by the urgencies of situations in which choices have to be made. Empirical science must be content with external relations among its terms and assertions, since experience is contingent and the relations it offers might in principle be other than what in fact they are. Mathematics alone secures logically necessary unities, but it appears that these relations are tautologies, holding not between mutually distinct parts but between part and subpart. In art alone are distinct parts related with a necessity that arises from the natures of the parts.

Generality in art is of a mixed sort. It was shown above that artistic representation is universal, since it is not a historical account of an individual limited in time and place and by the sheer contingencies of actuality, but an ideal account of how an individual of a certain kind exists and acts in certain necessary ways. It may be supposed, however, that art that does not represent is necessarily particular. A building or formal painting may seem to be as particular as the supporting ground or wall. But the status of every work of art as an essence detached from a given time, place, and causal context gives the aesthetic object an inherent generality. This generality is concrete rather than abstract, due to the high determinateness of art that yields the sense of the individual amid the universal.

Because of the concreteness, a work of art cannot hope for the universality of a scientific concept or law. The law of gravitation embraces individuals of many kinds throughout time and space; but the rashness of Lear and the innocent fidelity of Cordelia can be found only among men, and not all men are rash or faithful under the conditions of the king and his daughters. For this limit of extension in art there are compensations. Separation from a given time and place is achieved without loss of content, quality, and meaning. No universal is as vivid and compelling as the aesthetic universal. These characteristics enhance in art the moral function of the general, which is to promote both diversity and unity by enlarging awareness beyond the blindly immediate and egocentric.

The emotional relevance of form is attended to by art more thoroughly than by any other activity of man. This means that in art, form is more liberally received than elsewhere. Conversely, and only in art with any degree of system, emotion is taken as a problem for forming. It is neither neglected nor left to chance. This means that aesthetic experience is preeminent in the creation and ordering of the values of qualitative experience, which are infinitely diverse and subtle, conceptually elusive, and situated beyond the range of explicit choice: and which constitute the final challenges and rewards of moral experience.

The immanent interest of art is secured by the fusion of form and emotion, and it is part of the definition of aesthetic contemplation. No human activity is as self-contained and internally complete as the aesthetic experience. It does not contain the distinction of means and ends that is common in choice and conduct, or the temptation to applications that converts a pure science into a profession. From the closeness of relation between aesthetic experience and intrinsic value, action and thought are often called aesthetic when the interest in them is notably immanent.

The contemplative nature of art also indicates the role and limits of transcendence in art. As shown in an earlier chapter, the objectivity of aesthetic disinterest consists in the fact that attention is steeped in the object or form, which lies at a distance from the self. Objectivity extends especially to the emotion by virtue of its embodiment in the form. Something normally subjective, internal, and hidden becomes objective, external, and manifest. Transcendence in art thus has its ultimate basis in embodiment. But the direction of attention to the embodied emotion means detachment of self from self, as was also shown in the analysis of contemplation. The self contemplates the form and emotion apart from the usual stream of its interests; it puts aside its private history and becomes an impersonal self; it even distills its agency of awareness so that the process of awareness merges with the object. Here the self not only looks beyond itself to objects; it moves beyond itself, leaving much of itself behind. Transcendence thus appears to be singularly advanced. But the same detachment that promotes it in degree limits it in kind. The embodied emotion is not affirmed; it is not related to the tissue of emotion, desire, and action that the self has in its personal identity. It rides at a distance and the contemplative self with it, certain to cause no damage and certain also to make no contact with the responsibilities of the self. To this extent aesthetic transcendence is ideal rather than actual; it occurs in the imagination rather than in the will, or in an imaginary will rather than the actual will.

In contrast, moral transcendence involves the will in its irreducible, personal substance. In commitments assisted by the full resources of reason and discursive knowledge, it brings the actual self beyond the limits of the present moment of experience and desire. In prudence the self transcends toward the whole of its experience and interest in time, and in love it transcends to such totalities in other selves. The self before transcendence is integrated with the self after transcendence in an ever widening circle of commitments and responsibilities. In regard to its special objects or contents, then, aesthetic transcendence is amoral. But in its form it is moral. The act of contemplating, as distinct from the contents contemplated, is an act of transcendence of the actual self in the mode of commitment.

The final liberal trait of aesthetic experience is its freedom. The embodiment of emotion is a source of freedom in the self. In its negative phase, as liberation from passivity, aesthetic freedom is fully moral. It is in no imaginary fashion that the self is freed from the compulsion of primitive emotion. But the release is during the experience of embodiment, and there is no assurance that the emotion in a compulsive form will not return at some future time. Ethical freedom, based on conceptual insight, tends to make liberation more enduring. But that concerns the self after aesthetic experience rather than during it.

In its positive phase, aesthetic freedom has been shown to differ from moral freedom, and the difference parallels the difference in the modes of transcendence. The power of aesthetic freedom is not based on the assimilation of the emotion into the actual self, as it is in moral freedom. The power occurs independent of the integration of such special contents, in ways that were discussed earlier. The scope of this power is limited in comparison with that of ethical power, which engages the whole self in prudence and extends the self further in love. But for this deficiency in scope there is some compensation on another level. Ethical freedom denies some experiences while affirming others, since for each experience integration with an actual self is intended. But aesthetic freedom is entirely catholic: it censors no experience, but knows the essence and savors the vital force of each.

Because art participates in the several traits of liberal activity, it is moral in a high degree, which is perfect in the forms that define ideal morality if not in the materials. Liberal activity belongs to the aesthetic process itself, so that art is moral internally, without dependence on future consequences and contingencies. Liberal activity is a general characteristic of art, and thus the experience of a bowl and of a tragic drama are alike moral. The liberal nature of art has some of the advantages of the other proposed sources of moral value in art. Like entertainment, it is enjoyable, as is evident in the intrinsic value of all liberal activity and in the beauty of embodiment; but this pleasure is more active and has greater scope. Like wisdom it has results in the future. The composed vigor of liberal activity is a source of strength in life outside of art, and the liberal nature of art is a model for the creation and ordering of life as a whole. Here liberal activity and wisdom coincide: the most basic wisdom to be found in art is the understanding of liberal activity as an ideal to be pursued in every moment of experience.

Beauty, Love, and Eros

The relation of aesthetic experience to moral value may be understood further by a comparison of beauty with love, which is the ultimate good of morality and a major form of transcendence. Human love, or love of man for man, falls into several types. Brotherly love is love of a human being because he is human; it therefore extends without distinction to all men. Friendship is love of another by reason of special qualities that he is thought to have, or due to sharing of experience and value; because of these sources it is limited to a few. Erotic love is love combined with sexual interest, whether overt or sublimated; erotic love is distinct from erotic sensuality, in which sexual interest alone moves; and it is limited to one other person when it has the completeness that it ardently seeks. Parental love is love of those who have been brought to birth and will be helped to grow by the parents, and who thus have a special claim on love, in which alone being is created and conserved. Parental love has the motive force of erotic love without the erotic motor, and it extends to more than one person without dilution or competition.

In all of these types, love admits of two aspects. The lesser is the love of admiration, which is pleasure in the valued qualities of another. The greater is the love of benevolence, which is pleasure in the happiness of another. The opposite of admiration is envy, which is displeasure in the good traits of another and pleasure in his deficiencies; and the opposite of benevolence is malevolence, which is pleasure in the misery of another. The pleasure of admiration leads to a desire for the conservation of the admired qualities, so that admiration is not entirely contemplative. The pleasure of benevolence leads to a desire for the promotion of the happiness of the other, and a great part of the love of benevolence is concerned with means toward that end.

Admiration and benevolence may exist separately; they may coexist; and they may cause each other. We may admire intelligence or physical strength without taking an interest in the happiness of their possessor, and we may feel benevolence toward those who are wretched without being aware of any ground for admiration. But love of all types normally has in it a conjunction of the two aspects of love, and it is more secure for their coexistence. Admiration and benevolence engender each other. Given admiration, the pleasure we have in the contemplation of the qualities of a person leads to the idea of the person as the cause of our pleasure. With no forced gratitude we wish to reciprocate pleasure, thus taking an interest in the happiness of the other. The benevolence of friendship usually grows in this way. More subtly, the admired qualities usually are a source of value to their possessor, and the desire of the admirer to conserve them is at least indirectly benevolent. And benevolence opens the door to admiration. It removes prejudices and deepens observation so that actual values can be noticed and admired. As is well known, it also may lead to the creation of imaginary values in the loved person. But the summit of benevolence is the perception that what is most excellent in any person is his capacity for meaningful happiness. With this insight, admiration and benevolence do not merely exist jointly or interact: they fuse into a single pleasure and single desire.

Both aspects of love involve some degree of unity between the person who loves and the person who is loved. The unity increases as the two aspects are joined, or as the valued qualities and the conditions of happiness grow in number and in weight, or as the love is reciprocated. Because of this unity, the relation between persons who love, whether reciprocally or not, is sometimes described as beautiful. But beauty exists only where it is experienced, and the relation between the persons may not as such enter awareness. The person who loves directs his attention basically to the valued qualities or the happiness of the other person, and he may not consider the relation between the persons at all. But love embellishes itself ardently and ingeniously, and it is no artifice for friend or lover to reflect upon the relation and to value its unity. Here the candidate for beauty is experienced, but a second impediment arises. Beauty in the strict sense requires embodiment of emotion, and it is not likely that an emotion about the unity of the persons will be embodied in its object. The relation is too abstract to constitute a form suited to the embodiment of emotion. Beauty will occur only in the loose sense of a pleasurable emotion associated with an object, or it will be a transfer from the beauty of the person loved.

Admiration may exist without any sense of beauty in the person admired. The admiration of courage does not imply beauty in the possessor of courage. But if the emotional content of the admiration can find an object in which it can be embodied, the object will be experienced as beautiful. Courage in the abstract is not such an object; but courage as the concrete nature of a will that we seem to feel tangibly before us may perhaps qualify, and the courageous will may thus be beautiful. Of this sort is the beauty of moral character generally, as is the beauty of a sensibility that is felt to be ardent or imaginative or profound. The admiration of the psychical qualities of a person may thus, perhaps, be attended by beauty. But the case for beauty is much clearer when the qualities are physical, or more exactly, sensory. Admiration of the shape and color of a face, or of the entire body, may easily lead to beauty, for the emotion of admiration may be embodied in the indubitably concrete and sensuous form. It is not, however, correct to say (if the intent is analysis rather than something justifiably rhetorical) that the object of admiration is beauty. Beauty in the loved person does not precede admiration,

as intelligence or charm may; it is admiration itself in its most
fortunate development.

The capacity of admiration to generate benevolence here
operates at its highest degree, for the pleasure of the admirer now
is most closely identified with the person loved. Benevolence
thus grows from the perception of beauty in another. But it
seems that it would not, like admiration, be a source of beauty,
since it is directed toward no specific quality in which its emotion might be embodied. Its object is the happiness of the person
loved, and this appears to be too indeterminate and elusive, too
abstract, to constitute a form suitable for embodiment. But
benevolence provides a sympathetic awareness for which the
happiness of the other becomes vivid and close. To this it adds
two further resources.

Since benevolence is concerned with the general happiness and
not merely a specific experience of the person loved, its sympathy defines the individual selfhood of the other, in which
happiness flows and ebbs without ceasing. The vehicle of this
self is the physical person, which also is the source of communication between the two persons. Benevolence directed toward the
happiness of another finds his body a natural target. In this
concrete and sensory object the emotion of benevolence may be
embodied, and the loved person felt to be beautiful. Furthermore,
emotion experienced by the loved person may be externalized by
a smile, the shading of a voice, the movement of a hand, the
posture of the body. This emotion is not embodied for the person
involved, and it is not itself available to another for embodiment.
But benevolence brings into being in the second person emotion
that is identified with the emotion externalized. This emotion
can be embodied in the same bodily forms, and the loved person
felt to be beautiful in a given moment of joy or sorrow, anger or
fear, vitality or depression.

Thus a form that would not be pleasing to the cool survey of
an eye prepared only for admiration may be beautiful under the
warmth of benevolence. But to the extent that this is true, beauty
is subjective rather than intersubjective, and the form is imperfect
and embodiment unsteady. Then beauty suffers. And the friend,
lover, or parent may for his part feel that he has conceded enough
of his love to beauty, to the partial disadvantage of love. The
embodied emotion of admiration or benevolence is contemplated

at a distance, where it is detached from the self and from the commitments that the self has to the loved person. This is perhaps no matter for the love of admiration, but it is important to the love of benevolence. When benevolence sponsors beauty, it contemplates instead of moving toward the service of the other. But when benevolence contemplates itself, that is a good of understanding; and when it contemplates the emotion of the other, that is a good of sharing. Both goods favor love. And apart from the emotion embodied, the beauty that emerges is a fire that joins the two persons in the stream of commitment.

Much the same can be said of erotic love, which is distinguished from other types of love by the presence of eros. Eros begins with the pleasure of admiration, which here is directed toward the sexual being of another; the pleasure contracts into desire for union with that being; the desire represents itself as moving toward a dark ecstasy, a passage beyond the clear areas of self, pleasure, and consciousness; and the passage mirrors the concentration and transcendence of generation, though eros in its blind hunger does not specify that goal. For its overwhelming program eros enlists the whole range of nonsexual admiration and the resources of benevolence. In erotic love, eros stimulates admiration and benevolence, and these in turn leaven and deepen eros and prolong its life. Without benevolence and a range of admiration eros becomes sensuality, which passes from abstract fury through ingenious pampering into hollowness. Aspects of this vicissitude of eros are well illustrated in the relation of Erik and Fennimore in Jacobsen's novel, *Niels Lyhne*.[5]

The original direction of eros toward the body, in which generation takes place, is broadened but not basically changed in erotic love. The emotion of eros thus has a concrete, sensory form in which it may be embodied. Naked eros has no interest in embodiment; it presses for union and discharge. But erotic love, which grows under the influence of imagination, can find value in the imaginative act of embodiment. When the complex emotion of erotic love, with eros at its core, is embodied in the body of the loved person, erotic beauty comes into being. Here the transitive aspect of eros is removed in the act of distanced con-

[5] Jens Peter Jacobsen, *Niels Lyhne*, trans. Hanna Larsen (New York: The American-Scandinavian Foundation, 1919), Chap. xi, pp. 196–198.

templation. Erotic beauty, as distinct from bare erotic attractive-
ness, purges desire. The removal of possessiveness means the arrest
of commitment; beauty and love are again in opposition. But
the opposition is once more within a common value. In erotic
beauty the lover beholds with clear intensity the love that in the
stream of commitment is somewhat obscure, whether as hunger
or as satisfaction. This is a service to his love. And he beholds his
love not as his, but as identified with the person he loves in the
manner of a visual attribute. In thus investing with beauty the
beloved person, he renders as great a service as that person can
ask for in the name of love. If to be perceived as beautiful is the
ultimate wish of a loved person, which remains after all other
wishes have been satisfied in the human economy, then the
beauty which begins by arresting commitment ends by satisfying
the noblest need of love.

CHAPTER 13

Art and Religion

The Components of Religion

Religion may have four functions. It usually has beliefs, by virtue of which it is true or false and capable of alliance or dispute with philosophy and the sciences. It always has effects within the domain of emotion, volition, and action, because of which it is moral or immoral. It frequently has rituals, which are effective or ineffective in promoting belief and in making an impression on emotion, volition, and action. With equal frequency, it has an institutional fabric, by virtue of which it is efficient or inefficient in communicating and standardizing the preceding functions. The first of the four aspects of religion may be called theoretical in a broad sense of the term. The other three may be called practical with varying degrees of breadth. Of the three, the broadest consists of religion as made of effects upon feeling, will, and conduct. Here religion is a way of life, or systematic practice, to which institutions, rituals, and beliefs are means in an order of increasing importance. Of the four functions, then, religion as a way of life and religion as belief stand out with great emphasis.

Religious belief varies with the religion and therefore with the time and place. But four beliefs tend to define the essential program of much religious thought. First is the conviction that the nature of value is objective, universal, fixed: good and bad are not inventions or conventions of the individual or the group, but are discoveries of the nature of things. To this belief about the timeless being of values is added a second about temporal being or actuality: what is good tends to become actual. Realization of value may well be a progressive process embracing the whole of time: thus a teleology. Uniting the two assertions is a third about God, in whose being may be found the apprehension of objective good and the source of enactment in time of that good. The passage from the apprehension to the enactment presupposes the inherent goodness of the divine substance: a condition more concrete and powerful than objective universals, and more basic and powerful than reality in time. Fourth and last is a belief in human immortality, which is naturally conceived of by men as the condition of the maximum realization of human good. All of these beliefs, and belief generally in religion, are sustained by appropriate methods, which round out the nature of religion as theoretical. The methods are those of mystical experience, reason, and sensory and introspective experience, which are used for the origination of religious belief; authority, by which belief is propagated from one person to another; and faith, which seems to be not so much a method for arriving at belief as a method for believing without method.

Religion as a way of life can be defined on three levels. It promotes moral choice and action by providing through divine revelation authoritative and infallible precepts as to what is right and wrong, and by providing through fear of divine wrath and hope of divine favor incentives to observance of those precepts. Amid disappointment and death, it guarantees happiness for those who deserve it, either in the overall course of this life or in a future life. The assurance is itself a source of consolation and peace, apart from its fruition in specific events and goals. More deeply than in either of the foregoing ways, it influences life through a concept of meaning, which does not merely promote or secure goods available in principle without religion, but supplies a good which is uniquely religious and is a fresh dimension or perspective in life. In this concept are three aspects of the greatness of religious experience: an ideal of perfect value as the object of a perfect love; identification with being and resulting companionship with it; and a sense of general purposiveness which stands in sharp contrast with a pagan dispersal of the self in isolated moments, goals, and enjoyments.

It is commonly supposed that religion as a way of life depends on religious belief. Religious institutions have spelled out beliefs with dogmatic precision and rigidity in order to guarantee the purity and stability of religious practice. But religions vary more in their dogmas than in the kind of life they enjoin, and this indicates some independence of belief on the part of practice. Furthermore, in persons of critical or imaginative tempers, literal belief yields to symbolic belief as a foundation of the religious life. The Christian doctrines of the creation of the world, the fall of man, the incarnation of God in human form, and the death and resurrection of Jesus may be taken as symbols of considerably more abstract metaphysical and moral truths. And religious practice may be had when virtually all belief, literal or figurative, is foregone. Instances of the description and explanation of this final condition may be found in Santayana's *Reason in Religion*,[1] Dewey's *Common Faith*,[2] and in a proposal about mysticism that will be made in the following section.

However mystical experience may be had or described or interpreted, it offers itself as the center of religion. If used as a method for arriving at and validating belief, it surpasses the methods of reason and of sensory and introspective experience in two ways. It is better able to grasp the unique nature of deity, the main object of religious belief. Reason yields no data or elementary terms, but supplies relations which structure data from other sources. Sensation is rich in data, but it is limited to stimuli from physical objects, which alone can be received by the organs of sense. Introspection is confined to the individual consciousness that introspects. And mysticism gives to belief a vividness and conviction that are invaluable if belief is to influence the conduct of life.

But whether used with a claim to knowledge or not, mystical experience may embrace in its own fabric the most important part of religious practice, the awareness of meaning. Here are experienced at their human apex the ideal of perfect value, identification and companionship with what is felt to be most real, and the sense of comprehensive purposiveness. It is not only true that mystical experience may contain these values and, beyond that,

---

[1] George Santayana, *Reason in Religion* (New York: Scribner, 1926), Chap. xi.
[2] John Dewey, *A Common Faith* (New Haven, Conn.: Yale University Press, 1934), pp. 9–23.

impart them to the conduct of life as a whole. It is also true that whenever religion and life contain the sense of meaning, as distinct from the thought of it, they participate in mysticism in some degree.

So broad a function for mysticism follows from the general nature of mystical experience, which is an intuition, or immediate awareness, of the nature, reality, and presence of the holy: that is, of God or the divine character. The intuition may be found over a broad spectrum, which includes the intense concentration, introversion, and ecstasy of distinguished mystics of the East and the West; devout prayer; and a diffuse background of ideal sentiment which accompanies and guides the daily conduct of life, as in the inner light of Quakers. In all of these forms and degrees, the holy is felt to be present.

This feeling in turn admits of two stages, which may be called vision and union. In vision, God is present to mystical intuition as the red color of a rose is present to sensory intuition. The intuition as a process of awareness and the holy as the object of awareness are distinct from each other, but stand in direct confrontation with little or no distance, whether of symbols or of space. In union, however, the intuition and its object, the mystic and God, become one. The union may be primarily axiological: the complete agreement of the goals and will of the mystic with the divine purpose, as in the line of Dante: "And in His will is perfected our peace."[3] The union may be metaphysical and partial, as in the intuited indwelling of the divine spirit, or its influence, in the finite spirit of the mystic. In both of these instances, union is compatible with the individuality of the mystic and with the maintenance of awareness and intuition.

But union may also be thought to be metaphysical and total: the merger, rapture, and dissolution of the spirit of the mystic in the infinite spirit of God. In this return or ascent to the ground of being, individuality is annihilated, and intuition apparently ceases with it. Thus ethical, epistemological, and theological problems arise. For morality, the individual self is the greatest and the final good, and the major tasks are to unite the self internally through prudence and to unite all selves externally

[3] Dante, *Paradiso*, trans. L. Binyon, in P. Milano (ed.), *The Portable Dante* (New York: Viking, 1952), Canto III, line 85.

through love. In theory of knowledge, it is difficult to see how total union can be known at the time, when awareness has ebbed from its individual focus into the sea of being. Theistic theology, dominant in the West, asserts that God transcends the world and man and is separate from them in substance. Theism can accept vision and the two modified forms of union, but it rejects union which is metaphysical and total. The latter is acceptable only to certain forms of pantheism.

Some light on the union of the individual and God may be found in the distinction between the secondary and the primary content of mystical intuition. The secondary content consists of images, words, and concepts, such as the voice that spoke from heaven to Saul, the idea of social injustice that occurred to Woolman in a mystical experience, or the visual forms of the cross, Jesus, the Virgin, or a saint that have been present to many Christian mystics. Content of this sort is highly variable among mystics; it resembles the materials and forms of sensation and reason, which suggests a borrowing from these sources rather than the use of a uniquely mystical mode of apprehension; and it consists of symbols which either take the place of God, or stand between him and the mystic when he is felt to be present. For all of these reasons the secondary content is peripheral and dispensable in mysticism, and it is even inimical when it distracts attention from what is essential to the experience.

This is the primary content, which is more emphatic as concentration and introversion deepen; is quite constant among mystics who have advanced in these virtues; is founded on mystical intuition alone; and brushes aside all symbols. Unfortunately, the primary content is virtually indescribable, and description founders among analogies and in the darkness of the "negative theology." To the extent that it may be described directly, it may be spoken of as a primordial One, which is above all distinction. The One contains the fusion of power and value: it is creative love. This is the holy as experienced in developed mysticism.

The indeterminate totality of the One gives some warrant for the notion of the complete absorption of the individual self into God. An individual is determinate and limited, and the One may plausibly be taken as a model leading to the annihilation of individuality. But the One is creative love; creation is of determinate forms or beings; and love is of these objects. Here the One counters the tendency toward absorption into God. From the primary content, then, contrary moments or tendencies may be derived in regard to the union of self and God. But the moments may be reconciled.

Creation and love are supported by union in the two senses of the sharing of purposes and the indwelling of divine influence. And the indeterminate totality of the One does not imply absorption of the individual self into God. Indeterminate totality is a condition of the creator of all determinate beings. These cannot return to their source without nullifying the creative process. It is also the condition of a love that embraces all determinate beings without distinction or partiality. This love preserves determinate objects and individual selves, but looks on every object in a meaningful relation to a widening sphere of other objects, and in a similar relation to the fountain of all determinations. It may have an image in a human love. The human significance of the One, then, is not to be an invitation to absorption of the individual self into God, but to be a model for a human love which is total and impartial. This love is the immediate source of the religious awareness of meaning, and it sets limits to union which are acceptable to creator and creature.

Religion and Art

The comparison of religion with art in general, as distinct from the special kind of art that is usually identified as religious, reveals points of convergence and of divergence between the two activities. These relations may be found in emotion, sensation, transcendence, freedom, belief, and form.

The centrality of emotion in art is repeated in religion. When the self is united with the holy it experiences joy; piety, which is benevolence founded on gratitude for the source of the being of the self; and awe, which is admiration for an excellence that is total and, being beyond definition, wrapped in mystery. When the self compares itself with the holy, it feels humility and self-abasement. And when it is in a condition of alienation and failure, it experiences contrition, intolerable longing, despair, and spiritual dryness. The significance of these emotions is a model for aesthetic sensibility. But there are differences between emotion in art and in religion. The range of emotion in art is greater, since art may deal with any emotion whatsoever, provided that it admits of embodiment. Although the emotion in art is intense, its intensity is founded on subtlety and purity of perception; religious emotion has a greater and more naked intensity, due to the impact of totality on consciousness. Aesthetic emotion is contemplated disinterestedly in the condition of embodiment, while religious emotion is aroused. This is to say that in religious experience, as in fully moral experience, emotion is experienced with commitment of and by the self: and the commitment is greater in religion than in morality.

The community of art and religion in regard to emotion, which puts them in joint contrast to such activities as physics, diplomacy, banking, or tennis, is echoed in a lesser but still significant interest in sensation. Sound, color, light and shadow, moving shapes, and incense are well known in the rituals of public worship. The affinity of sensation with emotion has been understood by many churches, and it is surely no coincidence that the oldest and most populous of the Christian churches has made more use of this connection than any of its sisters. Beyond sensation and closely tied imagery, the concreteness and vividness of sensation have been achieved in a second degree in the imaginative constructions of parables, allegories, and myths. These give to religious belief an intimacy and emotional charge that are far less evident in the abstractly conceptual thought of philosophy. Religion thus has a marked interest in sensation and in thought that is close to sensation. But as it advances in depth it leaves behind sensation and imagery, parables and myths. Sensation is incompatible with mystical introversion, which puts aside the stimuli of the physical environment. Images and myths belong to the secondary content of mystical experience, which is transcended in the more advanced forms. Plotinus describes the mystic as having "risen beyond beauty; he has overpassed even the choir of the virtues; he is like one who, having penetrated the inner sanctuary, leaves the temple images behind him."[4]

But even here there is a sensuous character of special interest.

---

[4] Plotinus, *Enneads,* trans. S. MacKenna (London: Faber and Faber, 1956), VI. 9. 11.

Sensuousness is inseparable from experience in time: it belongs to the flow of consciousness and is specified in emotion, sensation, and imagery. A condition of sensuousness more concrete than emotion and more diffuse than ordinary sensation is evident in mysticism at any stage. It may perhaps be described as a filtering or sublimation of organic sensation, including that of eros. At a remove which transforms objects and satisfactions, the love of God draws on the erotic motor of the most concretely intense form of human love. Former sensualists are not uncommon among mystics, as Augustine and Francis of Assisi testify, and Santayana remarked with insight that "it is easier to make a saint out of a libertine than out of a prig."[5] Poets often pass from erotic love in their youth to mystical love in full maturity, and it is not hard to discern a common quality in the two stages amid differences of imagery and emotion. Spenser and Donne may here be cited, as may Eliot and Dylan Thomas several centuries later. Apart from these particulars of biography, the poetry of St. John of the Cross, one of the most profound and articulate of Western mystics, contains a holy sensuousness behind the images required for art. A measure of the excellence of mysticism may be had in the extent to which sensuousness is preserved, but shorn of local color and dependency.

Such separation involves transcendence of self. The mystical union of self and God is the ideal limit of the passage of self from its initial narrowness in the present moment and point of experience to its final and greatest breadth in the intuition and love of the whole of what is most real. The transcendence of religion differs from that of morality only in degree. Moral transcendence is from the present moment to the self as a whole, and from that self to other selves in human society. It embraces prudence and benevolence. Religious transcendence moves a step further to the whole of reality; it contains piety, which lies beyond prudence and benevolence but supplies a new perspective and strength for those antecedents. The same relation of the partial whole to the total whole is found between moral and religious freedom. When the self is identified with the holy, its former passivity to reality becomes a sympathetic activity, and the self rises to the apex of freedom. It was this summit that was envisaged in the description

[5] Santayana, p. 201.

of freedom in liberal activity that was made in an earlier chapter.[6] Because of the similarity in nature between the moral and religious forms of transcendence and freedom, the religious development of these attributes stands in the same kind of partial contrast to the aesthetic as does the moral. The contrast is between commitment, now total and "for eternity," and detachment. But the contrast does not impair the underlying common interest of art and religion in transcendence and freedom.

A further contrast between art and religion appears in religious belief. It has been seen that art has intuitive knowledge of emotion in the condition of embodiment, and that it may have discursive knowledge, or wisdom, about human nature and its values. But religious belief is directed beyond emotion and man to the foundations of being. It makes a claim to metaphysical truth, which art does not. It is no doubt natural to feel that a tree of Cézanne is more real than one of sense perception or of botany. But when the tree is so praised, it is not because it defines an independent reality, but because it defines through embodiment the subjective reality of human sensibility. It is sometimes claimed that the poet, for instance, has insight into reality which surpasses the accomplishments of sense experience and reason. But if a poet has such knowledge, it is not as part of his art or poetic function, but as something added to it. He may be a mystic as well as a poet, but he may be either without being the other; and his poetic art and imagination do not validate any metaphysical claims that he may make as a mystic. Emotional sensitivity, experience of self and man, imaginative richness, and formative power do not confer authority in the discernment of transhuman reality.

The gap between religion and art in regard to belief may be narrowed somewhat, and possibly eliminated, by two matters. From the side of art, it is justifiable to say that the artist may excel in knowledge of the value for human nature of the reality revealed in mystical intuition. The human wisdom which includes observant understanding of the role in human nature of jealousy and fidelity, rashness and endurance, may go a step further to the appreciation of the need of man for an attachment and security that have a divine object and source. Into this need

---

[6] Above, Chap. 12, "The Scope of Moral Experience."

the poet may have exceptional insight, which is not incidental to his genius but inherent in it. And from the side of religion, it is possible to regard mysticism as having no cognitive result or claim, but as being purely a conative act of worship.[7]

More basic than the question, whether the primary content of mystical experience is an object independent of the mystic and his intuition, is the question whether that content is an object at all. The indeterminateness of the One, and the closeness of the mystic to it, make it difficult to decide whether the primary content stands over against intuition as an object, as a red color does against the process of visual sensing, or is an attribute of the process of intuiting. Without damage to the importance of mysticism, it is reasonable to propose that the indeterminate totality of the One characterizes the love that informs mystical intuition, rather than a love in the nature of things to which the mystic's love is a response. Mystical intuition may be the love of love, and the appreciation of the unconditioned oughtness of love, without any discernment of the status of love in the cosmos. If this be accepted, then mysticism itself sheds all metaphysical belief, and the gap between art and religion on that account disappears.

There is a final difference between art and religion, which seems to be fundamental and stubborn. The aesthetic object is a form, in which determinate parts are unified to make a structured whole. But the holy as an indeterminate totality has no parts and no structure; it is formless. The holy is apprehended as formless because it is more basic than form and is the source of form. That which can create all form is itself formless: otherwise it would not create, but merely repeat itself. The holy must therefore lie forever beyond the reach of form, and art cannot grasp or communicate it.

Two attempts may be made to soften this contrast. One is to point out that art itself has an element of indeterminateness of structure, since organic unity means interpenetration of parts, and interpenetration means that parts cannot be fully distinguished from each other. But the interpenetration does not by any means dissolve parts into each other; and in art, the parts that interweave presuppose a creative act in which mutually external parts

---

[7] Compare Arthur Berndtson, "Cognition and the Mystical Experience," *The Personalist*, Vol. XXXI, Summer, 1950, pp. 272–288.

are handled with technique. The other attempt is to propose that though art can neither present nor represent the One, it can express the emotion of the mystic. Embodiment, however, makes an emotion determinate in the embodying form, while the emotion of vision or union must be as indeterminate as the object for which it is felt. This is all the more evident if the One is identified with the worship and love of the mystic: its indeterminate totality is that of the emotion of the mystic at the point of culmination. What can be expressed are approaches to this ultimate emotion, and lower emotions in the religious hierarchy. This is not adequate in relation to mysticism: but it brings art closer to the heart of religious value, and therefore of all value, than any human activity other than the mystical process itself.

Religion in Art

The comparison of art and religion has shown that art cannot itself be an instance of religious experience, since it differs from the latter fully in regard to form, and partially in regard to transcendence and freedom. But the survey also indicates that art has the means to take an effective interest in religion, by virtue of which many works of art, including some not usually so identified, may be called religious in a modified sense of the word.

The more evident of the means is the representation of a religious subject matter short of the holy itself. The representation may be of a person or thing, an event, or an idea associated with religion or, more usually, with a particular religion. In Christian culture, a painting or poem will readily be described as religious if it represents Jesus, a saint, or the cross; the creation, the Crucifixion, or the day of judgment; the eternal goodness of God; or the comparative imperfection of man. The art of the Middle Ages abounds in such subjects, and in no subsequent period of Western art have they been absent. But religious iconology and religious doctrine are not sufficient to make art religious even in the modified sense available to art. Without expression of religious emotion through these forms, the art is only nominally religious. And they are not necessary; for both music and architecture can have a religious character through the expression of religious emotion, without benefit or impediment from the representation of a

religious subject. The more important of the means by which
art has a religious concern is thus the expression of a religious
emotion.

The nature of religious emotion and the difficulty that art has
in expressing it were touched on in the preceding section. It was
suggested that in union the self experiences joy, piety, and awe;
in contrast with the holy it feels humility and self-abasement; and
in alienation from the holy it feels longing, contrition, despair,
and dryness. The history of religious art shows the occupation of
the artist in many media with religious failure and contrast, and
with fragments and symbols for the approach to religious consummation. These aspects of religious sensibility may stand apart
from each other, or they may be mixed or graduated into each
other in accordance with the complexity of religious experience
and the mutations of men.

The alienation of man in relation to the holy is shown in the
Crucifixion of Rouault (Plate 17). Man suffers no greater estrangement
from God than when he destroys the human symbol of divinity.
In colors of muted harshness, laid on as though flesh had become
bone of a somber light, Rouault shows the sorrow of this ultimate
loss. But the god is not eclipsed in death, for the line of the face
is strong. And the kneeling figure beside him shows that he is not
alone among men. Thus in the *Pieta* of Michelangelo in the
Florence Cathedral, the broken figure taken from the cross is held
with compassion, the gravity of which is fixed in stone.

From extreme alienation it is progress for the estranged to feel
religious guilt, which is founded on distance from the holy and
acknowledgment of dependence on it. The "Holy Sonnets" of
Donne express remorse for sin, the fear of death as the issue of the
sinful state, and undeserving hope for redemption through the
merciful love of God. Less assured of mercy is the *Requiem* of
Berlioz. Through the fierce energy of this monumental work, the
holy is heard to stand in judgment of all men. The soul fears a
wrath more powerful and terrible than death: one that awakens
the dead and renders a verdict on them for eternity.

The experience of humility and abasement, as the inherent
condition of the finite when it compares itself with God, is difficult to isolate in art, as it also is in religion. It readily moves
toward the states of union or alienation, in which humility is
piety or contrition, and abasement is awe or terror. In the Berlioz

Requiem, abasement before the divine splendor is edged with terror and loneliness. Whatever its virtue in faith and works, the soul falls in the void as it advances. Or humility may contain such transcendence of self that it borrows the radiant piety of union. In the *Madonna of Humility* of Fra Angelico (Plate 18), gentle lines, folding masses of mild blue warmed with muted red, and a background fixed in geometric repetition express the serene dedication of the mother.

Vision and union have their first intimations in aspiration, which lies between the struggles of alienation and the culmination of religious experience. There is no more systematic expression of aspiration than in Gothic architecture (Plate 15). The vertical theme found in the pointed arches of windows, doorways, and nave, in the rise of piers in interior walls and of buttresses against exterior walls, and in the height of nave and tower expresses the upward movement of the soul strengthened by the awareness of the holy. But the ascent often is agitated, as it may well be by the mystery that lies in the invisible heaven. The repetition of ascent, and the transfer of motion from one height to another, express both the agitation and the sustained ardor of flight. An audible sense of aspiration is common in the music of Bach, and the racing tones are charged with abasement from one pole and radiant vision at the other. In Van Gogh's *Crows Over the Wheat Fields* (Plate 19), aspiration flows into and through an ambiguous union. The grain swirls in a plenum of energy, as though to negate the realm of determinate forms. It meets the dense sky, which is similarly charged, though pressed against the fields. Here nature seems to be the restless image of the One. But the black forms of the birds are holes into darkness beyond the sky: rapture is demonic.

A moral union with God, in which the self knows directly the security and comfort of the holy, pervades the *German Requiem* of Brahms. The divine love, given tenderly and received with exaltation, is expressed in the soprano solo of the fifth part, "Ye who now sorrow." The immanence of God in nature is felt by Wordsworth in "Tintern Abbey":

> *And I have felt*
> *A presence that disturbs me with the joy*
> *Of elevated thoughts; a sense sublime*
> *Of something far more deeply interfused,*

> *Whose dwelling is the light of setting suns,*
> *And the round ocean and the living air,*
> *And the blue sky, and in the mind of man;*
> *A motion and a spirit, that impels*
> *All thinking things, all objects of all thought,*
> *And rolls through all things.*

Beyond these determinations of the personal and natural is the mystical unity of Rublëv's *Old Testament Trinity* (Plate 20). In great silence the three figures encircle the small table. Blue folds of the garment of the central figure break into jeweled angles. Against these glowing definites the surface of the table dissolves into a pool of light, which has no bottom. This is a very far reach in religious art, which is attained with difficulty and great reward. But it is possible to go a step further in difficulty and perhaps in achievement, to the formulation of a unity which lies entirely within the will and emotion of the mystic, without support from objective deity, from nature, or from man. This is the accomplishment of Beethoven's *Quartet in A Minor,* Op. 132. In the third movement, sound moves beyond its horizon into silence, and there is poised without weight in a calm air. Without fear or eagerness, and raised above every finite concern, the self dissolves into its measured, measureless joy.

Many of the aspects of religious consciousness can be traced in organic continuity in the poetry of T. S. Eliot. The poems of the volumes of 1917 and 1920, headed respectively by "The Love Song of J. Alfred Prufrock" and "Gerontion," are marked by satire, drawing room elegance, and imagistic insouciance, under which are discontent with erotic love and the church, contempt for self, and preoccupation with age. The nihilistic temper of the poems, untouched by any sense of restorative meaning, is evident in passages from "Prufrock":

> *I should have been a pair of ragged claws*
> *Scuttling across the floors of silent seas.*[8]

and from "Gerontion":

> *I have lost my passion: why should I need to keep it*
> *Since what is kept must be adulterated?*[9]

---

[8] T. S. Eliot, *Collected Poems 1909–1962* (New York: Harcourt, 1963), p. 5.
[9] Eliot, p. 31.

The Waste Land (1922) systematizes and deepens the perception of the spiritual void of the poet and the time. Beginning with the magical statement of living death:

> *April is the cruellest month, breeding*
> *Lilacs out of the dead land, mixing*
> *Memory and desire, stirring*
> *Dull roots with spring rain*[10]

it surveys the sterility of a life and civilization in which there is no love other than the meaningless urges of erotic sensuality. Despite the hints of rebirth through death, and the final advice to give of oneself, to sympathize, and to control self, the poem stands at the vestibule of religious awareness, since there is alienation without discernment of the holy as the object from which men are separated. Despair thus grows apace in *The Hollow Men* (1925). Discovering a shadow between idea and reality, conception and creation, potency and existence, the poem ends after an incantation similar to broken prayer with the statement:

> *This is the way the world ends*
> *This is the way the world ends*
> *This is the way the world ends*
> *Not with a bang but a whimper.*[11]

Discernment of the nature of the alienation, and the struggle to rise toward the holy through denial of the world and the opening of the self to divine influence, are expressed in *Ash-Wednesday* (1930). The self feels impotent to advance its own salvation, and yields itself in humble passivity:

> *Because these wings are no longer wings to fly*
> *But merely vans to beat the air*
> *The air which is now thoroughly small and dry*
> *Smaller and dryer than the will*
> *Teach us to care and not to care*
> *Teach us to sit still.*[12]

Though it has known the torments of love unsatisfied and of love satisfied, the self ascending the purgatorial stair still is distracted by eros and requires an extraordinary kind of strength to with-

[10] Eliot, p. 53.
[11] Eliot, p. 82.
[12] Eliot, p. 86.

stand temptation. There are moments of illumination. But the
time and place are not right for the discernment of truth. Still
in a condition of humility based on distance from the holy, the
writer ends the poem:

> Sister, mother
> And spirit of the river, spirit of the sea,
> Suffer me not to be separated

> And let my cry come unto Thee.[13]

The fulfillment of the religious process is the subject of "Burnt
Norton" (1935), the first of the *Four Quartets*. Time, or the mutual
exclusion of past, present, and future, is found to be unreal. It
is a "place of disaffection" where men are "Distracted from distraction by distraction." What is real is an eternal now charged
with activity, to which the poet has had access:

> At the still point of the turning world. Neither flesh nor fleshless;
> Neither from nor towards; at the still point, there the dance is,
> But neither arrest nor movement. And do not call it fixity,
> Where past and future are gathered. Neither movement from nor
>   towards,
> Neither ascent nor decline. Except for the point, the still point,
> There would be no dance, and there is only the dance.
> I can only say, there we have been: but I cannot say where.
> And I cannot say, how long, for that is to place it in time.[14]

The subjective aspect of the timeless experience is rendered with
great complexity:

> The inner freedom from the practical desire,
> The release from action and suffering, release from the inner
> And the outer compulsion, yet surrounded
> By a grace of sense, a white light still and moving,
> Erhebung without motion, concentration
> Without elimination, both a new world
> And the old made explicit, understood
> In the completion of its partial ecstasy,
> The resolution of its partial horror.[15]

---

[13] Eliot, p. 95.
[14] Eliot, p. 177.
[15] Eliot, pp. 177–178.

In these two statements of the objective and subjective poles appear several traits of union. The transcendence of change and of contraries at the still point indicates radical indeterminateness. The world turning upon the still point expresses creative power at the indeterminate center. Release from practical desire and from suffering attests to negative freedom in the experience. At both poles, reflecting the closeness of union, is a self-contained equipoise with positive freedom: power intense and composed.

Bibliography

ADLER, MORTIMER, *Art and Prudence* (New York: Longmans, 1937).

ALDRICH, VIRGIL C., *Philosophy of Art* (Englewood Cliffs, N.J.: Prentice-Hall, 1963).

ALEXANDER, SAMUEL, *Beauty and Other Forms of Value* (London: Macmillan, 1933).

ARISTOTLE, *Nicomachean Ethics,* Bk. VI, trans. by W. D. Ross, in the *Works of Aristotle,* ed. J. A. Smith and W. D. Ross, Vol. IX (Oxford: Clarendon Press, 1925).

———, *Poetics,* trans. by Ingram Bywater, in *Works,* Vol. XI, 1924.

———, *Politics,* Bk. VIII, trans. by B. Jowett, in *Works,* Vol. X, 1921.

BARR, ALFRED H., JR., *Cubism and Abstract Art* (New York: Museum of Modern Art, 1936).

BAUMGARTEN, ALEXANDER G., *Reflections on Poetry,* trans. and ed. by Karl Aschenbrenner and William B. Holther (Berkeley, Calif.: University of California Press, 1954).

BEARDSLEY, MONROE C., *Aesthetics: Problems in the Philosophy of Criticism* (New York: Harcourt, 1958).

BELL, CLIVE, *Art* (Philadelphia: Frederick A. Stokes, n.d.).

BERGSON, HENRI, *Laughter,* trans. by Cloudesley Brereton and Fred Rothwell (New York: Macmillan, 1911).

BERNHEIMER, RICHARD, "In Defense of Representation," in *Art: A Bryn Mawr Symposium* (Bryn Mawr, Pa.: Bryn Mawr College, 1940).

BOSANQUET, BERNARD, *A History of Aesthetic* (London: G. Allen, 2nd ed., 1949).

———, *Three Lectures on Aesthetic* (London: Macmillan, 1931).

BULLOUGH, EDWARD, " 'Psychical Distance' as a Factor in Art and an Aesthetic Principle," *British Journal of Psychology*, Vol. V, June, 1912.

BURKE, EDMUND, *A Philosophical Enquiry into the Origin of Our Ideas of the Sublime and Beautiful*, ed. by J. T. Boulton (New York: Columbia University Press, 1958).

CARRITT, EDGAR F., *The Theory of Beauty* (London: Methuen, 4th ed., 1931).

CASO, ANTONIO, *Principios de estética* (Mexico City: Porrua, 1944).

CASSIRER, ERNST, *Language and Myth*, trans. by Susanne K. Langer (New York: Harper & Row, 1946).

COLLINGWOOD, ROBIN G., *The Principles of Art* (Oxford: Clarendon Press, 1950).

COOPER, GROSVENOR, AND LEONARD B. MEYER, *The Rhythmic Structure of Music* (Chicago: University of Chicago Press, 1960).

CRANE, RONALD S., *The Languages of Criticism and the Structure of Poetry* (Toronto: University of Toronto Press, 1954).

CROCE, BENEDETTO, *Aesthetic*, trans. by Douglas Ainslie (London: Macmillan, 2nd ed., 1929).

———, *The Breviary of Aesthetic*, trans. by Douglas Ainslie, in *Rice Institute Book of the Opening*, Vol. II (Houston, Tex.: Rice Institute, 1912).

DEWEY, JOHN, *A Common Faith* (New Haven, Conn.: Yale University Press, 1934).

DUCASSE, CURT J., *The Philosophy of Art* (New York: Dial, 1929).

DUFRENNE, MIKEL, *Le Poétique* (Paris: Presses Universitaires de France, 1963).

EKMAN, ROLF, *Problems and Theories in Modern Aesthetics* (Malmö: Gleerups, 1960).

ELIOT, T. S., *Collected Poems 1909–1962* (New York: Harcourt, 1963).

———, "Hamlet and His Problems," *The Sacred Wood* (London: Methuen, 7th ed., 1950).

ELSE, GERALD F., *Aristotle's Poetics: The Argument* (Cambridge, Mass.: Harvard University Press, 1957).

———, *The Origin and Early Form of Greek Tragedy* (Cambridge, Mass.: Harvard University Press, 1965).

FALLICO, ARTURO B., *Art and Existentialism* (Englewood Cliffs, N.J.: Prentice-Hall, 1962).

FREUD, SIGMUND, "The Relation of the Poet to Day-Dreaming," "The Theme of the Three Caskets," and "The Moses of Michelangelo," in *Collected Papers,* trans. under supervision of Joan Riviere, Vol. IV (London: Hogarth, 1934).

————, *Introductory Lectures on Psycho-Analysis,* Lecture XXIII, in *The Complete Psychological Works of Sigmund Freud,* ed. by James Strachey, Vol. XVI (London: Hogarth, 1963), pp. 371–377.

FRY, ROGER E., *Vision and Design* (New York: Meridian, 1956).

GILBERT, KATHERINE E., AND HELMUT KUHN, *A History of Esthetics* (Bloomington, Ind.: Indiana University Press, 2nd ed., 1953).

GILSON, ETIENNE, *Painting and Reality* (Princeton, N.J.: Princeton University Press, 2nd ed., 1957).

GOODMAN, PAUL, *The Structure of Literature* (Chicago: University of Chicago Press, 1954).

GOTSHALK, DILMAN W., *Art and the Social Order* (New York: Dover, 2nd ed., 1962).

GREENE, THEODORE M., *The Arts and the Art of Criticism* (Princeton, N.J.: Princeton University Press, 2nd ed., 1947).

HANSLICK, EDUARD, *The Beautiful in Music,* trans. by Gustav Cohen (London: Novello, 1891); *The Beautiful in Music,* M. Weitz, ed.; trans. by G. Cohen (New York: Liberal Arts Press, 1957).

HARTMANN, N., *Ethik* (Berlin: de Gruyter, 1926); *Ethics,* trans. by Stanton Coit, 3 vols. (New York: Macmillan, 1932).

HARTSHORNE, CHARLES, *The Philosophy and Psychology of Sensation* (Chicago: University of Chicago Press, 1934).

HEGEL, GEORG W. F., *The Philosophy of Fine Art,* ed. and trans. by F. P. B. Osmaston, 4 vols. (London: G. Bell, 1920).

HOSPERS, JOHN, *Meaning and Truth in the Arts* (Chapel Hill, N.C.: University of North Carolina Press, 1946).

HUME, DAVID, *Of the Standard of Taste and Other Essays,* ed. by J. Lenz (Indianapolis, Ind.: Bobbs-Merrill, 1965).

JACOBSEN, JENS P., *Niels Lyhne,* trans. by Hanna Larsen (New York: American-Scandinavian Foundation, 1919).

JAMES, WILLIAM, *The Principles of Psychology,* Vol. II (New York: Henry Holt, 1890).

JENKINS, IREDELL, *Art and the Human Enterprise* (Cambridge, Mass.: Harvard University Press, 1958).

JORDAN, ELIJAH, *The Aesthetic Object* (Bloomington, Ind.: Principia Press, 1937).

JUNG, CARL G., "Psychology and Literature," in *Modern Man in Search of a Soul,* trans. by W. S. Dell and Cary F. Baynes (New York: Harcourt, 1936).

KANT, IMMANUEL, *Critique of Judgment,* trans. by J. H. Bernard (New York: Hafner, 1951).

KEATS, JOHN, *Letters,* ed. by M. B. Forman, Vol. I (New York: Oxford University Press, 1931).

KRIS, ERNST, *Psychoanalytic Explorations in Art* (New York: International Universities, 1952).

KUHNS, RICHARD, *The House, the City, and the Judge: The Growth of Moral Awareness in the 'Oresteia'* (Indianapolis, Ind.: Bobbs-Merrill, 1962).

LANGER, SUSANNE K., *Feeling and Form* (New York: Scribner, 1953).

————, *Philosophy in a New Key* (Cambridge, Mass.: Harvard University Press, 1942).

LANGFELD, HERBERT S., *The Aesthetic Attitude* (New York: Harcourt, 1920).

LEE, VERNON, *The Beautiful* (New York: Cambridge University Press, 1913).

LESSING, GOTTHOLD E., *Hamburgische Dramaturgie,* Vol. II, in *Sämtliche Schriften,* ed. by K. Lachmann, Vol. X (Stuttgart: Göschen, 1893).

————, *Laokoon,* in *Sämtliche Schriften,* ed. by K. Lachmann, Vol. IX (Stuttgart: Göschen, 1893); *Laocoön,* trans. by E. A. McCormick (Indianapolis, Ind.: Bobbs-Merrill, 1962).

LEVI, ALBERT W., *Literature, Philosophy, and the Imagination* (Bloomington, Ind.: Indiana University Press, 1962).

LIPMAN, MATHEW, *What Happens in Art* (New York: Appleton, 1967).

LISTOWEL, W. F. H., Earl of, *A Critical History of Modern Aesthetics* (London: G. Allen, 1933).

MANDEL, OSCAR, *A Definition of Tragedy* (New York: New York University Press, 1961).

MARGOLIS, JOSEPH, ed., *Philosophy Looks at the Arts* (New York: Scribner, 1962).

MARITAIN, JACQUES, *Art and Scholasticism,* trans. by Joseph W. Evans (New York: Scribner, 1962).

————, *Creative Intuition in Art and Poetry* (New York: Pantheon, 1953).

MCKEON, RICHARD, "The Philosophic Bases of Art and Criticism," *Modern Philology,* Vol. 41, 1943–1944, pp. 65–87, 129–171.

————, *Thought, Action and Passion* (Chicago: University of Chicago Press, 1954).

MEYER, LEONARD B., *Emotion and Meaning in Music* (Chicago: University of Chicago Press, 1956).

MORRIS, CHARLES, *Signs, Language and Behavior* (Englewood Cliffs, N.J.: Prentice-Hall, 1946).

MYERS, HENRY A., *Tragedy: A View of Life* (Ithaca, N.Y.: Cornell University Press, 1956).

NAHM, MILTON C., *Aesthetic Experience and its Presuppositions* (New York: Harper & Row, 1946).

NIETZSCHE, FRIEDRICH, *Die Geburt der Tragödie*, in *Werke*, Vol. I (Leipzig: Naumann, 1899); *The Birth of Tragedy*, trans. by Walter Kaufmann (New York: Random House, 1967).

————, *Der Wille zur Macht*, Bk. III, in *Werke*, Vol. XVI (Leipzig: Kröner, 1911); *The Will to Power*, trans. by Walter Kaufmann and R. J. Hollingdale (New York: Random House, 1967).

OLSON, ELDER, *Tragedy and the Theory of Drama* (Detroit, Mich.: Wayne State University Press, 1961).

ORTEGA Y GASSET, JOSÉ, *The Dehumanization of Art and Notes on the Novel*, trans. by Helene Weyl (Princeton, N. J.: Princeton University Press, 1948).

OSBORNE, HAROLD, *Aesthetics and Criticism* (New York: Philosophical Library, 1955).

PARKER, DEWITT H., *The Principles of Aesthetics* (New York: Appleton, 1946).

————, *The Analysis of Art* (New Haven, Conn.: Yale University Press, 1926).

PEPPER, STEPHEN C., *The Basis of Criticism in the Arts* (Cambridge, Mass.: Harvard University Press, 1945).

————, *Principles of Art Appreciation* (New York: Harcourt, 1949).

————, *The Work of Art* (Bloomington, Ind.: Indiana University Press, 1955).

PLATO, *Ion*, trans. by B. Jowett, in *The Dialogues of Plato* (New York: Random House, 1937), Vol. I.

————, *Phaedrus*, trans. by B. Jowett, in *Dialogues*, Vol. I.

————, *Philebus*, trans. by B. Jowett, in *Dialogues*, Vol. II.

————, *Republic*, Bks. III and X, trans. by B. Jowett, in *Dialogues*, Vol. I.

————, *Symposium*, trans. by B. Jowett, in *Dialogues*, Vol. I.

PLOTINUS, *Enneads*, trans. by S. MacKenna (London: Faber, 1956).

PRALL, DAVID W., *Aesthetic Analysis* (New York: Crowell, 1936).

RADER, MELVIN M., ed., *A Modern Book of Esthetics* (New York: Holt, Rinehart and Winston, 3rd ed., 1960).

ROYCE, JOSIAH, *The World and the Individual*, Vol. II (New York: Macmillan, 1904).

SANTAYANA, GEORGE, *Reason in Common Sense* (New York: Scribner, 1929).

———, *Reason in Religion* (New York: Scribner, 1926).

———, *Reason in Science* (New York: Scribner, 1928).

———, *The Sense of Beauty* (New York: Scribner, 1896).

SARTRE, JEAN PAUL, *Imagination: A Psychological Critique,* trans. by Forrest Williams (Ann Arbor, Mich.: University of Michigan Press, 1962).

———, *The Psychology of Imagination,* trans. (New York: Philosophical Library, 1948).

SCHILLER, FRIEDRICH VON, *On the Aesthetic Education of Man,* trans. by R. Snell (New Haven, Conn.: Yale University Press, 1954).

SCHOPENHAUER, ARTHUR, *Die Welt als Wille und Vorstellung,* 2 vols., in *Sämmtliche Werke,* Vols. II, III (Leipzig: F. A. Brockhaus, 1891); *The World as Will and Representation,* trans. by E. F. J. Payne, 2 vols. (New York: Dover, 1966).

SPARSHOTT, FRANCIS, *The Structure of Aesthetics* (Toronto: University of Toronto Press, 1963).

SPINOZA, BENEDICTUS DE, *Ethics,* trans. by A. Boyle (London: Dent, 1934).

STOLNITZ, JEROME, *Aesthetics and the Philosophy of Art Criticism* (Boston: Houghton Mifflin, 1960).

SULLIVAN, J. W. N., *Beethoven: His Spiritual Development* (New York: Knopf, 1927).

TEJERA, VICTORINO, *Art and Human Intelligence* (New York: Appleton, 1965).

THOMAS AQUINAS, *Summa Theologica,* Vol. VII (London: R. and T. Washbourne, 1915).

TOLSTOY, LEO, *What Is Art and Essays on Art,* trans. by Aylmer Maude (New York: Oxford University Press, 1946).

TOMAS, VINCENT, ed., *Creativity in the Arts* (Englewood Cliffs, N.J.: Prentice-Hall, 1964).

USHENKO, ANDREW P., *Dynamics of Art* (Bloomington, Ind.: Indiana University Press, 1953).

VASCONCELOS, JOSÉ, *Estética* (Mexico City: Ediciones Botas, 3rd. ed., 1945).

VIVAS, ELISEO, *Creation and Discovery* (New York: Noonday Press, 1955).

VOLKELT, JOHANNES, *Versuch über Fühlen und Wollen* (Munich: Beck, 1930).

WEISS, PAUL, *Nine Basic Arts* (Carbondale, Ill.: Southern Illinois University Press, 1961).

———, *Religion and Art* (Milwaukee, Wis.: Marquette University Press, 1963).

———, *The World of Art* (Carbondale, Ill.: Southern Illinois University Press, 1963).

WEITZ, MORRIS, *Philosophy of the Arts* (Cambridge, Mass.: Harvard University Press, 1950).

WELLEK, RENÉ, AND AUSTIN WARREN, *The Theory of Literature* (New York: Harcourt, 1956).

WHITEHEAD, ALFRED N., *Adventures of Ideas,* Chaps. 17 and 18 (New York: Macmillan, 1933).

WORDSWORTH, WILLIAM, "Preface to the second edition of the *Lyrical Ballads,*" *Complete Poetical Works,* ed. by A. J. George (Boston: Houghton Mifflin, 1932).

WORRINGER, WILHELM, *Abstraktion und Einfühlung* (Munich: R. Piper, 1921); *Abstraction and Empathy,* trans. by Michael Bullock (New York: International Universities, 1963).

Index

A

Abstraction, in music, 131–132,
    136–137
  in painting, 38–40
Action, 245–248
Activity, and contemplation, 88–89
  liberal, 247–250
  and sensation, 79, 82
  see also Freedom; Power
Aesthetic attitude, *see* Contempla-
    tion
Aesthetic experience, as art, 6–9
  basic factors of, 11
  as beauty, 9–10
  and contemplation of emotion,
    87
  definition of, 11
  diversity of, 3
  as expression, 10–11
  unity of, 5–11

Aesthetics, data of, 11–12
  and philosophy, 5
  possibility of, 4–5
  and science, 4
  theories in, 12, 101–102
  unity of, 3, 5–6
Albright, Ivan Lee, 9
Alienation, religious, 280, 283
Angelico, Fra (Giovanni da Fiesole),
    Madonna of Humility, 39, 281,
    Plate 18
Apollonian, 240–241
Appearance, 106–107, 251–252
  see also Image
Appreciator, 7–8, 87, 89–90, 168–170
Aquinas, *see* Thomas Aquinas
Archipenko, Alexander, *Woman
    Combing Her Hair,* 39, Plate 4
Architecture, 27, 33, 52, 281
Aristotle, 6, 242
  and criticism, 197, 214
  and tragedy, 230–236

B

C